20 Nov 2017

Molly,
Thank You
so much for
your help!
Enjoy!
Love,
— Glenn

a man wearing a dress

by Glenn C. Koenig

A Message Rain Book

a man wearing a dress

©2017 by Glenn C. Koenig
Version 1.0
September 2017

Published by Message Rain
Arlington, Massachusetts, USA
www.messagerain.com

ISBN 978-0-9985833-0-3

Library of Congress Control Number: 2017952080

Although the author of this book may offer opinions herein on matters of
health, medicine, law, politics, religion, spirituality, sex, or gender,
he holds no degrees or certifications in any of these disciplines,
so please don't take any of what is said in reference to these topics
as professionally qualified advice.
Please confer with a recognized expert
or other professional if you need.
Or perhaps talk with a shaman.
Ultimately, you must take responsibility for your own care.

Some portions of this book may not be suitable for young children.

This is all about

LOVE

What Is Love?

He said
I love you
in the movies
And they kissed

He said
I love you
without a sound
while lifting his mother, gently
from her wheelchair

She said I love you
only by her smile
as she served soup
to people
who had none

He entered the room
with the negotiator
from the other country
as if to say, I love you
and your people

She opened the box
to let the spider out
into its natural world
The spider never said
I love you
But this love was true

When he slowed his car
to leave a gap in traffic
he said I love you
with a wave of his hand

All across the world
millions say
every day
in this way
I love you

One brief moment
then each one's gone
not ever counted
on the evening news

Their numbers game
lists casualties
or winners
some Tuesday in November

But we elect
our *true* administration
every day
when we say
I love you.

I Don't Blame You

Really, I don't!

Look, I'm not perfect.
This book isn't perfect, either.

I probably could have written it a thousand different ways.
But I had to stop adding, fixing, revising, changing things at some point
And just say print it!
Give it to the people I'm writing it for.

So please remember:
We're all human.

Sometimes our emotions overwhelm us
Or we run out of time or money
Perhaps the weather turns on us
We don't have the energy
Someone resists us,
Because they just don't understand.

And yet, we have to create something anyway.
We have to come through in the end.

I give you
This book.

Not Everything

Not everything in this book is about me. Not everything is about dresses. Not everything is about men, or gender, or sexuality, either.

So, what *is* it about?

· A memoir of my life, growing up (and still growing).
· My experience of my sexuality and shifting gender identity.
· My commentary and vision regarding society and culture.
· Some poetry.
· A few surprises.

There is no formal introduction, foreword, or preface, so you can just start reading right from the start.[1] The pages are all numbered consecutively; there are no Roman numerals! The Table of Contents is at the back of the book. What they call acknowledgements, I call Credits instead. They are also at the back.

In the table of contents the small dots (·) to the right of each title indicate poems. Some poems are centered on the page, while others are left justified. I also capitalize and punctuate my poems intuitively, without regard to convention. This is all intentional; I just like them that way.

There's no bibliography page. I think bibliographies are largely obsolete; just use an online search engine to find what you need. There is no printed index, either. I may publish an index online later. If you're reading this in an electronic version, please feel free to use whatever built-in search functions are available.[2]

There are no formal sections or chapters, just stories, essays, and poems. Please feel free to read straight through or skip around if you like. I'm not the teacher, just the writer. It's yours for the taking.

---

[1] You could claim that this page is actually an introduction, hiding under a different title. Mea culpa. And yes, that's Latin, so you can look it up.

[2] I plan to publish a paper version first; then create an electronic version later on.

Day One

I was the first child born to my parents, late in the summer of 1950. When my mother went into labor, my father drove her to the hospital, a few towns away. At that time, almost everybody was born in a hospital, rather than at home or anywhere else.

On the delivery table, as my mother reported to me years later, they were administering ether to her. They were holding the mask close to her face (so that she was breathing in some of the vapors), but they hadn't pressed it on just yet, so she was feeling "woozy" as she put it. Her labor was not progressing as expected. She told me that she didn't understand which muscles to use to push and was probably slowing things down unintentionally by tensing the wrong way. She said that a nurse started pushing down on her upper belly, as if to help push me out.

Eventually, as her labor finally started to progress further, they put the mask more firmly onto my mother's face, and she lost consciousness. Meanwhile, the ether crossed the placental barrier, from my mother's bloodstream into my own. I was partly anesthetized in the birth canal and remained so after being born, while I was struggling to take my first breaths.

I was placed in a nursery so that my mother could "get some rest." I was brought in to her room periodically, for breastfeeding.[3]

§ § §

Recently, I had a dream. In the dream I was floating down a river that was rapidly moving. The banks of the river were high and I could not see over them. They seemed to be made of a dark gray colored rock that was rough and barren, like lava that had cooled recently. Suddenly the river came to an end with the banks curved all around, encircling it, like a dead end street. The water was disappearing straight down, like a giant drain. I plunged down with it.

I ended up in a cavern, underground, half-full of water. It was totally dark. I was treading water, with just my head above the surface. I had the idea that this was in a hidden cave of solid rock, somewhere near the sea. I panicked. How would I ever escape? No one would ever think to look for me here, so I would never be rescued. After a lengthy struggle, I would die here. My heart was pounding as I began to wake.

Lying there, still half-asleep, I started to imagine what it would be like if I were somehow rescued instead. What if two scuba divers, with headlamps, swam in from an ocean cave to do some exploring? They would look up and see my legs dangling and swim up to me. They would offer me some air to dive with them and swim back

---

[3] At that time, newborns were taken to a nursery to sleep in a crib while their mothers spent about a week in the hospital to rest in bed, before taking their babies home.

down into the darkness, and finally out into the open ocean. I would come to the surface, look up at the sky, and breathe on my own.

At first, I had no idea why I had had such a dream. What could it be about? Days later, it dawned on me: It was about my birth.

The following week, I was on the phone with a peer counselor who lives in another city. When it was my turn to "client," I described the dream to him. Then, in a sudden moment of inspiration, I asked him to describe how he might rescue me. I instructed him to tell me that he was cutting a very large hole in the rock above the cavern. He would pass a rope down to me, so I could grab onto it, then he would lift me up and out.

So, he started describing exactly that to me, as I requested. As I imagined looking up, seeing the sky through the large open hole, and being lifted up through it, I started to breathe big, deep breaths. It was as if I were drawing in the ocean air, standing on a beach somewhere, in the summer. Suddenly, I burst into tears.

I Deserved My Mother's

I wanted to sleep with my
mother
when she was 30 and I
was in the first few days
of my life.

Her body heat
The odor of her pores
Exuding her hormonal essence
into my breath.

But she put me apart
from her, at night
because it said to do that
in the book.

Living in the 1950s

If you read about the 1950s, you will probably see stories about the post-war economic boom, President Eisenhower, the Cold War, fallout shelters, suburban sprawl, and the military-industrial complex.

But that's only what the adults were doing. As a small child, I had no idea about those things. My earliest memories were of my immediate surroundings. Even as early as age two or three, I seem to remember quite a lot about the house we lived in, my toys, clothes, and family life. Even then, I was fascinated by how things worked. For example, I was given a little record player, which I eventually opened up to see what was inside. I am still fascinated by how much our world of technology has changed between then and now.

We lived in a small house with two bedrooms and a bathroom upstairs and a living room, dining room and kitchen downstairs. We had a basement with an oil burner[4] and air ducts, next to the chimney. Across from that, my father had a workbench along the wall. We had a small front yard, a small back yard, and a detached one-car garage, that my father and grandfather built themselves, just before I was born.

We had the usual appliances and furniture, but no dishwasher or clothes dryer, so my parents washed dishes by hand and hung the clothes on a clothesline in the back yard. We also had an AM radio and a primitive hi-fi[5] but no fireplace or TV set.

For the first few years, our telephone was on a "party line." That meant we shared one telephone line with another house on our street. If one of my parents picked up the phone to make a call, and they didn't hear a dial tone, they had to hang up right away. That's because someone in the other household was "on the line," talking to someone. If the phone rang in two short rings, we wouldn't answer it, because it was for them. If it rang in single longer rings instead, it was for us.

We had only the one telephone, connected by a brown cloth-covered wire to a tiny box on the baseboard molding in our living room. We couldn't unplug it, so we had to be in the living room to use it. The telephone company owned the telephone itself and all the wiring for it. We didn't have extensions in any other rooms, because they would have charged extra *each month* for each one. On rare occasions, when we called relatives who lived far away, we kept the conversation very brief. That's because it was a "long-distance" call so there was a charge for the first three minutes and an additional charge for each minute more. These charges were listed on our phone bill at the end of the month.

---

[4] An oil-fired hot air furnace.

[5] This consisted of a record changer and a loudspeaker sitting loose on a coffee table, with a vacuum tube amplifier and FM tuner on a shelf underneath. My parents told me that some day they would get a cabinet in which to mount it all. This was monaural, as stereo hadn't been developed yet.

When we turned on the radio, it would take about thirty seconds before the sound would slowly come on. It took that long for the vacuum tubes inside to warm up and start working. I remember looking through the little holes in the back of the cabinet and seeing the orange glow of the tiny filaments inside the tubes. We mostly listened to news and interview programs on the radio; we played music from records and a few FM stations on the hi-fi in the living room. This was strictly classical music; we never listened to jazz or blues.

The transistor radio came out for the first time when I was a boy. It was small enough to fit in your shirt pocket, but it was still a novelty item. We didn't really need one; when my father was working out in the back yard, he would just take our table radio out onto the back porch, plug it into an extension cord, and listen to baseball games while he worked.

We didn't have a television set until I was eight years old, after we had moved to our second house. Most of the other kids who lived nearby had a TV at home before that, so they talked about a lot of things in school that I knew nothing about.

The ballpoint pen was big news around then. I remember a picture in the newspaper of a scuba diver using one to write underwater, something you could never do with a pencil or a fountain pen. Those were the main ways to write manually before that, besides the typewriter, of course. People wrote letters and postcards more often because phone calls were so expensive, and a postage stamp was only two or three cents.

My family had only one car, a gray Plymouth two-door sedan. My father drove it to work on some days, with another man as a passenger, which they called a car pool. On days when he rode in the other man's car, my mother would have our car for shopping.

When my mother didn't have the car, she and I often walked to the local grocery store. I remember her pushing a carriage with my sister in it, as we walked along the sidewalk, headed into town. We walked down a stretch of Main Street where we could see out over a marshy area beside the small river that ran through town. There was a row of metal posts with two strands of heavy wire rope strung along them, to form a barrier to keep cars (and people) from falling down into the marsh.[6] I remember running my hand along the smooth surface of the galvanized wire rope, and patting the smooth metal covers mounted at the top of each post, as we walked along.

§ § §

When I was about one year old, my mother had the car one day and drove down into town with me in the front seat. There were no seat belts then; I was just sitting there

---

[6] As I write this, I realize that today, there would be a guardrail there to serve that purpose, but what I saw back then was before the interstate highway system, high-speed traffic, and guardrails as we now know them.

on a small booster seat, on the passenger side, next to her. If she had to stop suddenly, her "mom's safety arm"[7] would fly out across my chest to keep me from falling forward into the dashboard or onto the floor.

Anyway, on that day, she pulled up to the traffic light on Main Street. We stopped at the "T" intersection where Main Street ended at the Boston Post Road, which traveled directly through town.[8]

As the light was about to turn green, I started scrunching up my face and blowing air out my nose in short bursts. My mother was mystified. What the heck was I doing? I couldn't talk yet, so she didn't think of asking me directly. Was I pretending to sneeze or something? A few days later, when she had the car again, I did exactly the same thing when we stopped at that intersection.

Finally, after the third day, she realized what I was doing. Just before the light turned green, big trucks were pulling up to the light on the Post Road and stopping just as it was turning red. I was imitating the sound of their air brakes!

Mystery solved. She had to laugh about the whole thing. She thought I was so cute, doing that.

I don't remember actually doing this, at that age, but it doesn't surprise me in the least. I have always been fascinated by the sounds things make and how the texture of things feel when you touch them. I'm typing this book using a computer keyboard, but when I do the Jumble Crosswords in the newspaper, I use a ballpoint pen because I like how it feels to write the letters into the little squares on the newsprint. It just wouldn't be the same if I were to do it online using a keyboard.

Likewise, when someone is going around a sharp curve in a car, even if I'm the one driving, I sometimes make the sound of squealing tires, even though we're not going nearly fast enough to have the tires really do that. It's just a built-in "feature" of who I am, starting from before I could even talk.

---

[7] This was an instinctive reaction of parents, when stopping a car, to put their right arm out in front of any child sitting next to them, to block them from falling. As we now know, in a high-speed crash, parents are not strong enough to prevent a child from flying forward and being injured or killed, so we have children ride in child safety seats in the back seat instead.

[8] This is the local name for US Route 1. There was no interstate highway system yet, so traffic traveling from New York to Boston went right through communities along the Connecticut shoreline. The Merritt Parkway had already been built in the 1930s, but trucks were not allowed on it, so all the trucks had to come this way instead.

The Unexpected

When I was about twenty months old, my father took my mother to the hospital to deliver my first sister. My mother later told me that she and my father were not fully aware of what I could understand at that time, because I was just barely starting to talk. So they never tried to explain to me what was happening. They just dropped me off at my grandmother's house (my grandparents lived in the same town as we did) with some of my clothes and toys, and disappeared. This may have been in the middle of the night (whenever my mother went into labor), but I don't remember for sure.

In those days, women typically stayed in the hospital for an entire week after delivery, to recuperate. My father spent most of that time at home and went to work each day. So I lived at my grandmother's house for the entire time. Finally, my grandmother drove me home and took me upstairs to where my mother was sitting on her bed, with my sister in a bassinet nearby. My mother says that when we arrived, she smiled at me and said hello, but I looked at her as if she were a stranger and clung to my grandmother's skirt. It took several minutes for me to warm up and accept a hug.

Years later, my mother apologized to me for the way they handled this. Looking back, I don't really blame them; they just didn't know any better. But I sense that their sudden unexplained absence was a big shock to me at the time.

§ § §

Soon after that, as I began to talk more, life shifted in two significant ways.

One, I was toilet-trained around age two. I don't think I was ready, but with my sister still an infant, and my mother doing almost all the childcare (my father being at work all day), I think she reasoned that keeping two children in diapers was a daunting task. So I had to wear "training pants" which were very uncomfortable when I wet them. I was supposed to learn to hold it in and ask to be put on the potty instead.

The other shift was that, in my father's eyes, my starting to talk somehow signified to him that I should be able to manage my emotions with my newly developing intellect. When I acted out as a child, such as getting frustrated and throwing a toy on the floor, or refusing to do as I was told, he took it personally and often responded with rage. I remember being spanked sometimes, but I was never hit with any hard objects.

But that wasn't the problem. The problem was that his rages included threats of terrible harm. His level of energy, as evidenced by his very loud voice, the look in his eye, and the tension in his entire body, was very convincing! He would yell things like, "If you don't get up those stairs this instant, I'll break every bone in your body!!!" He stood at the bottom of the stairs and started to count to three. I was terrified.

It seemed to me that if I did one more thing wrong when he got like this, he would lose control and assault me to such an extent that I would end up in the hospital with broken bones or worse.

My reaction to this was to shut myself down as completely as possible. I would look down, not say anything, not move a muscle except as he commanded, and even breathe as little as possible, in case anything I did would finally push him over the edge.

But sometimes, even that didn't work. One time, just before bedtime, I was trying to button up the front of my pajamas. For some reason, he concluded that I was pretending to have trouble in order to get my mother to help me and delay going to bed. He started yelling and said if I didn't do it any faster, he was going to "slug" me. He raised his right hand, out to one side, ready to slap me across the face and started counting. I was crying and my mother was pleading for him to stop. I don't think he actually hit me, but I was so upset, I can't even remember exactly how it ended.

I was left wondering if indeed I had been pretending to have trouble, just to get my mother to help me. I stayed confused about my own motivations long after that. Years later, when I was in my thirties, someone said to me, "Who cares? You were only three! Perhaps you needed your mother's attention and didn't know how to get it any other way." I finally realized that I was actually having trouble manipulating the buttons. It had literally taken decades of self-doubt for me to finally understand that.

But back then, I really didn't know what to expect. I think somewhere deep inside, I remained worried that another scene like that might happen at any time. My mother tried to get him to stop by reasoning with him or calming him down. This had mixed results, at best. She was also afraid of him when he got like this, so she didn't have the courage to put her foot down and insist that he change his behavior in any significant way.

We ended up in a classic triangle, sometimes known as "persecutor, rescuer, victim" where the three people involved keep repeating the same pattern over and over again because they have no idea how to work their way out of it.

I remember a few times wishing he had actually hit me, so that I would have bruises to show someone else. That way, someone outside the family would believe me and get him to stop. But there was never any evidence.[9]

---

[9] In a way, perhaps that was probably for the best, because if he had actually attacked me physically, and I ended up injured, some authority might have broken up our family, and that would have been a disaster of even worse proportions. Of course, many times, in those days, officials took no action, which might have made things at home much worse instead.

I wasn't the only one who experienced all this. As my siblings got old enough, the same things would happen. I watched him fly into a rage at my sisters and brother at times, when he thought someone had "disobeyed" him.[10]

In spite of all this, he was a loving father to us at other times. He let me accompany him down to the basement where I could watch him work at his workbench, or play out in the yard while he was doing yard work. He showed great patience when it was time to teach us how to ride a bicycle, practice catching a baseball, plant seeds in our backyard garden or even when he was tucking us into bed at night.

§ § §

When I turned three, a very significant event occurred.

I got a tiny speck of something stuck in my eye. I don't know how this happened, but I woke my mother up in the middle of the night and complained to her that, "When I close my eye, I cry." I don't remember my exact words, but my mother remembers me telling her that. I remember what it felt like. When my eyes were open, I was fine, but when I tried to close them, there was this painful scratchiness in one eye, under my eyelid. It was so painful that couldn't keep my eye closed.

The next day, she took me to the eye doctor and he discovered a tiny speck on the surface of one of my eyeballs. He was able to remove it with a magnet, as it turned out to be metal or rust which had somehow lodged there.

But, there was still a problem. Although he was able to remove the object, there was a small surface infection where it had been. I remember sitting in the exam chair in his office. He told me to look at a spot way up on the ceiling while he tried to remove the infection. Being the careful little boy I was (for whatever reason - born under the sign of Virgo perhaps?) I noticed three little specks in the paint on the ceiling, any one of which could be the spot to which he was referring. I couldn't make up my mind which one to stare at. I had no idea that it didn't really matter to him, as long as I kept my gaze in that general direction and held still. But later, I felt guilty for not knowing which one he wanted me to stare at, and not having the courage to keep asking him until I understood.

Each time he tried to remove the tiny bit of infected tissue, I flinched or blinked. He explained to my mother that he would have to complete the work in the hospital, with me under general anesthesia. I don't remember any of that conversation, but later that evening, after dark, my mother took me to the hospital.

Unfortunately, the hospital at which the eye doctor had admitting privileges had a pediatric ward but no place for parents to stay with their children. So the hospital staff told my mother to go home after she took me there. She obeyed them and left

---

[10] Recently, when I discussed this with one of my sisters, she said they thought I bore the brunt of dad's rage, more than they did.

me there for the night. I was scheduled for the operating room at one o'clock the next afternoon, so I had nothing to eat or drink all night or the next morning.

I do not remember sleeping or even trying to sleep in the hospital that night. I have dim memories of having to say goodbye to my mother as she left. I have one image in my mind of lying on a table, on my back, and turning my head to see a green tile wall and someone wheeling in something that looked like a black 35-gallon drum, next to me.

My mother told me years later that she remembers standing in the kitchen that night, finishing up the dishes and realizing that she had done the "wrong thing" by leaving me there, but she could not think of what to do as an alternative by then (that late at night), so she finally went to bed. She has regretted this, and has since apologized to me.

When it was over, my parents came by later that afternoon to pick me up. I don't remember that, but I know I was wearing an eyepatch over that eye. I do remember being at home days later and my parents (and I think grandparents or great aunts) telling me that I looked "debonair" or "suave" wearing my black eyepatch.

This incident left me with a deep emotional wound, which still has some resonance for me, even now.

Early On

Before I was seven, we lived on a small street, near the center of town. Our street curved around with both ends connected back to Main Street, so there was almost no traffic. My parents had only been married for a few years when I was born. I was the first of four children.

Our house was surrounded by other houses with elderly people living in them, either couples or single women living alone, so I had no other children my age to play with. My mother ended up isolated in a similar way, as there were no other mothers around who were raising children my age for her to socialize with. I was given toys and I figured out how to amuse myself with them, while my mother cooked and cleaned, often with the radio on, tuned to a morning interview program on WOR, from New York City. Sometimes, she relaxed by reading "ladies'" magazines. She loved me and cared for me, but she was somewhat insecure about her new life as a stay-at-home mom, so she was preoccupied with trying to do a good job of it. My first sister was born before I was two, and another sister came along before I was four, so my mother stayed pretty busy.

§ § §

Our house had oil heat, but the people next door had coal. A big truck used to come to their house and back into their driveway. The driver would attach a metal chute to the back of the truck that led down into their basement coal bin. Then the engine would rev up, the dump body would lift up, and coal would start pouring down the chute. The coal made quite a racket as it slid and tumbled down in the metal trough.

I was fascinated with this process. The main staircase in our house did not have any carpet on it; it was just bare wood, and relatively steep. So I would take my box of little wooden blocks to the top of the stairs and dump all the blocks down the stairs, "Crasssssshhh!" to simulate the sound, the falling, the whole drama of the coal delivery process. My mother later told me that the sudden loud noise would startle her at first, as she stood working in the kitchen. Then she would remember, "Oh, that's just Glenn, dumping his blocks down the stairs."

§ § §

The theory in those days was that children needed consistency to feel that life was dependable. But it was clear that I was not meant for that!

Back when I was being potty-trained, the idea was for me to sit on the potty chair, on the floor in the kitchen,[11] at the same time every morning for "serious business." But I was never "regular" in that way. As a result, I ended up sitting on that thing for something like twenty minutes at a time, totally bored, and usually unproductive.

---

[11] Although this might seem like a strange location, this was the easiest place for my mother to check on me, as our only bathroom was upstairs.

By the time I was old enough to sleep in a bed rather than a crib, I remember lying awake (for probably an hour or more) on some nights, not feeling sleepy at all. When this happened during the summer, I would sit up and stare out the open bedroom window with my elbows on the windowsill and my chin in my hands. I gazed out at our empty street, under the dark sky.

There was a street light across from us, with a naked lightbulb under a white enameled reflector, shining down onto the pavement. It was very rare for a car to come along, but occasionally, I would hear the faint whoosh sound made by a car on Main Street as it passed by the end of our street. Sometimes, I could hear the high school boys who lived a few doors down, playing horseshoes and talking. I couldn't see them but I could hear the horseshoes go "thump" in the pit or "clank" as they hit the post.

The rest of what I could see – the houses across the street, the trees, sidewalk and plants – was all bathed in a faint bluish moonlight. I could hear crickets and other bugs making their sounds in the darkness. I remember sitting there, bored, but at least with something to look at, for what seemed like a very long time. Sometimes, I would go back to lie down, but still not sleep, so I would sit up again and look out some more.

By the time I was in my mid-twenties, I came to understand that I experience lunar cycles. A few of my friends seem to react quite negatively to me when I explain this. It's almost as if describing the effects of the moon turns me into some kind of religious fanatic or something! They say there are studies that prove the moon has no effect on human behavior. I don't know about their studies. All I know is what I experience, and believe me, the effects seem to be quite real!

Just before the moon is going to be full, about three to five days in advance, I'm more likely to be energized, need less sleep (or sometimes none at all, for the entire night), be more optimistic and creative, and have greater sexual energy. Then, once it's full, and for a day or two after, it is often payback time, where I might sleep for nine or ten hours for a few nights, or take naps in the afternoon, to catch up. This doesn't *always* happen, but it certainly happens a lot more often than not.

Looking back, it seems very likely that this started when I was quite small, although I had no idea about the possible effect of the moon's cycles back then.

The Erection

When I was about four years old, I was standing out in front of our house on a warm sunny Saturday in the spring. We had a small house with a small front yard with a little cement walk that led up to the front door from the edge of the street (there were no sidewalks). It was a warm enough day for me to be wearing shorts. My father was doing some kind of yard work nearby.

At some point, I remember that I had one of those little boy erections. I had no idea why my body was doing that. I felt the pressure, but no sexual euphoria that I know of. My shorts sort of poked out in the crotch area. I felt embarrassed, for some reason. I held my hand over the area and tried to push my penis back in, so it wouldn't show.

My father saw me doing this and asked me, suddenly, "What are you doing?" I don't remember how I answered, but he said not to do that; it would eventually go down by itself.

I remember feeling even more embarrassed after he noticed me doing that. So, I didn't say anything else.

§ § §

My mother told me years later that when I was around five years old, I told her that I wished I had a "flat wee-wee"[12] as my sisters had. I don't remember saying this, but it seems like something I might have mentioned. I don't remember what she told me, at the time.[13]

I'm not sure why I did or asked these things. I didn't really think about it. It was just a reaction to my own body, I guess. I don't think I hated my body, per se. It occurs to me now that I wanted a girl body a little more than mine, perhaps. As if being female would be a little better, or more comfortable or satisfying somehow.

---

[12] The children's bathroom language we used in our family for peeing, and as a noun for genitals.

[13] My mother recollects trying to reassure me, by telling me that I was going to grow up to be a father. Perhaps I didn't think that was very appealing? She also said that her parents told her that they thought my father paid more attention to my sisters than to me. They had heard him say that he thought little girls were cuter than boys. My mother now says she thought that little boys were more fascinating.

The World Outside

When I was four, my mother took me around to the other end of our street, to a nursery school run by an older woman in her own house. Although there were other children there, most of whom lived on other streets nearby, I had already developed a routine of occupying myself. I found a set of blocks in the back room and built things with them. Somehow, my focus was on my own designs; I don't remember collaborating with the other children that much. There I was, at age four, and I had already adapted to a life of isolation from other children, I guess.

The woman who ran the school didn't seem to do a whole lot to integrate me with the others. Mostly, she worked alone or had one assistant, and there were a number of us children, so I guess I "was a good boy" and didn't seem to need a lot of attention.

When I got to kindergarten, one thing they had in the classroom was a set of large blocks. They were actually small empty corrugated cardboard boxes printed with a graphic on the outside to make them look like a few rows of red bricks, complete with light-colored mortar between each row.

I had started to play with some of them, trying to build something, when the other boys in the room took them all away from me. I was upset to the point of tears, so I went to the teacher to complain. She counted out how many blocks there were and how many boys wanted to play with them, and then divided them proportionally. As I was playing alone, I received three such blocks. The other boys were playing together in a group, so they got the rest.

So, I sat there with my three blocks. What could I do? I put two down on the floor, side by side, and then put the third one on top of the other two, at which point, my building career was quickly over.

The other boys were playing "fort," but I had no idea what that was. You see, their houses all had TV sets, and this was the age of Davy Crocket and Western dramas, with gunfights, forts, cavalry, and cowboys and Indians plots. Because we didn't have a TV, I was clueless about all this. Anyway, I had no interest in pretend gunfights. I didn't know the other boys outside of school, so I wasn't friends with any of them.

I didn't seem to want to play with the girls either, I just wanted to build things (or draw things on paper). I had come from a long line of inventors, engineers and artists, so I guess this shouldn't surprise me. My grandfather had over 300 patents, but by the time I knew him, he worked alone in his brightly lit basement with metalworking machines, while my grandmother was upstairs doing the housework. He was very creative, but also very isolated. She played the piano sometimes, and had painted in watercolors earlier in her life, so there was a tradition of fine art in the family as well.

Without good models of adults with an active social life, I remained socially awkward throughout childhood. I was well into my 20s before that would really change.

Blue and Gray

When I was young, I remember a picture in the newspaper of a very old man who had just died. He was over 100 years old, so it made news beyond just a regular death notice in the obituary pages. In his picture, he wore a military uniform with a small, funny-looking hat, as if someone had sat on it, but he chose to wear it anyway. It said he had fought in the Civil War. I was so young, I had no idea what that was.

There was this thing called the Civil War and he had been a soldier in it. That hat was part of his uniform. The photo was in black and white, so I had no idea what color his hat and uniform were. Nor would I have known the significance of the color being blue or gray.

Just think. When I was born, the Civil War had ended only eighty five years earlier, well within the lifetime of that man! His life and my life overlapped, at least just a little. I'm still amazed by that!

No wonder there was still racism. One lifetime was just not enough time for people to recover from the horror of the war and change their attitudes as well. Just think, one whole segment of the population had been kept as slaves, treated as less than human, less valuable than other people. And many people believed this! And yet, as I grew up, I eventually came to understand that it was all a lie. The truth is, we are all equally valuable.

Two Paths of Fear

As a boy, I pondered what men and women had to do when they grew up. Men had to go into the Army and women had to go into the hospital to give birth.

I didn't like either prospect. They both scared me. I was born and grew up male, and in those days, I didn't see any choice. Of course, I was just imagining.

I only had vague images in mind at the time. I didn't really know what it would be like to be in the Army. My father was drafted after World War II was over, so he was never sent into combat. His stories were mostly about stupid things that happened because there wasn't much of anything for them to do by then. But the idea of going through training and what I saw in movies documenting the war was pretty scary.

My mother's stories of going to the hospital to give birth were not very good, either. She was administered general anesthesia during the process, which was scary for her and scared me when she talked about it.

Either way, I felt powerless. When I got older, somebody else was going to take over my life for a time and I wouldn't have any say in it.

My mother has been a homemaker for my entire life. She had worked at an advertising agency and later at a bank for a few years before meeting my father, but after I was born, I never saw her leave the house to go to a job, except for some volunteer work. So I had little concept of the challenges women faced in the workplace. As far as I knew when I was young, men went to work and came home for dinner. Women stayed at home and took care of children, did the shopping and laundry, and made the meals.

The New House

My mother wanted to have four children. By the mid 1950s, with three children already, it was clear that our little two bedroom house would be much too small. So my father, a mechanical engineer,[14] designed a new house for us, creating a complete set of drawings. He drew them on large sheets of paper while sitting in the easy chair in our living room. He put the paper on a large wood board that was originally used for kneading bread. The board rested on the chair's arms, above his lap. He used an architect's scale, a T-square, and triangles to line things up, as he worked.

I remember my mother, from time to time, standing next to him at one side, looking down at the drawings and pointing at things, as they discussed the details of how they wanted everything arranged. How big would the bathroom be? Can we fit two basins? Where would the light switches go? They seemed to cooperate quite well while doing this, sharing ideas and respecting each other's opinions and suggestions.

He took the drawings somewhere and they made blueprints of them, so they came out with white lines on a dark blue background. He also typed out all the specifications on a manual typewriter. I don't remember his doing the typing, but I do remember the pages formed kind of a book with a black cover, when they were done. Our new house was to be a split-level, a popular design at the time.

My parents hired a builder and had the house built on a piece of land they bought, a few miles north, in the same town. We didn't have enough money to finish it completely, so the slab level had a family room with unplastered gray wallboard on the walls, and a rough plastered ceiling that was also gray, since it was left unpainted.

That level also had our downstairs bathroom, which had only smooth, blank, white plastered walls, and a rough cement floor. There was a toilet off by itself in the far-left corner, and a small basin on the right-hand wall with a medicine cabinet, mirror, and two fluorescent lights, one on each side, that blinked when you turned them on. In the near left corner, a pipe stuck up out of the floor almost waist high, with some wadded up paper stuck into the opening at the top. That was where the shower was going to go someday. We stored boxes in the empty space where the shower and closet would eventually go.

I remember being afraid to use the toilet in that bathroom. I can't exactly say why. I think the emptiness of the room was part of it. The flush valve in the toilet would get stuck sometimes, so it would keep running long after someone had flushed it and left the bathroom, wasting water. Later on, someone would hear water running and one of us would have to go down there and jiggle the handle to make it stop. To me, it

---

[14] His degree was actually in aeronautical engineering. During World War II, he worked for Chance Vought, on the Vought F4U Corsair. After the war was over, the company moved to Texas, but he decided not to relocate. When I was young, he worked designing sewing machines at the Singer Manufacturing Company.

seemed as if the toilet itself was somehow defiant, as if it had a personality in a way, and I was afraid to approach it. If I was told to go down to stop it, I would stand only as close as necessary, reach over to touch the handle, then retreat and exit the room as quickly as I could.

I was afraid to tell anyone about this fear, so I kept it to myself. My father was irritated by my reluctance to use that bathroom or go down to fix the toilet, but that just made me more afraid. If he found out that I had an "irrational" fear, he might get angry and force me to go down and use it or even open the tank and tell me to reach down and settle the flush valve plunger by hand. The whole idea of this terrified me greatly, so I tried to hide my feelings as much as possible. Fortunately, he never found out, so he never made me do that, but I was afraid he would.

Years later, we had contractors come in and finish the bathroom in a bright yellow tile, with a shower, a closet, a new counter and basin, new lights, everything. It became my parents' master bathroom, so now it was outfitted with towels and toothbrushes. The toilet still sat in the corner where it had always been, but now in its own alcove of yellow tile, nestled in by the closet wall. Now, it seemed like a minor player in the scene. Somehow, after that, I felt a little less afraid to go down there.

Gravel Road

The Mack trucks
drove the dirt road
through the open field
beside our house
then way around back

A cloud of dust
rose up behind them
leaving an unwelcome layer
on our dining room table

We shut
the windows
that side of our house
all summer long

I was a boy
wearing shorts
and brown shoe laces
I ran down the road
on the hard dirt
to see where they went

A P&H shovel
bright yellow machine
black boom high
wire rope cables
over turning pulleys
diesel engine growling
dug gravel
from the hillside

The bucket fell open
into each truck
then swung back again
to dig another
until full

Then stop and rest
with soft low idle
until the next one
would come

An old man
in a shack
wrote paper receipts
for each driver
as they drove away

I sat with him
asked questions
He talked
We entertained each other

He had a riddle
to push a quarter
through the hole
in a piece of paper

But the hole was
too small
for a quarter to fit through
I had no idea

So he put his *finger*
through the hole
to push the
quarter along the
surface of the desk

Ha ha!
I was fooled
by word play
not physics.[15]

---

[15] I can't seem to find photos or videos of the smaller, older P&H diesel powered shovels, but if you search for "northwest cable shovel" you should get a video showing a similar machine.

Patriotic

Soon after we moved into our new house, we also got a second car, a dark blue Volkswagen Beetle. The house only had a one car garage, on the slab level, so the Beetle had to live outside in the driveway.

My parents were conservative Republicans, and my father wanted to fly the American flag[16] in front of our new house. So, he got a spent helicopter rotor blade from Sikorsky[17], and took it down to the basement, where it sat for a year or two. Eventually, he pried off all the ribs, stripped off all the paint and corrosion, and then sanded it down, primed it and painted it white. This was to become our new flagpole.

He and my grandfather dug a small deep hole next to the driveway, using a post-hole digger (a kind of double-handled shovel) and filled the hole with cement. They placed four pieces of metal into the wet cement, each protruding above the surface, with a hole at the top, carefully lined up so that the base of the flagpole could be bolted onto them, after the cement had hardened. The top of the pole had a little shiny metal ball that someone made with a lathe, and a pulley and cord, so you could raise the flag in the morning and take it down at night (in those days it was still considered improper to leave a US flag up all night, or out in the rain).

One morning, before school (I was probably seven or eight years old), I woke up and realized that it was raining very hard outside and I had heard thunder. I sat up, crawled over the covers down to the foot of the bed, put my elbows on the windowsill, and stared out at the rainstorm through the screen in the open window. The rain was coming down hard on the driveway and our cars, parked below.

Suddenly, "ka-BAAANG!" Lightning struck our flagpole with the loudest sound I had ever heard in my life! My ears were left ringing and the bright white streak left a greenish purplish copy of itself in my eyes. I heard my mother, down in the kitchen, exclaim, "What was *that*?" I jumped out of bed and ran downstairs to tell her.

---

[16] I think we should always call it the US flag; America is the name for two entire continents.

[17] After a certain number of flying hours, all helicopter blades are removed and replaced. My father had a degree in aeronautical engineering and had worked for Chance-Vought in Stratford Connecticut, right next door to Sikorsky. So he knew exactly where to get one that was otherwise going to be scrapped.

Housework

My father did many of the things typical of men in those days. He went to work every day at an engineering job, and he did most of the yard work and all of the repairs to the house. My mother did most of the grocery shopping and all of the cooking.

But in other ways, there were a few things that I took for granted that were not as typical. When company was coming, both my parents worked together to clean up. For example, my father had no problem vacuuming or scrubbing the bathtub while my mother was getting laundry done and preparing food.

Although we got a dishwasher just before we moved to our second house (it was on wheels, with a hose that attached to the faucet in the kitchen sink), many pots and utensils still needed to be washed by hand. It was just as likely that my father would be washing dishes as my mother. He even put an old apron on to protect his clothes sometimes. I remember him, many times, standing at the sink, doing this.

For awhile, he worked for the Singer Manufacturing Company, which had a factory in Bridgeport, Connecticut, where they made sewing machines. Around that time, they had just started to make a new model with a sleek new design. It had a flat top and came in some new colors (besides the traditional black with gold lettering). He was on the design team that worked on the zig-zag mechanism. They made a few prototypes in new colors, such as light yellow, pink, light green, pastel blue, white, gray, and black. The marketing department rejected the color gray, so they never made another gray one, besides that one prototype. Eventually, my father got to take the gray machine home.

I remember my father sitting at the sewing machine, perhaps on a rainy Saturday afternoon, down at the far corner of the family room. He was surrounded by piles of fabric and clothes that needed mending, making a pillow case out of the ends of a sheet that had worn out in the middle. He also made things from scratch. He made at least a few small aprons out of heavy white canvas with giant pockets in the front to hold clothespins, so that you could wear it outdoors when hanging up the laundry. He selected a cam,[18] and embroidered an image of a clothespin onto the front of each pocket, using bright red thread.

My father was never embarrassed or ashamed that he participated in housework like this. In fact, he was proud of it and never saw any reason not to be. As the result, I ended up with a sense that gender roles were not so cut and dried.

------

[18] In those days, zig-zag sewing machines came with a set of small black plastic cams, each about the size of a small cookie, with different shapes around the edge. You'd mount one on a spindle on the front of the machine, tighten the thumbscrew, and start sewing. A little pin rode up and down along the various bumps and curves as the cam turned. The pin made the needle shift back and forth to form a particular stitch pattern.

School Sucks

When we moved to our new house, it was the middle of May, and I was still in first grade. My little brother had just been born. I was about six and a half years old. There were only six or seven weeks of school left, but the principal of the new school told my mother that it was okay to take me out of my old school and put me in a class in her school right away. That way, my mother didn't have to drive me back to the other school every day, to finish up the year. So they took me in one day, and introduced me to a classroom full of kids I had never met, who had been there all year already. As I walked in, they were already sitting at their desks, looking up at me as I stood there with my mother behind me.

It was a social disaster. I was immediately "the new kid" in a class of children who had already had all year to get to know each other. Already bullied at home by my father, I had "victim" written all over me, so I was quickly made the target of teasing and bullying.

Even the school itself bullied me. In second grade, I had difficulty with what I refer to as "non logical'" thinking. We had an assignment to fold and then unfold a piece of tabloid sized newsprint paper, leaving it creased into eight squares. The teacher wrote a single letter of the alphabet in the upper left corner of each square. We were supposed to think of a word starting with that letter, then draw a picture of it in the box. If there was a "P" there, we could make a drawing of a pie or a porcupine, for instance.

But I could not come up with new words that started with the right letters, right out of thin air. I could only think of the same words every time. B for boy, D for dog, and so on. It seemed to me that using the same words over and over would not be good enough for what the teacher wanted. So, I sat there, stumped. Instead, I colored the same spot over and over again with the crayons, until the wax built up into a thick layer. It formed strange bumps when you did that, and I was curious as to why the bumps formed when the paper had started out perfectly smooth. Other times, I drew pictures of inventions I had in my head. I designed a machine that would tear up a road and lay down new pavement, all in one operation. I drew pictures of it, with smoke coming out of the engine's smokestack, and little stick-figure workers operating it.

The teacher punished me for not doing the assigned work by leaving me alone in the classroom to finish it while she took the rest of the children down the hall to lunch. This happened several times. I sat there, alone in the room, and struggled to come up with different words, but I was still no good at it. The stress of being told that I was being punished just made it all the worse. Often, I wasn't done until lunch was over. The other kids came back from lunch and went out to recess. I had to walk down the hall all by myself to have lunch during the next period, with the third and fourth graders.

I felt ashamed, humiliated, and scared. I was completely out of place, standing at the end of a line of bigger kids where I wasn't really supposed to be, having missed "my" lunch period. I often brought a bag lunch my mother had made for me, but I had to stand in line to buy milk. After I got my little carton of milk, I sat alone at a table in the far corner of the cafeteria and ate my lunch. I wanted to be as invisible as possible.

In general, I did not do very well in school. What I wanted to learn, they weren't teaching. What they were teaching, I often found uninteresting or pointless. I couldn't concentrate that well on "my" (their) work, so I got mediocre grades. I could do well on tests, so I got through, but often just barely. I lived under the constant threat of "being left back a grade," if I didn't "do better." That possibility seemed to be an almost unimaginably horrible fate. I had a hard enough time making any friends as it was, so being left back would have had me starting over, like another "new kid" in class. This threat hung over my head like a dark cloud throughout elementary school.

I remember later on, in junior high school, I was in the guidance counselor's office. Both my parents had come to school to meet with her. All three of them sat there and talked about me, referring to me in the third person. I just sat there and didn't say anything. My father said, "He's a bright boy, we know that, but he just won't do his work." And, "We wish we could find the key that would switch him on, somehow." They all nodded. I was right there in the same room and they barely looked at me.

I was as clueless as they were, at the time. I desperately wanted to do better. I didn't know why I couldn't do my work, I just couldn't make myself do it. I'd get home from school and the whole idea was just so overwhelming, I went out to play instead. I just procrastinated until it was time for bed.

My mother would call up the stairs, "Glenn, are you doing your homework?" A twinge of guilt would rush through my body. I'd say "Okay," out loud, so she could hear me answer. But it was a lie. I almost never did it.

Later in life, I came to understand that somewhere deep inside me, I was incredibly angry. Furious, really. Enraged! Angry that what I wanted to learn was ignored and what they wanted me to do was pointless, frustrating, politicized, poorly conceived, and hypocritical. The system was set up for conformity and obedience, the very opposite of the foundations of learning, which are freedom, curiosity, creative exploration, and critical thinking.

It wasn't until years later that I finally understood that there really wasn't anything wrong with me.

§ § §

Recently, I realized something else that hindered me. In our elementary school, there were three "tracks" of student capabilities. I don't know how the teachers and staff referred to them, but we all knew them as the "smart" kids, the "average" kids, and

31

the "dumb" kids. There were enough students for three classrooms of 23 students each for each grade, each in its own track.

I was always in the middle (or average) track classroom. Somewhere inside I realized an essential fact: If I did a lot better, they would probably move me up to the "smart kids" track. Once there, the work would be even harder, take more hours at home, and put more of a strain on me. The nuances of what literature "meant" (the hidden meanings, the metaphors, etc.) would get more obscure and even more difficult to discern. For me, in a more socially isolated family with a strong history of engineers, when it came to literature and poetry, I would feel more and more lost.

It didn't occur to me until now, decades later, that this contributed to what I came to call my "fear of success." Success, ironically, meant more pressure, more risk, more chances to fail. The rewards for working harder were perhaps some token acknowledgement (having my name mentioned at a school assembly, or being given a certificate of achievement). Such things seemed essentially useless to me. The real "rewards" seemed to be mostly negative: Expectations that I would work harder at more difficult assignments.

This fear ended up following me through life, leaving me to be frequently at cross purposes with my own desires for progress and accomplishment. What if I really became successful? Too scary. Too much responsibility. More expectations placed on me that I didn't feel up to meeting. My thought was, better for me to pull back from my big dreams and projects instead.

Of course, now that I've written this book, I do want it to be successful. There certainly are risks.[19] But even without those risks, I have had to constantly face a sneaky internal resistance to finish it. I often seemed willing to do something, *anything* else, but keep writing! I never expected it to be so hard to put this fear aside and get back to work.

I remember a scene from the movie, *Butch Cassidy and the Sundance Kid*, where the two robbers are stuck on a cliff and decide to jump into the river below. Even though it's risky, they do it anyway, because to stay behind would mean capture and certain death. That has remained a favorite scene of mine, ever since I first saw it.

Of course, my life is not nearly as dramatic as that! Still, I've come to realize that, on occasion, "staying behind" is not really a good option for me. Instead, I have to crank up my courage, take a risk, and "make the leap" to move forward.

---

[19] In many places here in the US, if I showed up in public wearing earrings and dress, I would risk being verbally ridiculed, harassed, or worse. In some cultures elsewhere in the world I would likely be attacked violently by a mob and perhaps even killed, right in the street.

School Triumphs

When I was eight, I got an electric train set for Christmas. The train just ran around a small oval track under the Christmas tree, but it was fun and I liked it. It was powered by a small transformer that produced a low voltage safe enough to energize the tracks without giving anyone a shock.

In fourth grade, the science book showed a diagram of a simple electric buzzer, so my father helped me make one on the workbench in our basement. It consisted of two metal pins, set into a wood base, with wire wound around each of them, and a piece of flat metal mounted to sit just above the pins. I used the electric train transformer to provide the electricity to make it work. Since the electric train ran on alternating current, the current in the wire caused the magnetic field in the pins to fluctuate, which in turn, caused the piece of metal to vibrate against the top of the pins. Success!

§ § §

When I got to fifth grade, they handed out the science books at the beginning of the year. Right away, I looked through the entire book to see if there was anything about electricity. There was nothing. I went right to the teacher but he only confirmed that we would not be studying electricity this year. I was crestfallen!

What we did have was a unit on the weather. There was a chapter about it near the end of the book, so we had to wait until spring to get to that. The science book showed how to make primitive weather instruments out of typical household items. We formed small teams of students, with each student on a team selecting one of the weather instruments to make and operate. I chose the anemometer, the instrument to measure wind speed. In the book, it was shown as a simple pair of thin wood slats, at right angles to each other, forming a horizontal cross with a small hole in the center. There were four waxed paper cups, one attached to the end of each slat. The whole thing was held up on a post and allowed to spin freely. One cup was red and the others blue, so that you could keep your eye on the red one as it spun around. That way, you could count how many revolutions it made in one minute, and thus how relatively strong or weak the wind was that day.

But I had a different idea. I drew a diagram of a wood framework, with a vertical shaft running up the center, supported by two real bearings. At the top of the shaft, I had two rods forming a horizontal cross with four metal cups, one at each end of each rod.[20] Down near the bottom of the shaft would be a wooden spool with a small copper strip attached to one side, two strips of copper that rubbed against the side of the spool, a battery, some wires, and a small flashlight bulb. Every time the shaft and the spool went around one revolution, the copper strip on the spool would come around to touch the two copper contacts, completing the circuit and causing the bulb to blink on and then off.

---

[20] See the Anemometer Wikipedia article for pictures of similar instruments.

I went home and showed my father my idea, and he agreed to work with me to build it. I was too young to use the table saw or the heavy tin snips, so he cut the pieces of wood and metal, and then helped me assemble it. I brought it to school and my group used it to record relative wind speed.

On the last day, when we went out on the playground to take measurements, it was bright and sunny, but much windier than it had ever been before. None of the other teams could get a wind speed number because the little cups were spinning around too fast to follow the red one with the naked eye. But our team was successful! I remember a girl on my team, leaning in close to the bulb, with her hands cupped tightly around it to keep out the sunlight, so that she could see it flashing. She counted off, "One, two, three, four, ..." while someone else looked at a wristwatch to measure one minute. I felt so proud!

§ § §

There were a few other high points, where I found a way to combine my intense curiosity and creativity with the school's curriculum, but mostly I just survived school with a constant low level of stress.

Socially, I was a boy who didn't really belong anywhere, not with the smart kids (who were in advanced English, math, and science classes), not over in the shop, with the kids who were headed for jobs in the trades right out of school (without any college), not in the gym or out on the field in athletics, and not hanging around talking with the girls.

Recess

I remember watching girls play on the playground when I was in elementary school, probably in third or fourth grade. They were pretending to be horses. One particularly tall girl had long hair pulled into a ponytail, so her appearance and her fantasy all seemed to fit together.

I didn't actually want to play with them on the playground, per se. But I didn't really like the kind of competitive play that the boys often engaged in, either. Sometimes, a few boys and girls played together on the swings, which I enjoyed much more.

One night I had a dream that I was over at the house of the girl with the ponytail. We had been playing together and then she said I had to leave and go back home, because she was feeling sick. I remember in the dream wanting to be just like her, even if it meant being sick myself. But I did as she asked and went home instead.

The Ocean Liner

Once I was dreaming that I was lying face down above an ocean liner with a swimming pool in the middle of the top deck. I rolled from one side to the other, but each time I rolled past the middle, I could feel the wetness of the pool against my torso. It was too hard to stay on either side, so I kept rolling back and forth.

I awoke in the middle of the night. I had wet the bed again. My pajamas were wet and the bed had a big wet spot in the middle. I had been rolling back and forth across it in my sleep.

I got up and went to get my mother. She came in and pulled the quilted pad out from between the sheet and the rubber sheet below and put a large towel over the wet spot. She helped me out of my pajamas, gave me a warm wet washcloth to wipe myself off, then I put on a clean set of pajamas.

I went back to bed, worried that the wetness under the towel would seep up through. But after realizing that I would stay dry enough, I eventually fell back asleep.

Nobody knew how to stop my bed-wetting from happening. There was even a device that would set off an alarm as soon as the first drops of moisture were detected, but we never got one.

We did go to the doctor, who prescribed some pills to take. When I took them, my urine came out a royal blue color. In the boys' bathroom room in school, the urinals were the old tall ones set into the wall, with the drain down at floor level. The other boys could see between my legs and observe the blue color liquid running down. I had trouble explaining why this was happening so they just judged me as even more weird than before. No one else in school had ever peed blue. It never occurred to me to just go into a stall and pee there instead.

Years later, my mother told me that when I was an infant, I was a very sound sleeper. I never seemed to move or roll over. She said that was convenient for her because there was little risk that I would ever fall out of bed. It turns out that very deep sleep is one of the causes of enuresis (bed-wetting).

I think I was twelve the last time it happened. I was at summer camp. It was terribly embarrassing.

Tree Tops

At our new house, there was a low stone wall along the edge of our front lawn, separating it from the sidewalk and the road out front. It was really just a row of loose stones piled on each other, without any mortar. It extended all along the road in front of the other houses and empty lots on either side. The only openings it had were for driveways.

In our front yard, along the wall, there were four or five large deciduous trees growing, a few maples and a linden. They were large enough to form a continuous spread of branches all across the front edge of our yard, extending out over the road to form a canopy with similar trees on the other side.

In warmer weather, I used to climb one of the maples almost to the top. I would climb as high as I could, until I was just below the branches that were too small to support my weight. I was probably about 40 feet high, certainly well above the highest point on the roof of our house. I took a camera up there once and took a photo of our whole house.

I must have climbed up there over a thousand times during the years we lived there. In the spring, as soon as the weather was warm enough, I would usually climb my favorite tree when I got home from school. I was very good at it and never fell. One time I decided to see how fast I could get up to my typical sitting place. I think I made it in something like 23 seconds.

From the top, I could see over the roof of our house, as well as over the roofs of other nearby houses. I could see beyond our backyard, over the dirt road that went to the gravel quarry, and even back to the trees that surrounded the pond behind that.

Although I never built a treehouse up there, the branches and leaves that surrounded me formed a unique kind of space - at once high up above the world, but at the same time, cozy and safe and secluded. This was my own personal place to enjoy. I remember the feeling of contentment I had there.

I was above and out of reach of the adult world. Above the traffic on the road below. Above our house. Above my room with my desk and my school books. Above school itself (although I couldn't see it from there). It was up to me as to when I wanted to come back down.

Occasionally, my sisters also climbed those same trees and enjoyed the view and feeling of being in a similar place. We could even talk back and forth from where we were, from one tree to the other. This was one of those times where we were just siblings and gender didn't matter. Almost anyone could climb a tree if they were strong enough and weren't afraid.

Boys and Girls

Looking back, I realize that I envied many things girls had. All infants are "cute" at first. They are held and fed and wrapped in soft blankets. People stare into the crib and smile at them to see if they'll smile back.

But as toddlers, girls were already considered cuter and got more hugs, kisses, and soothing words from their parents than the boys did. When they got older, it was more acceptable for girls to scream and giggle and show fear while playing. If a girl ended up in tears, she was more likely to be comforted. Boys were more likely to be told to stop crying. Girls got to cuddle with each other, be sweet to each other, and talk about feelings more openly.

In addition, girls got to dress in a greater variety of clothes, often in bright colors. They were told they looked "pretty," and encouraged to feel good about themselves as a result, whereas boys were supposed to look "handsome." But boys' clothes were a lot more plain and boring, so looking handsome did not seem nearly as good to me. The little jacket and tie I had to wear to Sunday school was like a uniform all boys had to wear. Being handsome seemed to mean that I would quickly fade into the background and never really feel special.[21]

Boys were discouraged from doing many of the things girls could do. You had to keep a lot more to yourself, in terms of both physical and emotional affection. Boys were expected to learn to respond to violence with violence (if they hit you, hit them back!). Early on, boys learned that you had to do certain things to "be a man" or prove you were a man when you grew up, whereas I never heard girls being told that they had to prove themselves to be "a woman." It seemed as if they would just grow up to become one.

I know that girls could be mean to each other sometimes, so it wasn't always that great to be a girl, necessarily. Of course, there was a pecking order among all children in school. Some were the popular ones, some were average, and some were outcasts. Sometimes that hierarchy seemed to be forgotten, at least based on my memory of doing oral reports in science in the sixth grade. Students were mostly supportive and asked reasonable questions, regardless of their social status.

If a girl wanted to wear pants, climb trees, play sports, or was interested in technical things, she might be called a tomboy but I think people in general were somewhat in awe of that. If a boy was interested in the things that girls usually did, he had to hide all that for fear of being labeled a sissy or "a girl" (as if that word alone, when applied

---

[21] Even today, when I watch the Academy Awards, the men are all wearing tuxes. All the fuss on the red carpet is about the gowns the women are wearing. I've often fantasized about being the first man to wear a gown on stage there. Of course, I'm writing a book, not making a movie, so I have no idea how that might happen!

to a boy, was an awful fate). So I guess some boys kept a lot of fear inside, lest they "step out of line" and not stay male enough.

Of course, for girls, things changed when puberty came along. Any girl who was a tomboy was likely told that she had better adopt more "feminine" ways or she would risk never "getting a man" and might never get married. There was a fear that not being married would be a dead end in life. Girls were taught that they had to be careful, lest they teased boys too much sexually. So, by then, I guess girls started to experience more fear. Dating was perhaps more of a tightrope walk for girls - they had to try to attract boys, but they were told "don't go too far!"

And yet, girls seemed to be able to confide in each other a lot, even after puberty. There was competition for the attention of boys, sure. But at the same time, I sensed a general mutual support system as girls got older - they could talk about their feelings toward boys, toward each other, and about other things in general. As boys, we were socialized to be strong and not be afraid and to keep our feelings to ourselves, lest we be seen as vulnerable. It was okay for boys to talk about sports or cars or intellectual stuff instead.

These were the things I observed growing up in the 1950s and 1960s. This was the era when the old "one size fits all" culture of uniformity was still the norm. Gender was "binary," as we now say. We had male and female. That was it. Any child who varied more than a little from that provoked a sense of concern among adults. People were afraid you'd grow up to be marginalized at best, or even ostracized as some kind of freak.

Remember, this was before the word "gay" had come into use to describe sexual orientation. The term we used was "homosexuals" and that entire topic was almost never mentioned, and when it was, there was always a tone of disdain. Sure, there were occasionally couples, such as two old women who lived together in a house, or perhaps two men, but they were just "old friends" who had "never gotten married"[22] or something. People made various excuses or used vague language. The idea that they might be "in love" with each other or have sex with each other was just put out of mind.

---

[22] They meant not married to an opposite sex partner, as marriage between same sex partners was not legal then.

Little League

One Saturday, when I was still in elementary school, I tried out for Little League baseball. I remember an adult was in the batter's cage, hitting balls out into the field. Each potential player had to try to field a few of them. When it was my turn, I waited until the ball hit the ground, then went in to grab it with my glove and throw it back.

We were put into three leagues: the "Major," "Minor," and "Cap" leagues. I ended up being in the Cap league. Boys in the Major and Minor leagues got real baseball uniforms; in the Cap league, we got T-shirts. Okay, I accepted that. I was disappointed but I wasn't all that gung-ho about baseball anyway.

My team went to practice one Saturday afternoon at a nearby baseball diamond. Just boys and their fathers were there, as girls were not permitted in Little League then.

During fielding practice, I was in the field when someone hit a high fly ball. From the sidelines, I could hear people calling out to me, "Run in! Run in!" So, in an attempt to catch the ball on the fly, I ran in right under the ball, looked up at it, and held my glove up to try to catch it.

My glove, however, was a bit too low. The ball came down directly into my left eye socket. BANG! Suddenly, all I could see appeared to be very bright fireworks on a black background. I fell to the ground, stunned, disoriented, and in immediate pain. People ran out from the sidelines to reach me. I don't remember what they said, but it was clear what happened and their responses were sympathetic.

I was taken home and someone called a doctor. As it turned out, a doctor lived on a street near us and he agreed to come over to look at it. He even arrived with the classic little black doctor's bag.

He looked at my eye and the surrounding area. He concluded that my eye was not damaged in any permanent way and no bones were broken. I would have to put something cold on it and wait for a few days for the swelling to go down, and the bruising would go away after that.

Someone suggested that when I went to school the following week, I should say, "Well, you should have seen the other guy!" – as if I'd been in a fistfight and had beaten someone else more severely. It was meant as a humorous remark, of course. They meant well. They wanted to prime me with something to say if I got teased or was asked probing questions. But the message behind that suggestion is now clear to me. It was more honorable to have been injured through violence than just by accident.

§ § §

Recently, I reflected on that experience. I wonder if perhaps that set me up for cluster headaches later on in life. The headaches were always on the left side of my head, but I really don't know if that incident contributed to them.

But what I now realize is that I naturally kept my distance from the ball, at first, because it was dangerous! I could have been hurt much worse (a skull fracture, perhaps?). I might have had a concussion from that (I probably did) but I didn't show any obvious symptoms, so I was never diagnosed. After all, in those days there were no CT scan or MRI machines, and the attention paid to head injuries wasn't nearly as intense as it has become more recently.

There was clearly a gender line of demarcation in sports. Girls played softball and field hockey. Boys played baseball and football. Boys were expected to take greater risks, go for more impact, and be exposed to injuries more often. Girls were expected to be better cared for and protected. This is not to say that there isn't danger in any sport, but that was the overall gender bias.

§ § §

I remember standing in the back yard holding my baseball bat. My father was pitching the ball to me so that I could practice hitting it. I was swinging as hard as I could. I really wanted to hit that ball into the next county. But I wasn't hitting anything. I got very frustrated.

My father suggested that I try to swing more gently and keep my eye on the ball a little more diligently. I still wanted to hit it really hard, but eventually I decided to try his suggestion. Well, then I hit one. It didn't go very far, just a short grounder. My father was happy that I had hit something and said that I was doing well.

But somewhere inside me, I was still frustrated. I was impatient. All I could see was the two options. Try really hard and hit nothing, or ease up and hit something but with little sense of satisfaction. It wasn't that my little ground ball would probably be picked up by the pitcher for an easy out. It was more that I was angry and frustrated inside because I desperately wanted to hit something really hard. That was what was missing.

A Nasty Surprise

At one point before I reached puberty, I was at a family holiday gathering at my grandparents' house. My cousins were there and some of us were playing in the backyard.

I had become engaged in a conversation with my cousin, a boy about one year younger than I was. He said he had to go to the bathroom, but we didn't want to interrupt our discussion, so we both went inside. It was just a small lavatory, off the back of the kitchen, but I was able to stand with my back to the window, facing him as he sat on the toilet across the room from me. We kept talking. Somehow, this didn't bother either of us. We really didn't give it a second thought.

Suddenly, there was an urgent knock on the door. My grandfather's voice came through from the other side of the door. He was loud and impatient. He asked if my cousin was in there. My cousin answered yes. I kept totally silent. Then he asked if anyone else was in there with him. My cousin answered that I was in there too. My grandfather's temper was on high by now. He yelled, "Glenn, are you in there?!?" I said yes. He yelled, "You come out of there this instant!"

I was confused. Was I doing something wrong? He was clearly furious! I opened the door, stepped out, and closed it behind me. He said, "Don't ever let me catch you in the bathroom with your cousin again! Do you understand me?!?" I nodded yes, but didn't say anything.

I walked back out into the yard. I felt stunned, frightened, and completely bewildered. What had just happened? My grandmother was out there and I asked her why Granddad was so mad at me. She stumbled over her words. She tried to explain that he didn't think it was right for more than one person to be in the bathroom at one time, but she really couldn't bring herself to explain directly that he thought we were in there to have to sex with each other.

Therefore, I remained confused about exactly what the problem was until much later. The idea that I would have any interest in sex with my cousin just never occurred to me.

§ § §

In spite of this incident (or perhaps in character with it), the whole topic of same-sex relations was almost never discussed. It's still a mystery to me as to exactly where my homophobia came from. One day while my father and I were doing something in the garage, I asked him what the word homosexual meant. He said a few things about anal sex, which I thought was disgusting, and that was it. Love was never mentioned.

Years later, in my early thirties, when I started peer counseling, I began to realize that I was about as homophobic as most people. I didn't hate anyone, or want to hurt anyone, but for some reason I was afraid of and put off by the whole idea. I just couldn't imagine myself having sex with other men.

Just as mysterious as the source of my fears seemed to be at the time, it was also a mystery as to exactly what motivated me to do something about my attitude toward it. Sure the peer counseling community recommended exploring the feelings. But somewhere inside, I wanted to work on it, too. So I did.

Swimming Lessons

When I was nine, after school on Friday afternoons, I had to go to my swimming lesson at the local YMCA.

My mother was convinced that everybody should learn to swim, just in case you ever had to, so she arranged it. I was terrified of deep water and I didn't want to go, but her idea was that if I learned how to swim, I wouldn't be afraid anymore.

School got out at 3:10 in the afternoon and I had to walk home from there. The swimming lesson wasn't until 4. We had to leave around 3:45 so my mother could drive me down to the Y. I spent the time in between sitting in my room, in dread. There was no way I could concentrate on doing homework! Not enough time, really, to do much of anything else. I felt as if I were in a dentist's waiting room or in a hospital bed just before surgery.

At the Y, we had to go to the locker room, change into our bathing trunks and shower before entering the pool room. This was boys only (the girls had a separate class). Everything seemed too cold. The shower was okay, I guess, but as we walked out into the pool room, still wet, the air in the room always felt chilly. The water was always just a little too cold.

There we were, a bunch of shivering boys, most of us skinny and not very athletic, sitting on a bench, being told how our bodies were supposed to float naturally, how swimming worked, and watching demonstrations by the instructors.

They started by teaching us the crawl stroke. The theory was, that if we learned that, considered to be the most difficult stroke, then all the other strokes would be easier to learn, later on.

First, they taught us to lie face down in the water and kick our legs rapidly, holding a rigid foam kickboard, in our hands, with our arms outstretched on the surface of the water ahead of us. Then we were supposed to learn how to give up the kick board and move our arms in a rotary motion, turn our heads to one side to take a breath, and then turn back, face down in the water, for each stroke.

I hated it. I couldn't see where I was going. I couldn't keep the different rhythms of my legs and arms going simultaneously. I was still afraid of the deep water. None of these techniques seemed to make any difference for me.

At the end of the last class of the season, we were supposed to jump into the water at the deep end, at one side of the pool, and swim across to the other side. The water there was six feet deep. One instructor was in the water, off to one side, in case anything went wrong, and the other was standing at the edge of the pool, as we stood in a line awaiting our turn.

When it was my turn, I was a complete bundle of denial. I jumped in and scrambled across, doing probably the worst version of the crawl stroke ever. I climbed out the other side, still tense and shivering and just about as afraid of deep water as I had ever been.

They said I passed, and gave me a "Minnow" badge to sew onto my swimming trunks. I took it, but I didn't want to wear it on my trunks. After all, having that badge visible would probably just get me into trouble as people would expect that I could swim in deep water.

Later that summer, I went to the day camp run by the Y. At the waterfront, they asked me to join the other boys, who had earned their Minnow badge, to go swimming out in the deeper part of the river. But I refused and stayed back in the shallow water, not sure what to do with myself.

The Swimming Lesson

Just before I turned eleven, my parents sent me to an overnight camp in Maine, on Long Lake, that lasted for eight weeks. I was pretty intimidated about being away from home for such a long time. I felt particularly out of place right at the start, as the trunk with all my camp clothes was delayed in shipment from home (my father had found a cheaper way to send it without realizing how inconvenient that would be for me), so I had to wear the same clothes for a few days until it finally arrived.

The counselor in my cabin taught waterskiing and had his family's own boat moored down at the waterfront, for that purpose. There were four main activity periods: swimming, boating, athletics, and crafts. Each day, we had four time periods, one for each activity, that rotated during the week. That way, you got swimming in the early morning on some days, and in the afternoon on others.

I liked crafts the best, and boating next-best. Athletics meant that sometimes I was stuck in the outfield on hot summer days, waiting until our half of the inning was over, as most of the boys couldn't hit a baseball out that far. I remember staring down at the grass and weeds around me, partly parched from the sun, feeling bored.

And then there was swimming. We had swimming lessons, but I don't remember much about them. At the waterfront, there were two docks, painted white, that extended out from the shore, with the shallow swimming area between them. There was a sandy area on the shore that extended down into the shallow area. There was a rope, with floats on it, that stretched across from the end of one dock to the end of the other, to divide the shallow section in the middle from the deeper water, farther out into the lake, sort of a classic arrangement.

There was also a large floating platform, off the end of the dock at the right, farther out into deeper water. It had a diving board, a high diving board, and a slide. It looked like fun when the other boys played on it during free swim, but I was still too afraid to go out there.

One morning, my group of cabins had swimming period in the late morning. There was plenty of time when it was over, before lunch, to walk up the long path, through the woods, up the hill to the dining hall. If you got back early, you could use the time to write a letter home or just sit and talk.

But that morning, my counselor (his name was Mac), who had been down at the waterfront with us, asked me to try something.

There was a little island, a little way off the dock to the left, and a few boats moored between it and the dock. Mac brought me out to the end of that dock, then he jumped into the water and swam a short way out to a boat mooring and turned to face me.

Then he asked me to swim out to him. He said he knew I could do it, that the only thing standing in the way was my fear. He said I could use any stroke I wanted. The dog paddle would be fine. It didn't matter. And I could take as long as I wanted before deciding to jump in. He said that when I got to him, I could grab onto him; I didn't have to tread water when I got there.

I stood on the end of that dock for what seemed like an eternity. I looked down at the water. Being a lake, the water was dark; the bottom wasn't visible. That actually helped as the depth of the water wasn't relevant, really, and not being able to see the bottom (as one would in a swimming pool) kept me from being distracted by that. But I was still shaking. I knew he was right, but I just couldn't jump. He said, "Take your time - only get in the water when you're ready."

I felt like I could almost jump in, and then I couldn't. I just stood there, leaning slightly over the water. This happened over and over, numerous times. I looked at him, then I looked down at my feet on the edge of the dock and then at the water between us. He said, "That's okay, whenever you're ready." I shivered and shook some more. I looked up and then down again.

Finally, the impulse to try it somehow upset the resistance that kept my feet on the edge of that dock. I jumped off the edge, into the water. I started doing the dog paddle, just as he said I could. I swam all the way out to him. And just as he said, I grabbed onto him and he held me when I got there.

I was still shivering and shaking but now it was with a completely different feeling. I was amazed at myself. I was all charged up. He said, "Now, do you want to swim back to the dock with me?" I said, "Yes, I think so." So, I swam back to the dock, with him swimming nearby, and climbed up when I got there.

We got our towels, dried off, and walked up the path through the woods to lunch.

The next day, we had a combined event with our sister camp, the camp for girls "next-door" to ours (just up the lake a bit). I remember being there and there was some time with nothing to do yet, waiting for whatever it was we were there for, to get started. It was a warm sunny day and I was wearing my swimming trunks.

I remember wondering whether I was really going to be okay swimming in deep water or whether what had happened the day before was just a fluke. There were no docks, just an open beach on that side of the peninsula on which the camp was situated. So I waded into the water until my feet barely touched the sand at the bottom. Then I pushed off and started to swim in a gentle arc, first out into deeper water a bit, then parallel to the shore, and then back in toward the beach again, until my feet could just touch down and feel the sand beneath.

It was remarkable. I wasn't afraid. I really could do it. I was amazed and pleased, and felt that tiny feeling of excitement inside, that little tingle you get when something new is going on and it's good.

47

§ § §

Later on, I realized the distinct contrast between what Mac did with me and the swimming lessons at the Y. The instructors at the Y were all about proper technique, competitive swimming, and a "get into the water" attitude.[23] Mac was all about a "come and join me in the water" attitude instead. His approach was that swimming was fun, and that the best way to deal with fear was patience and acceptance. It made all the difference in the world.

---

[23] Now, lest you get the impression that the people at the YMCA are somehow evil, I do not mean to imply that. Those swimming instructors were just doing what they were taught to do. Again, this was the world of the "one size fits all" standardized approach. Swimming was considered a competitive sport and proper technique was valued and judged at swim meets.

Boxing Lessons

Although I am not gay, I do have a strong feminine side. When I was a boy, I didn't really understand that about myself, but, looking back, I certainly was no good at most competitive sports (as boys were supposed to be), and I secretly envied the social interaction the girls seemed to enjoy with each other. As I mentioned earlier, boys could not be tender with or supportive of each other most of the time. We were each on our own to compete with others instead. I got teased and bullied a lot and once someone asked me if I was "a queer," a term with which I was not familiar (except from children's stories, where a "queer little old man" was mentioned, and which I thought just meant "strange"). So I was unaware of what they were referring to.

Because of my father's rages, I had become extremely afraid that someone's threats or expression of anger would lead to violence and I would be unable to defend myself. After all, I was typically smaller and weaker than they were. Some of the emotional scars of this have stayed deep within me for a very long time.

After we moved to our second house, and I walked into a class of strangers in first grade, it seemed as if I was already set up to be in the victim role, so the bullies took full advantage.

Being bullied was a source of much concern in my house. Both my parents had plenty of suggestions for things to say back to the bullies to defend myself against their taunts, but it really didn't do any good. I was frightened, and couldn't remember what to say. The real problem, my own lack of self-confidence, wasn't being addressed. Feeding me clichés to memorize did nothing to help.

One theory my parents had was that I just didn't know how to defend myself, physically. So, my grandfather helped them pay to send me to boxing lessons.

I didn't mind the lessons themselves so much. There were only a few boys in the small gym (situated in a small wood building, one floor above a car repair shop, surrounded by woods). We wore big fat boxing gloves and protective gear on our heads, so it felt safe enough to practice what I was being taught. When they said "no hitting below the belt" that meant that I was unlikely to be hit in the stomach, which was what I feared most. I didn't understand at the time that they really meant no hits to the groin, but as they didn't actually say that, I didn't really "get it."

But as you might be able to guess by now, all this technique really didn't help me out on the school yard. Bullying was mostly a psychological fight, not a physical one. I had pretty much lost before I got to the stage of hitting anyone else.

In a way, I was being bullied at home, by the other kids in school, and by the school system itself. I attended Christian Science Sunday school in those days, so there was no minister to approach, either.[24] My grandparents had a similar relationship, where my grandfather was the sensitive, easily upset and angered one, and my grandmother was the shy one who held back and tried to calm him down. Anyway, they were family, so whatever I might say to them might get back to my parents.

Even then, I didn't see any way that things could be changed, even if I were able to confide in anyone about how trapped I felt. The guidance counselors at school were part of the school system. They wanted me to get good grades like anyone else. It was clear that none of them or the teachers or other school officials did much of anything about the bullying. I think they just thought we'd all grow out of it.

So, I really had no port in the storm. No one really understood, or if they did, no one seemed to be able to change things in any significant way. Therapy, or its equivalent, didn't really exist. Back then, I remember my father saying that if you went to see a psychiatrist people would think you were sick (mentally ill) and you could lose your job and end up unemployable and destitute. That was the general attitude around that time.

I am, by nature, a non-violent person. Getting into a fistfight, when it finally happened (at my bus stop after school one afternoon, late in junior high), didn't actually solve anything at all. I ended up stumbling home in tears with the wind knocked out of me from being punched hard in the stomach. The next day, back in school, I was still the geeky boy who was stuck in pretty much the same status.

In spite of what I was told hundreds of times by my parents, "Just hit them once and they'll leave you alone after that," participating in that fight didn't really change anything.

---

[24] Unlike most other Protestant religions, Christian Science churches do not have ministers. Instead, volunteers read "the Lesson" at the front of the church every Sunday. The Lesson consists of selected paragraphs from the King James Bible and *Science & Health*.

The Bonfire

One night, in an empty lot behind our house, down by the pond, a bunch of boys had lit a fire and were standing around it. This was easily visible from the back of my house.

For some reason, I said something about how I wished I were able to go out to play with them, but I knew that at least one bully from the neighborhood was there and I didn't want to go.

My father decided that he was going to force me to go and fight the bully if necessary. My mother objected. But she could not stop him. He told me to put my jacket on (it was late fall, I think) and he was going to take me down there. I argued that I didn't want to go, but he was getting more and more insistent, so I had to.

When we got there, it was almost as if he were in the role of fight promoter. I can't remember what he said or any details except that I ended up in a fistfight with the kid who was the scariest bully at that time. That kid easily beat me up within a few minutes and the fight was over.

I was in pain and in tears, sobbing. My father was disgusted. I think he asked why I didn't use what I learned in boxing lessons, but I don't really remember. What I do remember was that I was practically crawling my way back home, still crying, in the darkness, with my father walking along nearby saying nothing.

§ § §

As much as this incident represents a family tragedy, it also seems to have something to do with gender as well.

I have often wondered if incidents like this contributed to my desire to identify more with girls. Certainly, my father never asked my sisters to do anything like this, although they got their share of teasing and bullying in school in different ways. Only boys were expected to defend themselves through violence. Although, admittedly, as far as I can tell, most boys would have just been terrified or miserable in such a situation, and thoughts about gender would never have occurred to them. I didn't really have any elaborate thoughts about how boys and girls were treated differently, at the time. I just had to live through it somehow.

Patriarchy

Unitarian Universalist (UU) principle:
"The inherent worth and dignity of every person."
(Practice this - it's hard!)

Thus:
Patriarchy is not a man
Patriarchy is not men
Patriarchy is a tradition
It is a way of thinking
Held by both men and women.

We're doing it with each other.
All of us.
And it will take all of us
Working together
To change this
And move to a new place.

And if you are a man
It's possible for you to have a life,
A good life.
A rich and rewarding life
Without practicing the damaging things
We call patriarchy.

And no matter who you are,
Please don't blame men,
As much as you might be tempted,
As hurt as you might be,
For the things that some men have done.

For, somewhere inside,
most men have been taught,
and many men still fear,
(and may even be terrified!)
that they will be nothing,
without patriarchy.

If we can show them
that we are all valuable, respected human beings
without patriarchy,
then it will be easier for us all
to move beyond blaming
and hurting each other.

Boy Scouts

When I turned eleven, my father took me to join the Boy Scouts. I joined a troop across town, but later, my father helped form a new troop closer to our home.

The Boy Scouts were perhaps my best overall social experience throughout my life in those years. We had troop meetings, but the most enjoyable parts were when we went on campouts and marched in the parade on Memorial Day each year. People along the sidelines always clapped when we came by. Although there was trouble between my father and me at times, we got along best when we were working together in the basement at the workbench, or at Boy Scout activities. He always came to meetings, and almost always went on camping trips with me, even in the winter.

I remember a dream I once had, where I was walking alone in a city. The streets around me were completely empty. There were intersections with traffic lights that changed from red to green, but no cars to respond. I kept walking until I reached the outskirts of town. There, I came across some railroad tracks and the street ended, so I stopped. From where I stood, I could see my Boy Scout troop, on the other side, just sitting there near an embankment, taking a break. In the dream, I didn't speak to them, and they didn't say anything to me, but at least they were there. Otherwise, I would have been completely alone.

In junior high school, there was a day when Boy Scouts all over the country were supposed to wear their uniforms to school. I think I was in eighth grade at the time. The idea was that people were supposed to suddenly notice how many of us there were, and be impressed by our uniforms and sense of belonging to something that we were proud of.

Exactly the opposite happened. Instead of inspiring respect, I was mostly met with derision and teasing. But it was too late. I couldn't go home and change. I had to wear it the entire school day.

Part of the uniform was a neckerchief that I wore around my neck, held in place with a slide under my chin, about where the knot in a necktie would be. The color and design of the fabric was the same for everyone in our troop, but the slide could be anything we chose. I had chosen one that was in the shape of our state with the word "Connecticut" in raised letters across the front. It was made of plaster of Paris with a small metal ring set into the back of it for the neckerchief to pass through. I had painted it so that it had a bright red border and the word Connecticut in gold.

In civics class (of all places), one of the boys grabbed it, pulled it off my neck and took it away from me. I asked for it back, but he held it just out of my reach. Finally, he handed it to another boy who pressed the metal ring against the edge of a desk so hard that it broke, cracking the plaster into pieces. He then handed the pieces back to me and said, "Oh, I'm sorry!" with that kind of insincere ironic tone that bullies have perfected over the centuries.

The Future

Everyone in Boy Scouts got a subscription to *Boy's Life* magazine, just by belonging to a troop and paying troop dues. There were articles about scouting activities, and display ads for tents and other camping gear.

In the back pages there were dozens of little classified ads for all kinds of things. Some of it pertained to the Boy Scouts directly, but most of the ads were for other things, such as comic book subscriptions, decoder rings, balsa wood glider planes, and the like.

I distinctly remember seeing one ad for a small device made out of red plastic with three little white dials mounted inside it. Each dial had tiny holes around the edge, numbered from 0 to 9. It was designed to add or subtract numbers. You could put a pencil point in one of the numbered holes, then use it to drag the dial around in a circle until it hit a stop. If you passed zero, it would "carry" to, or "borrow" from, the number shown on the dial to the left of that one. The headline said it was a "calculator." I think it cost 98 cents.

I remember thinking to myself, "Well, that's not a *real* calculator. I can't wait until they have *real* calculators!" What I wanted was what we eventually came to call a pocket calculator. But this was 1962! The kind of calculator I had in mind wouldn't be available until 1971, almost ten years later.

But somehow I knew we were going to have real calculators. I didn't just hope for one, I already knew they would exist. I knew approximately how small they would be, and that they would be inexpensive enough that I could have one. Perhaps I had seen articles in *Popular Science* magazine predicting their advent, but I was excited about the prospect and felt a little frustrated that I couldn't have one right then.

Somehow, in general, I've often yearned for something that is yet to be available or yet to take place in the future. Usually, I just know it will happen. I can't tell you exactly how I know, I just do. Perhaps it's my intuition. Perhaps I just look at current events in a different way, compared to most other people.

Playing with Numbers

When I was in seventh grade, the first year of junior high school, they started teaching the "new math." I was in the very first class to have it. The books were all brand new. My father wanted to help me with homework, but even *he* couldn't fathom some of the material, it was so foreign to him.

I struggled through it as best I could. But in my spare time, I was often daydreaming, doodling, and drawing pictures.

One day, I noticed something about the squares of numbers. You know, 3 times 3 (3 x 3, or 3^2) equals 9, $4^2 = 16$, $5^2 = 25$. I wrote them down in a column on a piece of graph paper. I saw that the difference between each of these squares was an odd number. Between 9 and 16, it was 7. Between 16 and 25, it was 9. Between 25 and 36 it was 11. Huh.

This seemed consistent as far as you went, up into larger numbers. Then I noticed that the odd number I had found was actually the two square roots added together. Aha! So the 7, (the difference between 9 and 16) was 3 + 4, the square roots of 9 and 16, respectively. And this was also consistent as I went up into larger numbers. Wow. I was fascinated by what I had discovered.

I wrote this down as $x^2 + x + y = y^2$. In my example, this would be 9 + 3 + 4 = 16. I thought this was so cool, I took it to my math teacher at school. He took one look at it and said, "Oh, that's called polynomials." I had never heard the word before. Right away he wrote it down as $(n + 1)^2 = n^2 + 2n + 1$.

Then, he told me that we wouldn't cover polynomials until next year. His tone of voice was pleasant, but he did not show much excitement at my discovery. He showed me a few other examples, and that was it. I walked out of the room, feeling empty.

This was in a "good" school, and he was considered a "good" teacher. But the annual curriculum reigned supreme, it seems. To him, my discovery was simply one year premature.

Years later, I was poking around on the internet and I came across an essay, "A Mathematician's Lament," by Paul Lockhart. I was quite heartened to find his support for what I had been doing! After reading it, I remained intrigued with his question about the area of a triangle where the apex is not directly over the base, like this:

I spent the better part of a week puzzling it out. I had a fantastic time doing it!

Compost Pile

At our new house, we had a sizable backyard. We got a rotary mower and had to walk it back and forth to cut all the grass. The part right behind the house had been seeded and kept as a traditional lawn. But a little farther back, it was pretty much wild field grass and other things. We mowed it all anyway.

We had milk and cream delivered to the house. We had a small insulated metal box on the back porch, with a hinged lid. We put the empty bottles in it, and a sign in the window as to how many bottles of milk and cream we wanted. Very early in the morning the milkman would come in a truck, take the empty bottles out of the box, replace them with full ones as we had requested, then drive off.

This service ran year-round. In the winter, when it was bitter cold out, the fresh milk was at risk of freezing, even inside the metal box. The insulation wasn't good enough to keep it liquid for very long. I remember my father getting up early sometimes, when he heard the truck come, and stepping out in his bathrobe to rescue the milk before it froze.

Way out in the back corner of the yard, where the land sloped downward a little, we had a compost pile. We kept a small plastic container in the kitchen sink, where we put food scraps, eggshells, orange rinds, and leftovers that had gone bad. When it got full or too stinky, someone would take it all the way out there and just dump it out on the pile. There was no organization to this otherwise. We didn't have a bin or a lid or anything to cover it. Birds used to come and peck at the seeds. In the winter it would just freeze, but in the warmer months, it would all slowly decompose.

On occasion, we had watermelon for dessert. We'd dump the rinds and seeds on the pile along with everything else. So, one summer, a vine sprouted. We realized that it was a watermelon vine. Soon, tiny melons started to grow along it. We learned that you can take a small container of water, sit it on the ground next to the vine, and keep at least one leaf dipped into it. This helps to hydrate the vine and grow a larger melon. Eventually, we had a good-sized watermelon on our hands.

Finally, it was time to harvest it. There we were, in the kitchen, and my dad was about to cut it open with a big knife. Suddenly one of us (perhaps my brother) asked, "What if we open it and it's full of old orange rinds, rotted vegetables, and egg shells?" We all burst out laughing! The mental image was so compelling. Why, of course!

Finally, Dad cut into it and sure enough, there was bright red watermelon inside. It was sweet and wonderful and we all enjoyed a slice.

Racism, Invisible

As much as I don't want to think about it sometimes, there is still some racism inside me. I don't want it to be there, but I know it is.

I was brought up in the 1950s and 1960s in a town that was almost completely white. Racism was invisible to me as a child because I seldom saw anyone with darker skin or other physical or cultural differences. There were a few Chinese restaurants, but that was about it. Everyone else was white, either Christian or Jewish.

There were no overt signs of racism. We had no "whites only" or "coloreds only" signs at drinking fountains, bathrooms, lunch counters, or hotels. There were no bus strikes, no demonstrations, no riots, no police with dogs and fire hoses, no visible housing discrimination. Everything was clean and neat and tidy and nice, so to speak.

However, by the early 1960s, it began to be clear that there was a revolution in race relations going on in this country. But that was on the news and it was in Memphis or Montgomery, not where I lived, right? That was in the South, where there was bigotry and violence. It was easy to think that. It all seemed so far away. Here in New England, things were calm, so we must be okay.

By the late 1960s, when Dr. King was assassinated, I still had little idea that we were all racists on some level. Now, I know better.

It seems to me that racism operates on both sides. In other words, those who think they are superior forget that they think that. Those who were brought up being treated as inferior sometimes forget that they think of themselves that way, too. There is often a lot of finger pointing, but honestly, I believe that we all carry it, more or less, because we've all grown up in a racist culture. It's quite insidious.

I don't know if I'll ever be completely free of racism. All I can say is that I keep thinking about it, keep working on facing up to my attitudes, keep discussing it with people who are not my same race. As a tall white man, raised in a middle-class Protestant family, I just expect that certain opportunities will always be there for me. It's very easy for me to forget that others may not have the same opportunities.

I'm not complaining, nor do I wish to blame anyone for this, exactly. And I'm not looking for excuses. As I see it, it's not my fault that I was born into a society that includes racism. But yet it *is* my responsibility, I believe, to keep looking for ways to challenge it when I find it within me. To stay aware of when it arises within me and in others. I want to continue to find ways, however I can, to do something about it.

In other words, my goal is to love everyone, and *act* on that love. My job is to understand the artificial limitations each person faces and help us all break through them.

We are all human beings under the skin. Sure, we come with a great variety of cultural backgrounds, history, and ancestry. We don't *all* have to like the same kind of food, dance the same dances, speak the same language, or carry on with the same cultural traditions. That's all fine. But at the same time, we're struggling to learn how to be more supportive of each other, figure out how to resolve differences of opinion that arise, and live in harmony.

My inclination is to talk to everyone I meet as if they are a fellow human being, with all the fears, triumphs, grief, joy, and other feelings I might have. And not just talk, but listen as well. No matter how young or old they are, or what their culture might seem to be.

Everyone's an individual. Everyone has a unique story. And yet, we're all in this together.

Blame Culture

I grew up with what I call "the blame culture." If something went wrong, the people around me looked for someone to blame for it. For example, my family of origin was almost always late when heading off on a trip to visit relatives. On the way there, in the car, I remember my mother saying, "If only you had ... (gotten ready earlier, helped pack, or whatever), ... then we'd be on time by now!" It wasn't just me; she was pretty much addressing everyone in the car. But just the same, I got the message.

Years later, looking back, I realized that this exercise in blame never improved anything. Next time we went on a trip, we were still just as late. Our tradition of blaming was essentially useless. But if it didn't improve anything, then why did we keep doing it? I was puzzled.

Eventually, I realized that assigning blame actually gave my mother a sense of security! If you think every bad thing that happens could have been avoided, then you can pretend that we humans should be perfect at all times! It's as if we should always be in complete control of everything. We should be able to anticipate all possible circumstances in advance and head off all problems before they even happen, right? So, anyone who doesn't perform flawlessly is just being lazy - or evil.

But, of course, that's not how life works! Most things in life "go wrong" because we can't help it. We're human, after all. We make mistakes. Our resources (time, energy, money, etc.) are limited. Communication is imperfect. Our emotions may overwhelm us. External circumstances can change suddenly, such as a change in the weather, getting sick, or losing a job, rendering our plans useless. We just can't anticipate every contingency. I realized that, most of the time, *we are all doing our best,* given the circumstances.

But to accept this about life can be really frightening! Think about it. Suddenly, you're faced with the question: "What if things can go wrong and nobody can prevent them?" This feeling of helplessness is often just too frightening! So we search for a way to comfort ourselves. We assign blame so that we can pretend that somebody was in control, or *should have been* in control. We even join others in fantastic conspiracy theories, a kind of "mass blame" effort.[25]

My first step was to start practicing the act of forgiving myself whenever I did something "wrong." Later, I came up with a T-shirt that says "I don't blame you" on the front, in hopes that I could help other people forgive themselves and each other.[26] It's a message from me to myself, as well; the process of "unlearning" blaming myself has been a struggle. I'm still working on it.

---

[25] See https://en.wikipedia.org/wiki/Conspiracy_theory, Psychological origins section, Humanistic Psychologists paragraph.

[26] The T-shirts are available here: www.messagerain.com/t-shirts.html

High School

When I got to high school, the bullying seemed to abate somewhat. People had better things to do with their time, and there was no more recess or a playground as a setting for idle trouble.

I still felt neglected by the school system. For example, I discovered that the few friends I had (more academically successful geeks than I) had enrolled in both geometry and algebra II, in our sophomore year.

I was never told that this course selection was possible, and by the time I found out, it was too late. I had been enrolled in geometry and a study hall instead. I was slated for algebra II the following year. I went to the head of the math department and asked if I could take algebra II in the summer and catch up with my friends who would be taking trigonometry the next school year. He flatly refused. The math department didn't offer accelerated courses in the summer and that was that.

So, I went over to the science department and discovered that I could take chemistry in the summer instead, so I signed up. I did surprisingly well at that. Apparently, the ability to concentrate on just one subject was a good idea for me, as opposed to the grand jumble of multiple classes in short time periods, during the regular school year.

This allowed me to take physics as a junior (one year ahead of most other students), so at least I was in the same class as most of those same friends. I did reasonably well in physics, partly due to my interest in it, and partly because the teacher was perhaps one of the best in the school, at least in the science department, anyway.

When I was a senior, this allowed me to take Advanced Placement (AP) chemistry, the only AP course I ever got into. However, I found the complexity of the math more difficult and I didn't do well enough to get college credit.

§ § §

There are a few places where I seemed to connect pretty well, socially. One was in the music department. I started out singing tenor in the Boy's Glee Club, but my voice cracked halfway through the year, so I moved over to the bass section. As a junior, I auditioned for and was accepted into the choir. Three or four times during the school year, we performed in big concerts, open to the public. Practicing was hard work for me, but I enjoyed the camaraderie and performing on stage.

Another place where I connected socially was in theater. I took a course in stagecraft and did relatively well at that. Our high school had an active drama department. We put on two plays per year. I worked backstage, preparing for *A Midsummer Night's Dream,* until one day I accidentally stepped on a support structure for some unfinished scenery and fractured my right foot. I ended up on crutches for weeks and had to drop out of the backstage crew for that production.

Down for the Count

In high school we were required to take gym class every year in order to graduate. This was all competitive athletics. Alternatives, such as dance, meditation, or New Games, were not included or hadn't been developed yet.[27]

When I was a junior, I was in gym period one morning in wrestling class. The gym teacher we had at that time was actually the wrestling coach for the entire school (2000 students). This class was only for the boys. Girls did not have wrestling then.

In wrestling, opponents were chosen by weight class. So, I was paired up with another boy, both of us skinny lightweights. We wrestled on large dark blue mats in the lower gym, downstairs from the main gym. A large white circle was printed on the surface of each mat to show the edge of the ring.

At one point, I was in a ring, wrestling with an opponent. Each of us was struggling to get the other one down to the mat. We were both on our knees, but upright and facing each other, trying to push the other down. He was able to push harder, so I fell backwards and he landed on top of me.

As he landed, I heard a sound, kind of a dull pop. It was distinct enough that he stopped right away. So did I. The coach came over and asked impatiently, "Why'd you stop wrestling?" I said, "I think I broke something." My opponent said he heard a sound, as well. The coach did not seem to give this much credibility.

The other boy got up while I lay on my back, on the mat, for a few moments. I said I didn't want to continue with the match. So the coach said, "Well, alright, why don't you go over to the side of the mat and rest until you're ready to go back in."

Now, you have to understand, I did not want to do wrestling. In fact, I didn't even want to be in gym class at all, most of the time. When I was a boy, the term "skinny" applied to me. I was anything but athletic, not very strong and poorly coordinated. I always came up underweight on the doctor's chart when I had a physical exam.

In addition, I was slow to get changed into my gym uniform and then also slow to shower and get dressed at the end of the period, so I was always rushing, on the verge of being late. More to the point, I didn't really enjoy strenuous physical exercise that much, gross motor movement, and most of all, physical competition. I was afraid of getting hurt, so I didn't really throw myself into it fully.

Some boys who didn't want to be in gym would forge hall passes or doctor excuse slips to get out of going. I was too honest and afraid of being caught to do that, so I always went to class.

---

[27] New Games was started by Stewart Brand and others in the mid 1960s, in California, around the same time that I was in high school. *The New Games Book* was published later on, in 1976.

Anyway, I got up, went over, and lay down at the edge of the wrestling mat on my back with my knees up and my feet flat on the mat. After a few moments, I decided to take both hands and place my fingertips at the top of my breastbone, right in the center of my body, just below my neck. I slowly moved my fingers outward, toward my shoulders on each side, feeling each clavicle (the so-called collarbones) as they extended out from the top of my breastbone. On the right side, I followed the clavicle all the way out to where it met my right shoulder. On the left side, it was very different. The clavicle just ended part way over in that direction. Over by my shoulder, I could feel what seemed like the other end of it, still attached to my shoulder. The skin was not broken; there was no blood. So I looked pretty normal.

But I was suddenly very frightened. This did not seem right at all. I was confused, but it began to dawn on me that that bone was broken and I had no idea what to do next. I started to feel nauseous.

Shortly, the wrestling coach came back over and asked, "So, are you ready to get back in?" I told him I didn't think so, I didn't feel right. I may have repeated that I thought I broke something, but he didn't bother to check it out. Instead, he told me to just go up to the locker room and get dressed. His tone of voice told me that he didn't necessarily believe me, but he didn't want to bother arguing about it.

I got up and walked slowly out of the room. I went up the half-flight of stairs to the locker room level. At the left side of the passageway, there was a single classroom desk just sitting there (essentially a chair with a writing surface attached at the right side). I was feeling so sick, I just sat down in the chair, and let my head rest on my right hand on the desk surface, with my face down. By then, I felt very sick.

A few minutes later it was the end of gym period. All the other boys rushed up the stairs past me. A few of them asked, "Are you okay?" I mumbled something but I don't remember what. None of them stopped to inquire further. They had no idea I had suffered a major injury. They were intent on showering and dressing before it was time to head to the next class. When they were all gone, it was quiet again, and I was left sitting there alone in the passageway.

Finally, the senior boys' gym coach (head of the department) came by. I happened to be sitting right across from his office door. By now, I was pale and in a cold sweat. He took one look at me and realized that I was in shock. He asked if I could walk and I said I thought so. He gently helped me up, back down the stairs, and back into the lower gym. There were weight training machines around the perimeter of the room, so he got me to lie down on the seat of the quadriceps machine. It had a large padded surface on top, so I could lie down with my legs propped up at one end.

He took his jacket off and put it over me, to help keep me warm (classic first aid for victims of shock). He asked if I would be okay lying there for a few minutes, as he was going upstairs to call a doctor.

I don't remember a lot after that. Eventually, he came back to get me and I ended up in a car with my mother driving me to a doctor in the next town. There, the doctor took X-rays, shot the whole area full of Novocain, and pushed the ends of the bone back to touch each other. He used adhesive tape (massive amounts of it!) with a piece of aluminum (as a splint) buried within the layers of tape to keep the bone at the correct angle. My left arm and shoulder were completely immobilized! My left upper arm was taped against my body, with my forearm across my chest. My left hand stuck out between the layers of tape, just below my chin, as if it were some kind of useless vestigial appendage.

I spent the next four weeks like that, while it healed. I had to lean my whole body down to pick anything up that needed two hands. I had to take sponge baths during that time (no showers or regular baths). Eventually, they took all the tape off (ouch!) and I had my left arm in a sling for awhile longer.

And, no, I didn't have to go to gym class for that whole time! By the time I returned to gym, the wrestling unit was long over.

§ § §

Over the years, I have worked on the emotional toll this trauma took on me. I never cried or expressed myself very much while in pain during all this. I was following the "be a good boy" admonition back then, and didn't make a fuss. I had blocked the natural expression of the terror, pain, and anger that I felt. Somewhere inside my being, I continued to hold the pain and fear, waiting for an opportunity for my feelings to come out.

Recently, over the past decade or so, I have sought out safe spaces to do the intense emotional work that seems necessary to express and release the feelings I still had from back then.

If I had followed that wrestling coach's wishes and tried to wrestle some more, the edges of that broken bone could have punctured my left carotid artery, the one that carries blood up the side of my neck to my brain. If that had happened, most of my blood supply would have hemorrhaged out and I would have died within a few minutes.

So this is the second time that one of my teachers should have been fired for incompetence (or worse).[28] But that coach continued to work there. Perhaps if I had spoken up more insistently about how dangerous it was, something would have happened. But this was still the world of "one size fits all" and the power of authority in institutions. The risks of making a fuss were high. I didn't even realize how intimidated I was.

---

[28] The first time was back in second grade when I was left alone in the classroom because I couldn't finish the assignment.

I am very glad, in spite of all that, I had enough personal strength to say "no" and refuse to get back into the wresting ring. And I'm thankful that the senior coach came by and knew what to do.

I think about how girls were not exposed to such physical danger. Not that the girls' gym class was any picnic. I'm sure there are many stories about the horrors of it all for them as well. I remember some of the girls telling me that nobody liked the little one piece "jumper" gym suits they had to wear.

But the real crime here is not just that. The important issue is how our culture had trapped both boys and girls into rigid expectations. I'll bet anything that our wrestling coach knew darned well that I didn't want to be there and he was disgusted by that. I imagine that he wanted everyone to fit the mold he himself was cast in - a tough, muscular, competitive man, ready to enter into physical conflict and defeat his opponent.

He probably thought that I was lying about being injured, just to get out of class. That's why I think he never took my injury seriously. To him, I was likely nothing more than a wimp, afraid to get in there and put my all into it.

How tragic that is! How many young people today are still being bullied by the school system itself, as they are forced (by law) to participate in activities or classes that they have no interest in, and are in fact potentially injurious to them, both physically and emotionally.

When are we going to learn that our children are often smarter than we are? Why aren't we trusting them to decide what and how to learn? When will we accept that it is up to us, as adults, to give them whatever support we can, rather than force them through the maze of our standardized curriculum.

Fortunately, I see little sparks of change, as some alternatives are slowly developing.[29]

---

[29] See www.self-directed.org for example.

Interpretation

Do not let
an English teacher
tell you what
this poem means.

The invisible implications
The improbable surprising insight
Buried in the few lines
that no student
has anticipated.

Really!
It's just a poem.

The Garage

Our second house was built with a one-car garage on the slab level. Eventually, my parents saved enough money to build a two-car garage off that end of the house and convert the former garage space into a large bedroom. By this time, my sisters and I were all in our teens.

When my father designed the new garage, he designed a rectangular pit in the floor, under one of the two cars. The pit was about two feet deep and just narrow enough for the car's tires to straddle it when driving in. Normally, we placed heavy wood planks over the opening, which covered the entire trench. The ends of the planks fit into a groove around the edge of the pit, so that their top surfaces were flush with the surrounding floor. We did this to keep from falling in when walking around or in case someone drove in at a slight angle, so the wheels of the car wouldn't fall in.

We bought a mechanic's "creeper" - a short wooden panel on caster wheels, with a small cushion for your head, at one end. One of us could climb down into the pit, lie down on our back on the creeper, and scoot around to see any part of the underside of the car just by looking up. We often used a trouble lamp on a long cord for light.

My father did all this because he liked to change the oil in our cars himself. It also allowed him to make a few other minor repairs and check on things that might need attention. He didn't save much money doing this, since gas station oil changes were relatively cheap, but my father liked doing it himself and he liked being able to choose the quality of the oil and parts.

But there was also another reason. This was an educational tool. And not just for me and my brother. He also showed my sisters how to change the oil in a car and learn what the various parts of a car were and how they functioned. In fact, both my parents had the idea that everyone should know how to use basic tools and be handy around the house.

Sure, sometimes while upstairs, he would send one of us children on a "tool run" to the basement ("Can you go down and get the Phillips screwdriver from the workbench drawer?"). But he was always open about what he was doing, and willing to explain how to do it.

I don't remember any workbenches or extensive tool collections in the basements of my friends' houses, at least the ones that I saw. They just used their basements for storage or perhaps a play area for the kids. So my friends only learned about tools and cars in shop class in school, and that was only for the boys. Recently, one of my sisters told me that she was lucky to have had the experience when we were younger. This is another way in which my father ignored typical gender norms.

The Latest Thing

At the start of my senior year in high school, in 1967, I had another unpleasant surprise. When I had to decide on electives at the end of my junior year, I came across a course called "Computer Math." The description did not really interest me that much. I pictured students sitting at desks in a classroom, studying different numbering systems with different bases, such as binary, octal, or decimal.

When the year started, however, I was in the science building one afternoon after school, and I discovered a few math teachers in a tiny room, all standing around a Teletype machine.[30] One teacher was sitting at the keyboard, and another was standing over him smoking a pipe, holding a booklet, saying things like, "Now type 'LIST,' ..." When he did that, there was a slight pause, then the machine began typing furiously, line after line.

It turned out that "Computer Math"[31] involved writing programs on a real computer! It used the BASIC language, which had been developed only a few years earlier at Dartmouth College. My high school didn't actually have the computer. What they had instead was an account on what they called a timesharing system, situated in another city, but connected to our Teletype machine by long-distance telephone lines. When we wanted to use it, we had to turn it on, then dial the appropriate phone number (with an actual telephone dial right on the front panel) to get connected. Then you'd hear a series of tones as the circuit was established. Finally, you'd type "Hello," and it would respond by typing back "Ready," on the next line below.

Some of those same friends of mine who had gotten ahead in math classes two years earlier were already enrolled in the class. But by the time I discovered all this, it was too late to enroll, just as before.

But I was very excited about it. I borrowed a booklet from one of my friends and read it. I stayed after school and waited until the other students from the class had finished with the machine and then wrote and ran my own programs. It took some practice, but I charged ahead, staying after school numerous afternoons. Sometimes, I was so wrapped up in what I was doing that I missed the late bus and had to call my mother to come get me. She was somewhat annoyed when I did this, but she relented and came to pick me up anyway. We lived only about three miles away.

---

[30] An ASR-33

[31] The course was likely given that name to differentiate it from courses in the business department where they taught business typing, keypunching, and accounting machine plugboard programming. They actually had an IBM 402, on which they printed all our student class schedule slips.

Life Path and the World Around Us

Although I didn't do well in AP chemistry, and my grades in other classes were often mediocre at best,[32] I was still convinced that I should go to college and be an engineer of some kind, probably electrical. Very few places had computer science programs back then, so choosing that as an area of study didn't occur to me.

My life plan from there on was pretty much a carbon copy of what my parents had done 30 years earlier. Now, I and others my age were expected to do the same. I was to be the little engine that could, chugging along on the typical railroad track of life. The station stops were: Graduate from high school, go to college, and get a degree. Then get a job, find a "girl," and get married. Save up for a down payment, get a mortgage, and buy a house. I would end up married, with a steady career, a few children, two cars, a lawn mower, and a family dog.

Although I was not really aware of it at the time, there were signs inside me and in the world around me that perhaps things were not going to go that way.

My parents were conservative Republicans. They had supported Barry Goldwater for president in the 1964 election. The message I got from my parents was that they knew the "right" way for things to go, but things were not going that way. The student demonstrations, the rock 'n' roll music, the long hair, and the drug use, all seemed to indicate that we were headed in the wrong direction or society was breaking down completely. They thought we should fight harder and just win the damned Vietnam War, rather than withdraw from it.

They blamed a lot of this on our principal adversaries in the Cold War: The Soviet Union. To them, "the Communists" must somehow be subverting our youth and causing all this trouble. After all, Nikita Khrushchev, the USSR's Communist Party leader in the 1950s, had famously stated, "We will bury you." He predicted that the West would not have to be conquered by war, but would rather "... fall like over-ripe fruit into our hands." Years later, when President Ronald Reagan called the Soviet Union the "Evil Empire," my parents were in complete agreement.

At first, I went along with their lead. I was too young to vote in 1964, but in 1968, I voted for Richard Nixon, the Republican presidential candidate. I had a lot to learn.

Meanwhile, there were hints that my own life was about to diverge from that world of culture and politics. The first one was what happened in my senior year English class, of all things.

---

[32] The one exception was when I was a sophomore in geometry class, where I got straight A's. I just had a knack for it. The teacher even asked me to help the other students go over exam questions that they had gotten wrong, after the exam papers had been graded and handed back. That was two years before the computer math class I missed, when I was a senior. The part of my brain that was good at the logical steps used in geometry proofs seemed to come in handy for writing computer programs later on.

A Shock to the System

When I was finally a senior in high school, a strange thing happened. I was placed in an English class where the teacher (Ms. English was her name, coincidentally) didn't refer to her class as English! She preferred to call it "Communications."

Well, okay.

She even came to class one day with a copy of Jefferson Airplane's album *Surrealistic Pillow*, and played a track from it called "My Best Friend." She did this because she thought it was so beautiful and communicated just as well as any prose or poetry read from a book.

I hadn't even heard of the band before that, but I liked the song.

She also told us that she didn't agree with issuing grades herself, so at the end of each marking period, she had a separate conference in her office with each student individually. Together, the two of them came to an agreement about what that student's grade should be.

That seemed like a nice idea.

At my high school, there were no final exams during the last semester of senior year. Instead, you had to do a project of some kind. Ms. English told us that her students the previous year had such a great time doing their projects at the end of the year, that they wished they had been able to do more than one! So she decided to have each of us do a project at the beginning of the year, as well. She started by inviting us to think of an idea for a project.

Wait a minute, ... what?

I felt as if I had stepped off the edge of a cliff into a free fall. I mean, here was my entire tradition in school being interrupted by a concept so totally different that I had no idea what to make of it. I was so used to being assigned some homework to do, then *not* doing it, then being shamed or humiliated in class for not having it done when it was time to hand it in. I would end up feeling terrible about that and wondering why I was so hopeless. At the end of the grading period, I ended up with mediocre grades and concluded that I was ruining my life and I couldn't help it.

And here was this teacher telling us we could pick any project we wanted and just do that. I was completely lost. The Buddhists might say I had achieved perfect Zen at that moment because my mind was totally blank. I was so rattled that I tried to transfer out of the class! I went to the office to do just that, but they said it was too late by then (a few weeks of the first semester had already gone by) and I'd have to stay put.

So I went to the teacher and asked her what I should do. Perhaps she could give me some idea of a project assignment. She told me to meet her after school, in the cafeteria, where she'd be working on some papers, and we could talk it over.

I showed up and she started asking me questions about my life. What did I like to do? Did I have any hobbies? I told her my hobby was electronics. There was a pause. Then she asked me if there was anything specific that I was doing related to electronics. I told her I was building an FM tuner.

She looked at me for a moment and then said, "Okay, you wanted an assignment, then here's your assignment: describe for the class how to build an FM tuner." I agreed, but inside, I was immediately taken aback. Sure, I could describe it well enough, but I didn't expect that anyone else would be interested. Who would care about that?

But this was to be the assignment. I had asked for it. Now I had to figure out what to do. I went home and thought about it. Soon, I was making notes and drawing diagrams on big pieces of paper. I took the parts I had already purchased - resistors, capacitors, diodes, and other components - and stuck them all into a block of stiff plastic foam, so I could take them to school and hold it up in front of the class. I had already made a tiny circuit board for part of the circuit that I had designed and etched. I had even soldered some of the components onto it.

The day came when it was my turn to present all this. I put my diagrams up on the chalkboard with masking tape, described how you etch a circuit board in detail, and so on. The other students sat and listened. When I was done, it was time for questions.

Much to my surprise, some hands went up. One student said he didn't quite understand how the etching process worked, so I tried to describe it in different words. Then there was another question. And another. Finally, one boy at the back of the class asked a very interesting question, "How much will it cost when you get done building this?" I said about $35. Then he asked, "What would it cost for someone to just go out and buy one that was already built?" I said it would probably be about the same, $35. Finally, he asked, "Well, then, why are you bothering to do this?"

Before I could answer, a girl sitting in front of him turned around and said to him, "Because this is what he *likes* to do! He enjoys building things like this." She wasn't upset with him for asking the question or anything; it just seemed obvious to her, so she spoke up. A few other students nodded in agreement.

After that, I took down my presentation and went back to my seat. An unfamiliar warm feeling went through me. It took a few moments for all this to sink in. Here were others, who were not only interested enough to ask questions, but who understood and cared! Other people who I *thought* wouldn't have given me the time of day were actually interested in something I had a passion for, even if they didn't share that passion themselves. Wow.

My idea of transferring out of the class was gone. I went ahead and wrote short stories, participated in other projects, and ended up doing a senior project that consisted of a slide show with a tape recording for a soundtrack. The theme of the piece was anti-smoking.

I had wanted to make a movie, as some of the other students were doing, but my family didn't have a movie camera or a tape recorder.[33] I had to use my mother's Kodak Retina 35mm camera to take the slides and use one of the reel-to-reel Wollensak tape recorders the school had.

After I showed my project in class at end of the year, the other students applauded. The teacher said, "And this is from a young man who thought he couldn't do anything in this class at the beginning of the year." She was clearly proud of me as well.

§ § §

This was, of course, just one class. What I didn't realize at the time, was that all of education could be like that. There didn't have to be rigid assignments and "cookbook" questions at the end of each chapter, assigned books to read, etc.

You see, as soon as I got to junior high school, where they had a useful library, I had been learning about electricity and electronics on my own. Alas, nobody in the school system had ever given me a grade or any credit for doing that. I did it all after school or at home. I was already a self-motivated learner.

It seems to me that most children are inherently self-motivated learners. I wish school systems would stop pretending that students need to be "motivated" to learn, and instead encourage their natural curiosity and creativity a lot more.

---

[33] Home movie cameras in those days used 8-millimeter movie film, three minutes per reel, that you had to take to the camera store to be developed. They didn't have sound built in, so students who wanted sound had to use "dual system." That's film industry language for separately recording the images (in the camera) and the sound (using a portable tape recorder). I remember some students showing their film in a lecture room in the science building. One stood at the projector in the back, and the other sat at the tape recorder down at the front. With their hands at the controls, they did a little countdown, "Three, two, one, go!" and started them both going at once.

The Price of Integrity

In December of 1967, the film *The Graduate* came out.[34] Pretty soon, it seemed that everybody had heard about it. Back then, movie theaters had only one screen, and most suburban towns only had only one movie theater. When a movie came out, it might take a while before it reached your local theater, because it played in theaters in other cities first.[35] Finally, it was booked for a theater in the next town over from ours, so my parents said we could go see it, some time in February of 1968.

This was just before the current motion picture rating system was devised, but as the film had "adult content," we decided that only my parents, my sister (the older of the two), and I would go. It was a week night and we went to the second showing. Although we seemed to be chronically late for most family trips, we got to the theater early.

We walked into the lobby and bought our tickets. The first showing was still running, with only a few minutes left. My father asked the young woman through the box office window if it made any difference if we went in anyway. She shrugged her shoulders and said she didn't know. So we went in, sat down and watched the last few minutes of the film. Of course, the frenetic action and the ending didn't seem to make a lot of sense. When it was over, we sat there until it started again.

When the story reached the point at which we had entered previously, my father started to get up to go. My mother got up with him, as did my sister. One of them whispered to me, "Come on, let's go." At first, I was taken by surprise. I didn't know what to do. I said something like, "Okay, I'll be there in a minute."

In a flash, I had an idea about what was happening. My father was an engineer and had lived through the golden age of Hollywood. To him, the plot was the main reason he went to see movies. Stories had a beginning, a middle and an end, typically all tied up neatly. The depth of character, the complexity of feelings, etc. expressed in a picture were not as important. As for the plot, he knew what would happen, and watching it over again was just redundant to him.

But, I just couldn't make myself get up and leave. By then, I was thoroughly wrapped up in the energy of the story. Here was a young man, Benjamin, who had been manipulated and then bullied by all the adults around him and he had finally had it. He exploded with energy as he finally decided to go for what he truly wanted. The

---

[34] Spoiler alert: I describe the theme and some of the plot of the film as I tell this story, here.

[35] The film industry only produced a limited number of prints, so each print was typically shipped from one theater to the next, in rotation, so that most theaters showed most titles if you waited long enough. If a film proved to be more popular than expected, there was a rush to produce more prints to serve more theaters, as each print had a limited life, due to wear. See: https://en.wikipedia.org/wiki/35_mm_film

excitement of his sudden commitment to himself was overwhelming. I stayed glued to my seat until the very end.

I grabbed my coat and walked briskly out of the theater. I walked to where the car had been parked but it was gone. My father had driven off with the others without me. I had a sinking feeling in my stomach. What would I do now? I was seven miles from home, I had no money, and there was no public transportation anyway. It was a cold winter night, so walking that far didn't even occur to me.

I returned to the theater lobby and asked to use their phone. They let me call home but there was no answer, as they hadn't even gotten there yet. So I stood around in the empty lobby, waiting until I thought they were back. When I tried again, my mother answered. She tried to explain why my father had left. He had to get up early for work in the morning, we had already seen that part of the movie, etc. But I could tell by her voice that her explanation was only half-hearted.

We paused for a moment. What would we do now? She agreed to come back to get me.

§ § §

In a way, I had done something similar to what Benjamin had done in the film. Sitting in that theater, I realized in a flash what I wanted to do. The story I was watching was parallel to what I had just started to feel about my whole life. The world around me had bullied me all along. I hadn't quite understood what was behind my own passive resistance before then. Suddenly, I staked out my position by staying in that seat and drinking in the elixir of the brisk liberation going on, up on the big screen in front of me, until the very end.

§ § §

Recently, I asked my mother what she remembered of the incident. She told me that when they got outside the theater, she had argued with my father, but could not dissuade him. She says she actually felt sick to her stomach. She could not imagine how I felt, as she sat next to him in the car on the way home. I didn't ask about her response to me on the phone, once they got home, but I think it was likely due to my father being nearby as she answered my call.

As I have mentioned before, my father was usually a reasonable and thoughtful person. But if he decided that someone should do something, and they resisted him, he somehow took it personally, and reacted irrationally, lashing out in extreme ways. Later on, the topic was dropped. Perhaps he was secretly ashamed of his own actions and didn't want to revisit the source of his anger.[36] It took my mother years to learn how to stand up to him when he got this way, long after my siblings and I had moved out of the house.

---

[36] Very recently, my mother reported to me that many years later, my father admitted to her that perhaps he shouldn't have abandoned me at the theater.

Do Not Read

Do not read
my poems
the way they do
at some
poetry readings

where they
have a voice
that trails away
with an ironic tone.

Do Not!

with a rhythm
that sings along
line after line
until my mind
is numb
with an overabundance
of imagery

of birdbaths
and autumn leaves.

Enough!

I love you.
I truly do.

But please give me,
... give *my poetry*
some punch!
then stop
(for a pause just a bit too long),

then speak out loud
to startle them
and make a face
that goes with it.

But whatever you do
Do not!

Higher Education

I finally graduated from high school and left Scouting, having attained Eagle Scout (accomplished only three weeks before the deadline: my 18th birthday!).

I liked making things and learning about electricity and electronics, I liked math and science better than English or "Social Studies" (history) in school, so I decided to go to engineering school to become an electrical engineer (an EE, for short).

I was accepted at Rensselaer Polytechnic Institute (RPI), in Troy, New York. My father had even graduated from there, with a degree in aeronautical engineering, so he already knew something about the place. Of course, it was now the late 1960s, thirty years later. Much had changed.

When I got there, it slowly became evident that I was in trouble. The freshman class was overcrowded because of the draft for the Vietnam War. If you could get into college, that postponed the draft, because undergraduate students could get a "deferment." The draft board code for this deferment was known as a "2-S." So a lot of guys went to college, but some of them didn't necessarily belong there. At least not at age 18. Also, in New York, unlike in some other neighboring states, the drinking age was 18, instead of 20 or 21. Many of them started drinking for the first time in their lives, without any supervision or mentoring. The results were not pretty.

I say "guys," because in those days RPI had originally only enrolled young men and had gone coed only a few years before I got there. So the college reserved two huge dorms up on the hill for women, leaving all the other dorms and fraternities for men only.

But the real source of my trouble was that I was not prepared for the math. Electrical engineering was not so much about building things and soldering wires and watching things light up or pick up radio stations, etc., as had been my hobby. It was a lot of very hard math. It started with calculus, and that was a very different animal from any of the math I had done before that. I could sort of get the concepts, but it required a lot of memorization, because I couldn't derive the formulas in my head intuitively, as I had done previously. "The integral of the sine is the cosine." Well, you just had to remember that. If you tried to figure it out during an exam, you'd never get through it in time. But that was not my learning style. I was more of an intuitive person, and memorization was very difficult for me.

My grades started out poor and got worse. Fast-talking professors, using chalk on blackboards, covered an entire wall of the room with equations. For most of us, we could either watch and try to understand, or take notes as fast as possible, but not both. If you were a notetaker, as I was, then you were left reading your notes later, trying to figure out what it all meant. If you were a "watch and learn" type, then you had nothing for reference later when it was time to study for exams.

The one highlight for me was the RPI Computer Society, an extracurricular group that met once a week, after classes. At that time, RPI only had five courses that had anything at all to do with digital computers and one of them was a management course. In those days, management was the major you switched to if you couldn't "hack it" as an engineer, so the word was spoken with a tone of derision.

But I was very excited about digital computers. RPI had a giant IBM mainframe computer by then, a System 360, model 50, with an extra core memory unit. It had card readers, printers, tape drives, disk drives, the works. It was all situated in a large room with a raised tile floor, bright fluorescent lights, big glass windows, and its own air conditioning system. There were glass doors with signs that said, "No Admittance – Authorized Personnel Only!" Only college staff assigned to the job could run the computer. It ran around the clock, 24 hours a day.

Students (and those of us in the Computer Society) were given a user number which allowed us to write programs, type them into punch cards, then submit the decks of punch cards to be run through the computer. We had to place our card decks in large gray metal trays on a table in the keypunch room and wait. Every once in awhile, a staffer would come out of the machine room, pick up the trays of cards and take them in to be run. A few hours later, we could return to the building (Amos Eaton Hall) and retrieve our card decks, along with a few sheets of green-striped paper wrapped around them, with the printout of whatever our program had produced.

I went to the student bookstore and bought the IBM FORTRAN reference manual (not the programmer's guide) to learn how to write programs. The reference manual was just the commands in that language, one to a page, with a description of what each one did. It didn't say anything about how to write a program. But I didn't care. I jumped right in. I began to hang out in the dorm room of one of the upperclassmen who had started the RPI Computer Society.

Meanwhile, back in my regular classes, at the end of the first semester, I got all Cs and one D. The second semester, I got all Ds and one F. Oh, and one I (incomplete), in mechanical drawing. I was placed on academic probation. I went home for the summer with the partly finished drawings, which I had to finish in order to change my "incomplete" into a real grade. I dreaded it so much, that I kept putting it off.

This was the summer of 1969. Woodstock took place that summer, but I barely had time to notice. My family was getting ready to move to another state. To save money, we took frequent trips to the building site of our new house to do some of the work ourselves, on the partly-built structure. We installed extra insulation between the rooms and painted all the trim before it was put up. We made so many trips, we all knew the route by heart; such as the places where Interstate 80 wasn't finished and you had to get off and take route 46 instead, then get back on 80 later on.

When she was driving, my mother would throw the toll money into the hopper in the exact change lane and just keep driving while the alarm went off and then silenced itself a moment later when the mechanism finally counted all the coins (and arrived at the correct total). This was something of a game and we all relished watching her do this.

Meanwhile, my father threatened not to send me back to school at all unless I finished those drawings! These were the most difficult ones at the end of the class, of course. Finally, with little time left, I struggled and struggled and got them done as well as I could. Three days after we moved, I went back up to RPI to start my second year.

It didn't take long before I was completely demoralized. I barely went to class. I became more and more frightened and depressed. Frightened because, if I couldn't do this, then what would happen to me? I only had this one single life plan in mind, and here was my "little engine that could," derailing and tumbling off the tracks. I had no alternative, no "plan B" for my life. Maybe I'd even get drafted. There was already word of people moving to Canada to avoid the draft. But even if I weren't drafted, I had no idea what I would do. I joked about suicide at the time, but I never actually made any attempts.

Even worse, in my first Engineering Science II class that semester, I found myself sitting in a lab in the Russell Sage building surrounded by other students and a whole host of analog computers. I had never seen an analog computer before. The professor was introducing us to what were going to cover that semester and he said an astounding thing. He pointed out the window, across the lawn, at Amos Eaton Hall, where the IBM digital computer was housed. Then, he said, "That machine will never do any real engineering." And he meant it![37]

I was speechless. I really had no idea if the IBM machine could "do real engineering" or not, but what I did know was that I was much more excited about what you could do with it than the dusty old analog computers sitting in that Engineering Science lab. I just knew that digital computers was where it was happening and that analog computers were all but completely washed up. It was just a matter of time. I can't tell you how I knew this, exactly, but I knew it with every fiber in my body. I was not about to sit around and learn this stuff.

This was the beginning of the end of my time at RPI.

---

[37] A few years later, I learned that he was dead wrong. Digital computers could do plenty of real engineering, and were already doing so in the military, the space program, air traffic control, and many other industrial applications.

The Dawn

And then, an amazing thing happened. It's almost as if my cry for help was heard on some level of the Universe that can change things.

Around that time, there were plenty of students sitting at card tables in front of the Student Union building with petitions for others to sign. You could demand an end to the war in Vietnam, or ban nuclear weapons, or support various other political causes. Having been brought up by conservative Republicans, I usually didn't sign anything.

But one day, I approached a table with a sign that said, "Keep Dr. Waterman." I asked them what it was about. It turned out that he was a professor in the humanities department. The department head was planning to fire him in order to hire more research staff instead. Dr. Waterman turned out to be a very popular guy. He had open office hours for students to talk with him, even if they weren't enrolled in any of his courses. I didn't want to sign the petition without knowing more about him. I also had gotten nowhere with the psychologist at the student affairs office about my "crash and burn" academic trajectory. So, I went to Dr. Waterman's office and made an appointment to see him.

When we talked, I discovered that he was the first person in my life who could paint a picture of what life might be like if I weren't at RPI anymore. My little engine that was derailing could actually take any of a number of different tracks and not end up in a wreck!

I told him that I was worried - if I dropped out, wouldn't my last semester of all "F" grades block me from going to college anywhere else? "No," he said, "Those credits just won't transfer. You only get credit for the courses you passed." In fact, if I wanted to return to RPI someday, it would likely be a non-issue. Meanwhile, he suggested, I might enjoy a sense of accomplishment by working at a job for a while instead. Perhaps I could try that for a year or two and then think about college again later.

Then I asked, "What about the draft?" He said that from what he could tell, Congress was likely to end student deferments at some point anyway. Thus, deciding to stay in college would be pointless if I really wanted to do something else. The draft was still likely to be there, one way or the other.

I walked out of his office feeling about 20 pounds lighter than when I had walked in. I don't think anyone before that had ever really understood my concerns in life like that.

The next time I saw one of those card tables with a petition to keep him on, I signed it right away. Later, it turned out that they fired him anyway.

Uncle Sam Calls

I dropped out of classes at RPI and spent all my time writing programs to run on the digital computer until the semester was over. The biggest one I wrote played a particular game using dominoes.[38] I returned home and eventually got a job at the Prudential Insurance Company (aka "the Pru") in Newark, New Jersey. I commuted by train to work every day.

My mother was worried that I would be unhappy in life if I didn't get a college degree, because many job opportunities would be closed to me. So she took me into New York City, to the career testing lab at New York University (NYU). They had me take a series of tests over a three-day period, in order to assess my aptitude in a number of areas, as well as my relative desire for various careers. The result? I was found to be interested in many lines of work, but almost all of them would require a college degree. This was clearly the result that my mother was hoping to hear!

I was in the first draft lottery, and although my number was relatively high (183), each draft board received separate quotas every few weeks. So, they had to call enough men to fill them. As a result, some draft boards ended up calling numbers more rapidly than others. Although the lottery was supposed to make life more predictable for men of draft age, there was still a lot of uncertainty for many of us.

During that spring, I decided to enlist, instead of getting drafted, in order to get an assignment (an MOS[39]) having something to do with computers. I'd have to sign up for three years, but I thought that would be better than ending up in the infantry, in the jungle. I went in and took the tests, and talked to a recruiter.

Around that time, the Pru hired a new employee for our department. He had just gotten out of the Army and told me stories about his time in the infantry, including tours of duty in Vietnam where he had engaged in combat. When he learned that I planned to enlist, he told me not to do it. He said there were too many ways they had to mess up my plans and I'd end up in the infantry anyway. And I'd be in for three years instead of two.

I listened, but I was too afraid to take his advice. When the day came for me to enlist, my father took me down to the induction center in Newark. He came into the building with me because I wanted him to help me review the contract I was about to sign. However, nobody tells you what will happen next. It's just, "Okay, everybody go into room six and take a seat." Then they closed the door and handed out the contracts. A sergeant at the front of the room started going over a checklist with us. Was your name on the contract spelled correctly? Your address? And so on. Meanwhile, my father was still out in the hall. He had no idea that this was the moment of decision.

---

[38] See *Scientific American*, December 1969, Martin Gardner's column on Mathematical Games.

[39] Military Occupational Specialty, a code number for job assignments in the Army.

Now what should I do? I looked at my contract. I couldn't remember the MOS number for the enlistment that I wanted, but the contract said, "Administration Group 70." That didn't seem right. I thought it was 74 something.

By that time, we had gotten all the way down to the bottom of the form, where the signature line was. The sergeant at the front of the room said that if everything was in order to go ahead and sign it. I had the pen in my hand, just two inches from the paper. Then I stopped. Instead, I raised my hand. I said I had a question. He asked, "What's the matter?" I told him that I was uncertain about the MOS number on my contract. He sounded unpleasantly surprised. "Well, why didn't you speak up before?" he asked. But there was nothing he could do. Unless I signed it, he had no actual power to make me do anything. "Go see the career counselor across the hall," he said, with a tone of disgusted resignation.

I left the room and found my father, still waiting in the hall. We walked across the hall into a little office with a Command Sergeant Major sitting at a desk. Sure enough, the contract was wrong. I had been about two inches away from giving them three years of my life for any of a variety of dull, boring clerical jobs. They offered me a different MOS, having to do with computer equipment repair, but the training was so lengthy, it would have required my enlisting for four years. So, I said no, and we walked out of there and went home.

When we arrived back at the house, my mother was standing at the front door. She did not look surprised. She said, "Something told me that you weren't going into the Army today." She later told me that she had gone up to take the sheets off my bed and put them into the laundry, but something told her not to bother, so she left them alone and went off to do other chores.

By that time, my draft board was almost up to my number. I went back to visit everyone in my department at the Pru to tell them I hadn't enlisted after all. The new employee said, "See, I told you!" Then he repeated his advice: "Just let them draft you. Don't sign up for anything. Don't volunteer. Do as little as possible – only do what you're told." Then he said, "If you desperately want to get out, just pee in your bed every night no matter what, and you'll be out within a month." Yuck. I couldn't imagine doing that, considering that I had been a bed-wetter when I was younger.

All I could do was wait for the inevitable. By the end of August, they drafted me.

It started out innocently enough. Down in Newark, at the induction center, there were only about a dozen of us going in that day. Soon, we were on a bus that took us to the airport. Then we were all put on a plane to South Carolina. I had never been on a plane before that. And I didn't even have to buy a ticket, right?

Reception processing was pretty routine. It lasted a week. We joined hundreds of other draftees. Everyone got haircuts, then was measured for and issued uniforms (fatigues, dress shirts, boots, slacks, brass, the works). Then we each mailed our civilian clothes home in a cardboard box. We took tests in big rooms full of desks, got inoculations, and got to see movies at the PX theater in the evenings.

Finally, we had to head off to another part of the base for basic training. I got two more inoculations with a serum "gun" in both arms at once and had to drink a pink, gooey liquid out of a tiny paper cup right after that. I almost threw up. One of the shots was tetanus, and my arm became quite sore.

The whole demeanor of those in charge shifted. The lazy pacing of reception processing was over. Now we had to run everywhere, each carrying all our gear in a huge duffel bag. It was my birthday that day, but nobody noticed. I decided to disown my birthday for a few years after that.

The whole thing was a big shock to my system. I had lived at home or in a college dorm all my life. During holidays or the summer, I had always returned home to my parents' house. When, I dropped out of college, I lived at home while working. Now, I had no idea when I would get to go home again. I called my parents on a pay phone, in tears. Couldn't they do something to get me out of the Army? But there was nothing they could do except try to calm me down and help me get through it.

One of the first things we did was bayonet training. We were trucked out to an open field of peach-colored sand, surrounded by woods. A drill sergeant hollered out commands while standing on top of a big wooden platform in the center. We were all spread out at double arms' intervals, each with an M16 rifle, with a bayonet affixed at the muzzle. These were real bayonets, dull green in color, but with a very sharp point. We had them covered with scabbards (a hard plastic cover), so that no one would get hurt accidentally.

We had to practice moves, such as the "forward thrust," and the "parry," and yell out with a blood-curdling cry at the top of our lungs, for each move we made. Of course, there was nothing to make contact with. The enemy was all in our imagination. In my imagination, I pictured what I would be doing in actual combat, in full Technicolor CinemaScope. Where would this knife enter the body of the other human being? In his stomach? In his throat? Right through his eye?

Inside, I recoiled from the horror of this. Back at the barracks, I pondered it all. My entire idea of what the Army was going to be like had shifted. My father's stories of a stupid, pointless time, spent waiting until release, was replaced by a new reality. I was being prepared for a war to be waged on an extremely personal level. They were going to order me to kill people who were standing right in front of me.

As I thought it over, I realized that this was just the beginning of an entire process for me. I began to question all kinds of things. Since I had gone to Christian Science Sunday school growing up, I sought out the church representative who came on post[40]

---

[40] A civilian who lived nearby, who came onto the Army base where I was stationed, for this purpose.

every Sunday to conduct services (ironically, in the hospital chapel!). He agreed to discuss my dilemma with me. Every weekend, I left post and went to his house to talk. The church did not have a policy of nonviolence, per se, but they did agree to support service members in their personal decision, whatever it turned out to be.

After many long talks together, I decided to apply for noncombat status. I would apply to remain in the Army but be exempt from any direct role in combat. One day, while serving on KP,[41] I took a break to go use the latrine.[42] I stopped into the orderly room on the way back and asked to see the company commander, a captain. I was invited into his office. He stood up, and I saluted. He was actually much shorter than I was, so I was looking down at him.

I told him that I wanted to apply to be listed as a conscientious objector. He looked up at me and said, "Before I hear your request, I think you should know that they will make you a medic and the death rate for medics in Vietnam is definitely higher than that of the infantryman."

I stood there in silence for a brief instant. Then I said, "Okay, but that's not why I'm doing this." He said, "Well, alright, then. See the company clerk. He will give you the correct form. You are dismissed." I saluted again and walked out to see the company clerk.

The form I had to fill out was seven pages long. It had a lot of very difficult questions for me to answer. As I understood it, the law said I had to have a "spiritual" objection to killing, not merely a "moral" one. In the past, only people who belonged to certain religions, such as the Quakers, could apply. But that turned out to be a violation of the First Amendment to the US Constitution (favoring some religions over others by the state), so it was changed.

I sat at a large manual typewriter in a spare room in one of the barracks, pondering my answers and then typing them onto the form. As there were no copying machines available, I had to hit the typewriter keys hard enough to make one original and five carbon copies legible. Each time I made an error, I had to peel the pages back, one by one, to erase it.

I also had to be interviewed by a chaplain, a psychiatrist, and a "disinterested" officer (someone not in my direct chain of command). Their reports, along with the form I had filled out, were all put together and sent to the Pentagon, where the decision would be made. Meanwhile, I continued to have some training, but my rifle was turned back in to the weapons room, and I was exempted from hand-to-hand combat training. The policy at that time was that I was presumed to be a legitimate

---

[41] Kitchen Patrol, an informal term for working in the kitchen and dining hall as assigned duty for a day.

[42] There mess hall had no bathrooms - trainees had to walk back to the barracks.

conscientious objector the moment I applied, unless personnel at the Pentagon later decided otherwise.

Once the others in my basic training company graduated, I was now on what they called "holdover status." I never knew what I would be doing, day to day. On some days, I had no duty at all. Other days, I had to work in the kitchen or help the captain do the payroll. I had to move into an extra barracks while a new company of men came in to start training for the next eight-week cycle.

The Army had just gotten rid of the pass system, so I could go into town whenever I did not have any assigned duty. I went into a bookstore and found a book called *How Children Fail*, by John Holt. I read that and then returned to buy other books of his, as well as similar books by other authors, all of which gave me a whole new perspective on the standard educational system.

As I read, I began to realize that the entire conventional school system had cheated me out of nearly 12 years of my life! They had used shame and humiliation in order to "motivate" me to learn. Of course, I was eager to learn, but I already knew what I wanted to learn. I had no use for their techniques, curriculum, and priorities. I was angry. I was furious! I wrote numerous letters home explaining how angry I was. The few ways in which I had done well in school were overshadowed by the emotional train wreck my so-called "education" had been.

Although the test results at NYU had suggested that I needed to go back to college to get a degree, I was in no mood to return to school *ever again*.

§ § §

Early the following year, word came down that I was approved for noncombat status, so I was exempt from being ordered to kill or injure anyone. I served out the rest of my time as a clerk typist at a few different posts here in the US. Fortunately, I was never sent overseas, to 'Nam, so now I'm considered a "Vietnam-era veteran."

I ended up working as a clerk at the US Military Academy at West Point. They had a mainframe computer with timesharing terminals and plotters in various buildings. This was well before the internet, as we now know it, came into use. So I wrote a FORTRAN program to help streamline operations in an office I was working in. They also had a craft shop, where I built myself a desk to keep in my quarters. (I still have the desk. I'm sitting at it now, as I write this book.) I also saved up some of my pay and bought a used 1967 Volkswagen Microbus in classic red and white.

In late 1971, word came down that a number of other men who had been drafted just before I was were to receive "early outs." This meant that they would be released from active duty before serving the usual two years. The word was, President Nixon was trying to reduce the size of the Army. I missed out on the first batch, but I was included when they announced another round. I was released from active duty in early 1972, after only eighteen months of service. That was the minimum to get full GI Bill benefits.

After that, I was given my job back at the Prudential. The law said they had to hire me back if I had been drafted, so they did. Rather than a desk job, however, I was assigned to work as a computer operator. Now, I was a guy with a badge who worked in a huge room full of computers with bright fluorescent lights and glass doors with signs that said "Authorized Personnel Only." The room occupied the entire eighth floor of the building, known as the Eastern Home Office. A woman in a glass booth checked my badge as I entered each day (there were no chip cards for IDs as we have now).

As important as I might have felt at first, working in a room full of big computers, my job turned out to be rather mundane. I spent months on set-up crew, where we gathered materials onto wheeled carts jobs to be run by the second-shift 1401 operators. We used job sheets in ring binders to guide us as we pulled specific tape reels from the tape library, program card decks from shelves, blank card stock and preprinted forms from the stockroom, then parked the carts near the machines when we were done.

Eventually, they trained us in Autocoder[43] (even though we were never supposed to actually write programs). Finally, I was put on a machine, an IBM 360 Model 30. It was running in 1401 compatibility mode, as they called it. So, I spent the day mounting tapes on tape drives, disk packs in disk drives, card decks into hoppers, and paper forms into printers; hitting a "start" button, waiting for the job to complete, and then unmounting all that stuff before starting the next job. This is what they used to call batch processing.

Years later, I described it as if I worked in a laundry. You take in the dirty laundry, wash it, and take out the clean stuff. It was just about as exciting, after the initial appeal wore off. And no, it didn't pay that well, either. So, I lived at home with my parents, and commuted back and forth by train, just as I had before.

Meanwhile, the question of college hung in the air.

---

[43] Autocoder is a computer language for programming the IBM 1401 line of computers. The 1401 is still one of my favorite computers ever, even though I could never hope to own one! Fortunately, the Computer History Museum in California has restored two 1401 computer systems to demonstrate to the public, so if I really want to, I can fly out there.

College?

While working at the Prudential the second time, I began to ponder what to do about college. I remembered the results of the testing back at NYU. Sure, my mother wanted me to go to college, but after the experts at NYU had weighed in, this became much bigger than just my mother's wishes. It was as if the entire world required me to get a degree if I wanted to have a reasonable life.

Given my experiences in the education system so far, I really had to think this over. Finally, I came up with an approach. "OK, world, … I'll go to college under one condition: That I find a college that passes *my* admission requirements. And if I don't find one, then fuck 'em all, I'm not going to college!"[44]

This turned out to be a brilliant approach. Suddenly, I had given myself priority above all academic institutions! After all, I'm the customer. It's *my* money and *my* life that we're talking about here! Clearly, after graduation, I'd be on my own. There were no guarantees. I couldn't go back for a refund if things didn't turn out well. So, I had to make sure that any institution I considered measured up to what I really wanted.[45]

I decided that instead of visiting three colleges on one road trip (as I had done with my parents the first time around), I would visit one college at a time and stay for three days, preferably while students were there. What's a few extra gallons of gasoline and a little extra time, when it comes to making such an important decision in life! And by now, I had my own car.

My mother had met a young woman teaching in a summer program at the local high school. She had been to Goddard College, in Vermont, had graduated, and was about to head up a new office[46] at a small college down in North Carolina. I went to talk with her, and she recommended I check out the college she was planning to work at.

So I got into my VW Bus and drove all the way down there. I stayed three days, as I had planned. But I didn't really like what they had there, so I drove back home and pondered what to do next. It occurred to me, why not go to the source? That is, if this woman thought her experience at Goddard was so great that she was trying to

---

[44] Years later, I realized that my experience in applying for non-combat status in the Army, along with what I had read about the flaws in the education system contributed to my new attitude. I had a new sense of personal power and resolve when approaching other institutions later in life. For the first time, I began to realize that I was more important than they were.

[45] I recommend this approach to *anyone* considering college, at any age. It's your money, your life, your learning process. Make them show you how they are prepared to fit your needs, not the other way around!

[46] She was starting an Off Campus Field Service (OCFS) program there, kind of like a co-op program, where students gain experience working or teaching in the surrounding community, before graduating.

replicate part of it at another college, why not visit Goddard itself? So in July 1972, I drove up to have a look.

When I arrived, the admissions office had already closed for the day, so there was just a sign that said to go up to "CL" dorm on the Northwood campus[47] and stay in one of the rooms reserved for prospective students.

As I walked up to the front door of CL, I noticed two things. First, there were two people standing there having a discussion about something. I stopped to listen to what they were saying. I found the discussion fascinating. Both people were making good points, but also seemed to be good at listening to the other person. After awhile, it suddenly struck me that this was not two students; one was actually a faculty member!

I was impressed. There was no sense that one person held any air of superiority over the other by virtue of their role at the college. They were just like two colleagues having a great talk with each other.

The other thing I saw was a tiny bit of graffiti. Someone had carefully scratched a few words into the dark brown wood on the outside of the building near the door. It read, "This is college?" Right under that, it said, "This is college!" After living in that dorm for three days and talking to a variety of people there, I got what this meant: Many of the usual trappings of college were absent, and yet what was going on was engaging, exciting, unconventional, challenging, and often amazing!

I realized that this was where I wanted to go.

---

[47] At the time, in order to better facilitate the process of community governance, Goddard was separated into two campuses, Greatwood and Northwood, with a path through the woods connecting them. A third one was planned but never built. Each campus was planned to have no more than 250 people.

At Goddard

After 12 years of public school, a year and a half of college at RPI, six months working a low-level job, a year and a half in the army, and another nine months of work, I finally arrived at Goddard College as an undergraduate student. Because of their trimester system, I was able to start in January of 1973. I was 22 years old.

At the time, Goddard's resident undergraduate program (RUP) was still going strong. Here was a college with no grades, no exams, no core requirements, and no majors. All credit was obtained, per trimester, by written evaluations prepared by the student, the faculty member teaching each course in which the student enrolled, and the student's academic advisor.

Thus it ended up as place filled with people who had found traditional academic institutions incompatible with their learning style. These were people who had rejected the adultism and conformity so typical at other places of so-called "higher learning."

When I arrived on campus to move into my room, I observed many returning students enthusiastically greeting each other. Two people would see each other, run toward each other, exclaiming the other's name, and almost collide as they joined in an emphatic embrace. I would hear them talking in excited voices, "I didn't know you were going to be here this term!" And "What dorm are you in? Are you in CR again?" And so on. I felt a bit envious. I had never experienced a close friendship like that.

This reaction was particularly intense at Goddard due to the flexibility of the trimester system. Students could freely choose their own academic calendar, scheduling resident terms, non-resident terms, and vacation terms in any order they desired.[48] So you never knew if you would be on campus with someone again, unless you both arranged for that on purpose. Later on, I realized an important lesson from this. Expanding individual options can work against community cohesiveness. With people scattered this way, it was more difficult to practice Goddard's form of community governance, based on large in-person meetings.

Although I had read all the literature from the admissions department, and had even visited Goddard during the summer of 1972, once I actually started my first term there, I discovered something I had not anticipated. The feeling I had was hard to describe, but here I was, surrounded by people with listening and communication skills that I had rarely ever experienced before. They were more likely to put effort into "relating" to each other and to "deal with" issues that came up between them (a whole new language to me). Somewhere deep beneath it all, I think love was the underlying factor.

---

[48] Each trimester was about three and a half months long, similar in duration to semesters at other colleges, so they covered the entire year, except August. If you wanted to spend a vacation term skiing instead of at the beach, you could just take the Winter/Spring term off.

I felt as if I were two feet tall in a land of giants. There were people who listened patiently to me, when I could not find much capacity to listen patiently to them. My stories (of my life up until then) just seemed to tumble out of my mouth, almost out of control. Whereas I had survived the first 22 years of my life feeling as if no one really understood who I was, here I seemed to be surrounded by people who were finally "getting it."

There were a great variety of people there, of course, some more sensitive and understanding than others. And there was a lot of political rancor at the time, as the original college president, Tim Pitkin, had resigned a few years earlier, and subsequent administrators had made many changes since then. Some students were very upset with some of these changes, to say the least, and spoke up about it at community meetings.

§ § §

During my first term there, I began to sense a great amount of grief within myself, about the trials of my life so far. It soon became clear to me that although these feelings were rather pronounced at times, I was physically unable to cry.

I cannot tell you exactly why this was, but I certainly remember being shamed and ridiculed by my father when I started to cry after experiencing an emotional reaction to something when I was younger. Perhaps I had already absorbed the social conditioning that almost all boys received, where "crying is for girls." That statement carries two terrible sexist messages. First, that girls are somehow inferior to boys because they are more likely to cry when hurt or in grief. But second, that boys are denied a natural human process that is a significant step in healing from trauma.

One night, I was up very late, feeling particularly upset and alone. Because of a quirk in the Design & Construction program in which I was enrolled, I ended up in a single room. I had been recording some video earlier in the day, and had all the equipment in my room before taking it back to the Learning Aids Center the next morning. So I plugged everything in, propped the camera up on a stack of books, threaded a reel of tape into the record deck, taped a Tensor lamp to a mic stand so that it would shine straight down in the darkness, and started the machine recording.

I sat in the darkness, just out of range of the light, where I was invisible to the camera. I moved my hands into and out of the stream of light, where they seemed to appear and disappear in the image being recorded. I began to use my hands to express my feelings as best I could. I made a fist. I shook my finger at an unseen antagonist. Finally, I bowed my head down into the light, face down into my open hands, and pretended to cry.

I wanted to actually cry, but I couldn't, so this was the best I could do. When I played it back, it almost seemed real. But crying was still stuck for me. I thought of that recording as kind of a journal entry, but in video instead of with pen and paper.

Sex and Drugs and Rock 'n' Roll

I need to go back a bit here to say a few things about sex.

When I was much younger, around the age of eight, I had a blue plastic raincoat. It was made of translucent vinyl, with reinforced seams and snaps up the front. I remember one day when no one else was home, I took it out of the coat closet, took all my clothes off and put it on. I got quite sexually aroused.

I had no idea what sexual activity was or why this piece of ordinary clothing had this effect on me, but I had two reactions. One, I really liked the feeling. Two, I couldn't dare let anyone know about this. I was years away from puberty, so I still had a lot to learn, that's for sure.

I now know that my reaction to the raincoat's material is called a fetish, or a class of human characteristics known as a "paraphilia" as described in the *DSM-5*.[49] But back then, it was just a strange secret I had to keep. As I was so socially isolated, I never really dated during my school years. So my fetish was my only sexual outlet. All during the rest of school and into college, I kept this secret, in fear that if anyone found out, I would die of embarrassment, or be taken in for some kind of evil aversion therapy.

When I first got to Goddard College, I happened on another, more classical sexual outlet, but with an unusual twist. I discovered masturbation in the shower. Of course, millions of teenage boys (and yes, girls) had made use of the shower for this purpose in the past, probably starting right after the shower was invented (along with a bathroom door you could lock from the inside!). You might assume that I had figured this out long before this, but my fetish had been a sufficient substitute until then.

But what's important is the fantasy I discovered in the process. I became aroused by imagining that my body could be magically transformed from a male body into a female one. Sex reassignment surgery was rare (or at least rarely discussed) at the time. Instead, I just fantasized that someone would wave a magic wand and my penis would be replaced with a vulva, I would grow breasts, my beard would disappear, and so on.

It is only recently that I have discovered that someone has proposed a name for this phenomenon: "autogynephilia."[50] Recently, autogynephilia has become somewhat

---

[49] The *Diagnostic and Statistical Manual of Mental Disorders*, fifth edition, published by the American Psychiatric Association. It now says that a paraphilia is "… not ipso facto [a] mental disorder, …" unless it causes, "distress or impairment to the individual," or, "[entails] personal harm, or risk of harm, to others." As I was not "impaired" by this, and was not doing any actual harm to myself or others, I did not officially have a "disorder,"according to the *DSM*.

[50] See the Wikipedia article entitled, "Blanchard's transsexualism typology," and related references.

controversial, now that the gender identity revolution (for lack of a better term) is going on. But rather than delve into detail about that here, I will continue my story and say more about it later on.

At the time, Goddard College was known for its tradition of experimental education, but it had also gained a reputation as a place where people more openly experimented with drugs and sex. During the late 1960s and early 1970s, the word on Goddard was that it was one of a number of places around the country where "it was happenin'," as we would say. The admissions department could get by with very little overt publicity, as potential students learned about Goddard from their friends and just showed up to apply.

Students lived in coed dorms, from the first trimester through the ninth. Even some graduate students lived in the dorms. Since many people didn't start at Goddard right after high school, the ideas of "younger" or "older" or "freshmen" or "sophomore" were irrelevant. Someone might say "I'm a '5,' this term," indicating what trimester they were in, but that was only if it came up in conversation.

The housing office staff did not assign a man and a woman to the same room unless they both requested each other as roommates. But, sometimes, two people "fell in love'" after the term started. Sometimes they negotiated with their originally assigned roommates to switch rooms. (One term, I ended up with a woman as a roommate because my original roommate moved in with her original roommate so they could push their beds together and sleep together. My roommate and I kept our beds apart and even agreed on a "knock first" protocol before entering the room.)

With all this going on, it was easy for me to feel like the "last virgin at Goddard" during my first term.[51] It seemed as if I wasn't "getting any" while everyone else must be. Of course, this was far from true, but logic escaped me. As the term went on, I felt more and more desperate.

Desperation is a funny thing. The more you feel it, the more it shows, and the less likely anyone is going to be attracted to you. That's just one of the ironic (tragic?) things about life and relationships. The more you need tender loving connection, the less likely you'll get it.

The dorm I lived in was a "cooking" dorm, which meant that the typical student lounge on the first floor had been converted into a kitchen and dining area. With only sixteen of us living there, all working on the same Design & Construction course, we became very close. As the term went on, it became more and more clear to my dorm mates that I was a long-suffering virgin. I secretly had a crush on one woman in my dorm, but she was rather shy and I was also, so we never connected romantically.

---

[51] Before Goddard, I had never had sex with anyone, gotten drunk, smoked weed, or taken any other "recreational drugs" of any kind, even though I had already been to college and served in the Army.

Finally, there were only two weeks of the term left. We had to finish our coursework, write our evaluations and get them signed. We had to make plans for leaving and think about what we were going to do next term. People who had grown closer during the term seemed to pull back into themselves as they prepared to go. In the midst of all this, I forgot all about my virginal status. The idea of starting a relationship so late in the term seemed impossible.

For my video production course, I had volunteered to record a dance performance for a student who was about to graduate. She needed the videotape to submit as part of her senior study project. Over the preceding few weeks, I had met with her a few times to review the dances she was going to perform.

The big dance concert was in the Haybarn Theater, one week before the end of the term, on a Saturday night. In those days, the equipment I needed was quite heavy and bulky.[52] Besides the video tape recorder (VTR), I had to bring a separate video camera, tripod, video monitor, reels of tape, cables, and an outlet strip.

When it was all over, the dancer helped me load all the equipment back into my VW bus, and rode with me back to my dorm on Northwood. Once there, she helped me carry it all upstairs to my room, where it had to stay locked up until Monday morning when it was due back.

I went off to park the bus for the night, and came back to find her lying on my bed. "I'm too tired to walk all the way back to my apartment in town," she said. "Can I just sleep here tonight?" I hadn't expected this, but I said okay. I went off to brush my teeth and came back to find her already under the covers, fast asleep.

Now this was a single (twin) bed, barely wide enough for one person. And I usually slept in the nude. I stood there wondering what to do. If I climbed into bed with her while naked, wouldn't that be a bit presumptuous? Finally, I decided to leave my blue jeans on, and squeeze into the bed, lying on my side. I could barely keep from falling out of bed, but by some miracle I settled onto my precarious strip of available mattress and fell asleep after awhile.

The next morning we both woke up a little early, as this was April and the sun was already up by 7 AM. As we were both still in bed, she slipped her hand down under the waistband of my jeans and said, "Why don't you take these off?"

My virginity ended that very morning.

---

[52] This was the era of the Sony portapak, a portable reel-to-reel, EIAJ-1 standard black and white videotape system. I had to use the bigger AV-3600 studio deck, for its one hour recording capacity, as I had also agreed to record other dancers performing that night.

Dance Class

In my elementary school gym class, when it was time to divide up into teams, the coach selected two boys who were known to be good athletes as team captains. The two captains stood before the rest of us, taking turns picking one boy at a time for each team. Often, I was the last one left to be picked, so nobody even had to call my name.

Once I got to junior high school, I wanted to join the gymnastics club (an after-school activity). I liked that both boys and girls participated, but I was not strong enough to do most of the events, so I was allowed to join as an "alternate." I think this was a way for the coach to acknowledge my enthusiasm for it, and allow me to practice, without actually competing against other schools at meets. There was no dance program there, and there wasn't even a gymnastics team when I got to high school, but something about the grace and creativity of the movements and the limited sense in which both boys and girls got to collaborate in something appealed to me.

The first term I was at Goddard College, I had a single room, as I mentioned before. The second term, however, I had a roommate. He was enrolled in a modern dance class that term. One afternoon, he returned to our room, opened the door, and found me with my stereo turned up, moving about the room in a wild improvisational frenzy.

I had started doing this back at my parents' house, after I dropped out of RPI. I felt lonely and isolated back then, especially on nights when the rest of my family was downstairs, watching *Medical Center* on TV, a program I detested. I would close my bedroom door, put Led Zeppelin's first album on the turntable, turn it way up, and practice my crude form of dance therapy to the blues they were singing. This was my way to express the anger and frustration that was pent up inside me, even though I didn't fully realize it at the time.

Anyway, my roommate said something like, "If you can move like that, I'm taking you to dance class with me!" I was reluctant at first. My first question was, "What will I wear?" In those days, students wore leotards and tights to dance classes. He tossed a pair of black tights at me and said, "Here, you can borrow these." Thus my connection to the world of dance outside my own bedroom began.

I enjoyed that first class enough to sign up for the rest of the term. Of course, I couldn't continue with his pair of borrowed tights, I had to obtain some dance wear of my own. In order to see what was available, someone lent me a Capezio mail order catalog. I discovered that most of the pages were devoted to women's dance wear, in a variety of styles and bright colors. For men, there were just two pages at the back. The one leotard for men was a tank-top style, with the neck and arms cut way down, presumably to expose as much chest and arm muscle as possible. There was one style of tights. You could have black, white, or pearl gray. Those were the only colors.

If you were a man but you wanted to order a short-sleeve or long-sleeve leotard, or something more colorful, you had to order one of the women's styles instead. First, you had to know your dress size, for that was the only way they sold them. After looking at some measurement charts, I surmised that I was a "16 - 18" in a leotard, and had to order tights in a large, to make sure the legs were long enough.

This disparity of clothing availability reflected the great gender imbalance in the dance world back then. Not many men ever took dance classes, even at Goddard. In the class I attended, there were about four men and perhaps twenty women. When the packages I had ordered arrived in the mail, the tag inside the neckline of the leotards said, "Women's, 16-18." I put them on and went to class.

But as I was wearing them, something unusual was happening inside me. This was not an erotic feeling, exactly. Fortunately, I did not become sexually aroused (which would have been quite visible in dance wear!). Instead, I had kind of a soft wonderful feeling, more in the center of my body. I felt, in a way, hugged, but not just by the physical cling of the stretchy fabric. In a strange way, I felt loved. Somehow, wearing the same things that the women in class were wearing gave me a sense of belonging, more so than just by being in the same class together.

Now, as I may have mentioned, I was brought up with a great amount of self-doubt. After awhile, I began to wonder: Was I was taking dance classes just because it was a good reason to wear these clothes and experience this feeling, or because I really wanted to learn modern dance? I vacillated on this for quite some time. After years of wondering, I finally arrived at an answer. The answer was, "Yes." I liked dancing *and* the dance wear, and it was all okay. It was all good.

At the time, I went on to take more dance classes, at Goddard and in the Boston area after graduating. Within a few years, the manufacturers of dance wear changed the wording on the tags from "women's" to "adult." So, even back in the 1970s, a shift toward gender equality was already taking place. I got more and more used to wearing dance wear in class (and occasionally on stage) and concentrated more on my dancing.

Feminism

In the early 1970s, what's now referred to as "second wave feminism" was in full swing. The Boston Women's Health Book Collective had just published the first edition of *Our Bodies, Ourselves* in 1971. *Ms.* magazine had started publishing that same year.

When I arrived at Goddard, two years later, all the dorms were coed except one. A group of women had decided that Aiken dorm would be the Women's Dorm, with no men allowed. Not only that, there were three or four courses that were open only to women students. They were talking about roles for women in society, the development and growth of women's consciousness-raising groups, and so on.

I wanted to talk about all that stuff, too! I felt very left out. There were no special dorms or courses for men. Anyway, I wanted to be in a group of both men *and* women talking about those things. What about the things I had to endure as a man? What about playground bullying and fistfights? What about the draft?

One day, I overheard part of a discussion among a circle of women in an adjoining meeting room (where they had left the doors open). I heard one woman say, "Well, every man is capable of rape." I didn't hear anyone else disagree. I remember thinking, "How could that be? I would never rape anyone." I loved women. I wanted all the best for the women around me and for women in general.

But I grew up judging myself as guilty before being proven innocent. That woman's remark cut deep. I was shocked, hurt, and confused. I felt terrible and upset. Now I've come to better understand how incredibly frustrated and angry many women were back then. Even now, men are often seen as the enemy when it comes to progress for women. I think we're still trying to tease apart how men and patriarchy are not the same thing.

The next term, Sally Binford, a faculty member that year, offered a course on gender roles in society, that was open to both men and women. I enrolled right away. I think there were about five men and sixteen women in the class. I remember class meetings where we sat on chairs in a big circle, and started to learn about each other's experiences. I felt honored and amazed to be there, to listen a lot, ask some questions, and be able to share a little from my perspective.

Another term or so later, someone finally offered a class open to men only, to study what was going on for men. I think there were about a dozen of us who enrolled. The graduate student who led it assigned readings in anthropology, including works by Margaret Mead and others. We met a few times a week to discuss the topics that were covered.

About halfway through the term, however, we reached a turning point. One day we had sort of a crisis meeting. The grad student posed the question, "Who actually completed the reading assignment?" Only two students raised their hands. The rest of us sat silent. He was somewhat irritated. "Why are you still coming to class if you're not going to read the selections? How can we have a reasonable discussion on the topics?" Everything stopped. At first no one was quite sure how to answer that. Slowly, we started talking about it, and we began to understand why.

Men had a tradition of approaching topics from a logical, analytical, or theoretical perspective. But one book, *Unbecoming Men*, which was recently published, was an account of things that came up in an early men's consciousness-raising group. So, the question became, "What about us?" Why just read about the emotional impact of being raised male in a book written by other men? Why aren't we talking about *our own* feelings, instead? We have plenty of experience to draw on, right here among ourselves!

So, at that moment, we changed everything about the course. We stopped holding class in the Manor Lounge and adjourned to the grad student's apartment down in Plainfield. Essentially we turned the class into a men's consciousness-raising group for the rest of the term. It took us a little while to get going, but soon we began to trust each other more and open up about what we were going through.

We even compared notes with some of the women's groups that were meeting around the same time. We discovered that each group needed a facilitator, but their roles were slightly different. In either case, the facilitator needed to help keep the conversation focused on personal experiences and feelings, rather than veering off into "safe" topics. For men, the safe topics were sports or cars or technology. For women, it was fashion or cooking or gossip. Either way, the facilitator had to catch group members in the act and steer things back to what they were avoiding.

We also discovered another difference. The facilitators in the women's groups often had to stop too many women from talking at once. Whereas for men, when it came to feelings, the conversation would sometimes just die out, leaving an awkward silence. So, the facilitator's job in mens' groups was much more to draw people out.

During that term, my parents came up to visit me. I convinced my father to attend one of our meetings. I think it was the only time in my life where I realized that he looked frightened. He didn't admit it, of course, but he seemed very uneasy. He kept asking little questions about what exactly we were going to do there, in a tentative sort of way.

I remember climbing the stairs up to the second floor apartment where we met. Once inside, after a few minutes, my father had figured out how to handle it. He was a walking encyclopedia of clichés and trivial facts, so he settled into that role, reciting familiar quotes, etc., when it was his turn to speak. I was disappointed, but later I realized that I was expecting a lot from him. Talking about his inner fears and feelings was just too far beyond his comfort zone. My guess is that he was also experiencing some homophobia beforehand, but I never asked him, so I never really knew.

The Decline of Civilization

By the time I got to Goddard, the angry demonstrations of the late 1960s had given way to a new sense of optimism. The first Earth Day and *The Last Whole Earth Catalog* both debuted in 1970. We were talking about cleaning up the environment, ending pollution, growing organic food, composting, solar energy, and so on. I was enrolled in the Design & Construction program at Goddard my first term. The idea was that the people who were going to live in a building should be directly involved in designing and building it.

Then, in the fall of 1973, during my third term there, the first oil crisis happened. Although Goddard is situated in rural Vermont, we were well aware of what was happening. We saw the newspaper headlines and our food prices started to rise.

Goddard had started to experience a decline in student enrollment. Because almost all of the college's income came from tuitions, budgets had to be cut in response. A few faculty had to be let go. Goddard dropped its unusual trimester system and went over to conventional semesters. A few academic deans resigned and new ones were appointed who seemed to have a much more conventional attitude.

Over the next two years, I watched as the focus of the entire student body shifted. Instead of an open exploration of the arts, for instance, students worried a lot more about whether they'd have a job after graduation. Mind-expanding drugs, such as cannabis and hallucinogens, gave way to mind-numbing drugs such as alcohol and pills. In the world around us, progressive rock music started to fade as disco and punk rock took over. I felt as if I had discovered life on a wonderful tropical island, only to have the ocean start to rise and swallow it up.

After I left Goddard in May of 1975, I spent some time at my parents' house in New Jersey, then went back to the Boston area and found a job as a software engineer. Eventually I found a group of roommates, moved into a house in the fall, finished writing my senior study, and returned to Vermont to graduate, officially, in December.

I still had many friends at Goddard, so I drove back up to Vermont on occasion, and spent the weekend "crashing" in someone's dorm room. I went "tripping" on two different occasions during that time. I only took half a hit (of mescaline the first time, then blotter acid the second time), sensing that I wasn't ready for anything more. It seems that I made a good decision; I enjoyed the effects, but didn't have so much that I "freaked out." After all, it seemed to me that these are very powerful drugs!

After that, I told various other people that I only wanted to take hallucinogens, "about twice every reality." A few people asked me, "What's a reality?" I couldn't exactly describe what I meant, but I told them, "I'll know it when I see it." However, inside, I began to sense that this brief period of optimism was now drawing to a close. I realized that it would be quite some time before we would have another one, although I was certain that eventually, we would.

Asking for Help

I used to sit in the living room in our group house in the late 1970s, talking about my feelings and emotional challenges with my roommate Paul. One day, he said, "I think you have some problems that just can't be solved by the two of us sitting here talking." He suggested that I seek out professional counseling of some kind.

I had resisted the idea long enough, I thought. "Okay, How do I start?" I asked him. He gave me a phone number to call for a referral. Later that evening, I noticed a tiny cramped feeing in my solar plexus. I didn't think much of it and went to bed.

Around 3 AM, I woke up with my heart pounding. My arms and legs, all the way out to my hands and feet, were all pins and needles. I felt extremely light-headed, as if I were about to faint. I was terrified!

Thoughts raced through my mind. Was I having a heart attack? What if I became unconscious, but continued to act, like some people do when they take sleeping pills and then sleepwalk to the refrigerator without remembering a thing? My room was on the third floor, so what if I stepped out of the window without being conscious of what I was doing? I'd hit the concrete below and probably die.

I was this close to going downstairs, waking up Paul, and having him take me to the hospital. I went back and forth in my mind, trying to decide, for what seemed like an eternity. Then I realized something. I had been sitting there for at least five minutes wondering what to do, yet I hadn't died of a heart attack. I noticed my heartbeat, although still rapid, wasn't pounding quite so much. The tingling sensation in my arms and legs wasn't quite as pronounced. I felt less faint.

Slowly, a feeling of exhaustion began to take over from the panic. I began to sense how truly tired and worn out I had become. By some miracle, I eventually lay back down, shut off the light, and went back to sleep.

The next day, I got up and called the number. They told me that the first opening was sometime next week. Next week?!?? I needed to talk to someone now! I pleaded with them, but that's all they had. Finally, I said okay and made an appointment. Then, I remembered that someone I knew practiced Gestalt therapy, so I called him. Yes, he had an opening in a few days. So I made an appointment with him, and canceled the other one.

In the years since, I've worked with psychologists, independent social workers, and others. I took a class and attended some workshops and started peer counseling as well. I learned that what I experienced that night is called an anxiety attack (or panic attack). Feelings of fear that I had suppressed came to the surface right at the point when I had decided to make a big change in my life. I was going to ask for help, even though what I often got in the past was no help at all, and often just made me feel worse. I had courage after all.

Suburban Life

Living in our group house, I ignored our local town government for a few years. A booklet called a "Warrant" came in the local newspaper each year, but I ignored it. I had no idea what "warrant" meant. The first page was in the form of a letter from a clerk to a "constable," telling him to post notice in public places in the town. What? The language was so archaic! There was a list of polling places, and a list of "articles," but it was not really clear to me what we were supposed to do with all this.

During that time, my housemate Paul and I were in the habit of having frequent discussions about politics and culture, sitting in our living room. One day, I told him that I was tired of just the two of us sitting there, talking. After all, what good were we doing? We were all talk and no action, right? Our spoken opinions never left the room! I challenged him (and myself) to actually go do something. He agreed.

A few days later, we were talking about the upcoming election for governor. He held up a copy of the *Boston Globe*, opened to a two-page spread for me to see. One side was a full-page ad for Ed King with a full-page ad for Frank Hatch on the other. He said, "I think we can agree which of these two candidates we support, right?" I said, "Okay, what are we going to do about it?" He decided to call the phone number right away and ask.

So here we were, two progressives, supporting Frank Hatch, who was a "moderate" Republican. In fact, a number of people who were registered as Democrats had decided to cross party lines and vote for Frank, because they thought Ed King was a such a poor-quality candidate.

The campaign office put us in touch with a local organizer in our town, Dick Smith, and he gave us leaflets to deliver door-to-door in another precinct (as ours had already been covered). Later on, in the election, Frank Hatch lost and Ed King became governor anyway.

The following January, we each received a letter in the mail from Dick Smith. He spoke of the importance of local government and how he hoped that younger people such as ourselves would get involved. There was an invitation to attend a meeting at a home nearby and he promised that a surprise guest would be there.

Paul begged out, but he urged me to go without him. So I went. When I arrived, I was impressed by two things. One was that there were about four men and twelve women attending. I thought that was a pretty good ratio! The other thing was that *nobody smoked!* A political meeting where there were no smokers in the mid-1970s was a remarkable thing, to me!

What didn't impress me was the surprise guest. It turned out to be Michael Dukakis. Mike Dukakis had been the incumbent governor but had just lost to Ed King in the Democratic primary! There he was, in that living room, telling us that he was going to run for governor again in four years. My first thought was, "This guy is a loser – he just lost in the primary; what makes him think he's going to win next time?" Of course, I liked what he said about some of the issues. I thought he was a reasonably good person.

Well, I couldn't have been more wrong about his prospects! It goes to show how well I could read politics at the time (not!). Mike Dukakis not only won in the next primary four years later, he won in the general election and served as governor for two more terms, becoming the longest-serving governor in Massachusetts history and eventually running for president of the United States.

But what was more important to me at the time was that I got an earful on how local representative government worked in our town. That spring, I collected signatures and got on the ballot for Town Meeting Member in my precinct.

Now, this is no high office, mind you. It's strictly volunteer. My town had 21 precincts with twelve representatives elected by the voters in each precinct. That meant that there were 252 of us to be elected. We were called "Members" – there's that archaic language, again – like Members of Parliament in the UK. Indeed!

We met in town hall as Town Meeting which is really a unicameral legislature. That's sort of like a House without a Senate. We voted on all the by-laws of the town, all the budgets, zoning laws, and so on. Of course, only about half of the 252 members actually showed up at most meetings, but we almost always had enough for a quorum.

The meetings were long and involved many specific details, both financial and legal, but I was fascinated enough to run for re-election when my first term was over. I almost never had any opposition. Typically, there were just enough candidates to fill the slots available.

Our town government was nonpartisan, meaning that nobody ran as part of a political party. So there was no overt party organization to support anyone's candidacy. Each person ran on their own, essentially. That also meant that were no "sides of the aisle" during the meetings, at least officially, but after a while, it was pretty clear which side of an issue certain people were bound to come down on.

Besides my contribution to public service, this was also a real education about how government works, firsthand. I saw people behave badly and I saw people do astoundingly good things as well. I saw the meeting get stuck on something, and I saw it eventually get itself unstuck and resolve the issue. Sometimes, I got up to speak, after carefully pondering what I wanted to say. I wrote numerous little outlines of my speaking points in the margins of the printed reports I had sitting in my lap.

I even drafted a by-law and got it passed, with the help of a colleague. We found a way to eliminate permits and fees for yard sales, which the town had previously required, yet still leave the town recourse in case anyone tried to run a business from their yard (by trying to have a so-called yard sale every weekend!).

The most important thing I learned was this: In any legislature, let yourself make up your mind during the session, not before you walk in the door. Be ready for new information, surprises, and new perspectives.

In the long run, I served for 16 years. Finally, in 1995 I decided not to run again. I made my decision after the series of meetings was over for that spring, so I never got up in front of the room to say goodbye. For the next few years, people kept assuming that I was still "on Town Meeting" and were surprised that I wasn't actually there to hear the debates anymore.

Now that I understand politics better, I know that you never just disappear like that. Instead, you get up in front of the hall at the last meeting of the year, stand up tall, and tell everyone that you are stepping down after many long years of service. Then you thank the Board of Selectmen, the Finance Committee, various other officials, and the rest of the elected members in the hall, all for doing a great job, and say that you hope they keep up the good work. You explain that you are going to do other things for the public once you leave office.

Now, as much as that might sound like the typical semi-pompous political speech, I have another take on it after my experience there. You don't thank all those people purely out of self-interest (in hopes that they will support you later on, as a candidate for some higher office, for example).[53] You thank them because debating and voting on legislation is hard work! Even in those days, there was plenty of drama and emotion in that hall. It takes a lot of patience and focus to sit and listen, note the important points made by others, understand the numbers and the legal language, and not get too embroiled in the drama yourself.

Of course, when I decided not to continue at Town Meeting, I was still too close to it all to realize all that. Even after all that time, I was still too naïve for it to occur to me to get up and say those things before departing.

In the long run, I left because I had begun to think that some of the things I wanted to do would best be done outside of government, rather than from within it. Legislatures, especially, are places designed to deal with this year's details rather than implement a long-term vision.

---

[53] Run for higher office, you say? After serving as a lowly Town Meeting member? Well, according to Wikipedia, "[Michael] Dukakis began his political career as an elected Town Meeting Member in the town of Brookline." And he's not the only one who took a similar path.

A Job's a Job

The only full-time job I have ever held for longer than a year was at a little company called CSE in the late 1970s. I wrote computer code in assembly language for various projects. Although we didn't have the kind of cubicles found in some offices, my life was a little like Dilbert's.[54] No, the boss where I worked wasn't as classically clueless, as in the comic strip, but computer technology was changing rapidly, and the older men who owned and managed the company were slower to adapt than the younger employees (my fellow software engineers). We were still using punch cards to key in our code, while many other companies had already changed over to teleprinters or display terminals.

In spite of that, I soon developed a good sense of accomplishment while working there. However, after a year or two, I began to see my life as a series of rising and falling waves of satisfaction with the work. Over time, I experienced a slow downward trend, with the peak of each wave a little lower than before, and the trough in between a little deeper.

One day, while I was working on a difficult project that was supposedly very top priority, we were all asked to stop whatever we were doing and start work on a huge proposal that had just come in, instead. For a week and a half, we worked all day and all evening, even through the weekend. I remember having sandwiches or pizza for dinner while there, then going home and directly to bed. The next morning, I would just shower, have a bowl of cereal or something, and drive back to work.

We had no word processors, so this was all handwritten stuff, typed up by women staffers, handed back to us for corrections and amending, then more retyping, back and forth. They were actually using scissors and double-stick tape to cut and paste various paragraphs onto backing sheets that were then copied onto regular paper for the final document.

Finally, on a Tuesday afternoon, the overnight service truck came to take it all away in a box to send to the customer. We all just stood there, kind of spaced out from lack of sleep. There was a large room in the back, slated to become a new hardware design lab, but it was still empty except for some chairs and a ping-pong table that someone had brought in. I remember playing ping-pong and then sitting out while others played. Somewhere inside me, I experienced a strange feeling.

I was on salary, so we didn't get paid overtime. We were just expected to work extra hours when requested. So they offered "comp time" instead. "Go home and take a few days off," I was told.

The next morning, when I woke up, I realized what the strange feeling was. I was going to quit my job. It was as if a very small voice deep inside me was saying, "I

---

[54] The comic strip character created by Scott Adams.

quit!" At the same time, I was in a panic. I remember pacing back and forth in my living room. What would I do instead? I had no plan, no idea, even. Yet my small inner voice was completely resolved. I could not turn back.[55]

Finally, on Friday, I went back into work. I told my boss, Charlie, who only a few years older than I, that I wanted to talk with him in his office. After he closed the door and I sat down across the desk from him, I told him I wanted to resign. "I had a feeling you were going to say that," he said.

I explained that I was giving plenty of advance notice. It was late October and I said I wanted to leave by the end of the year, over two months hence. I explained that they had me on a project with such pressure to write code that I had had little time to write any documentation. So, if they wanted me to write the documentation, there was plenty of time to have me do that.[56]

He leaned back in his chair so he could reach the calendar hanging on the wall behind him. He lifted up a few pages and looked at it for a moment. Then he said, "Why don't you quit on January third of next year? You'll get more paid holidays that way."

We both laughed. I said okay, sure.

---

[55] Later, I found out that this stage in life is sometimes referred to as one's "Saturn Return."

[56] They never did give me any more time to write the documentation. It's funny how managers typically lament that nobody writes enough documentation, but then they neglect to budget time for the engineers to actually write it!

Charging Ahead

I decided to take some time off and think about what to do next. I spent the next few months at home. I made up my mind that I would be a self-employed video producer. I had plenty of savings, since I had kept my expenses low and put money away.

I used some of the money to book a trip to the UK. I had never traveled outside the US before, so this was a big thing for me to do. I didn't go with a tour, but alone, setting my own itinerary. I used a guidebook in the "*Let's Go ...*" series, published by the Harvard Student Agencies. But even then, there were things I wanted to see that weren't in the book. I had seen Jacob Brownoski's series, *The Ascent of Man*, on PBS. I wanted to see the Iron Bridge, mentioned in the series, as I am fascinated with the history of technology.

I took the trip in April. I had one backpack and a BritRail pass, along with some money and my guidebooks. I stayed in London for a few days, then took a side trip to Coalbrookdale to see the Iron Bridge as I had wanted (even though the guidebooks didn't list it). I then rode further north, along the west coast to visit the one friend I knew in Manchester, in the Midlands. I went up to Scotland as far as Oban, and then traveled back down along the east coast, stopping at the railway museum in York on the way. Back in London, it was around Easter time and I was able to take in a performance of Handel's *Messiah* at the Royal Albert Hall.

Once back home, I started working on setting up my self-employment. I decided on a name, "Open Eyes Video," because I wanted to help others make their way into the future with their "eyes open," (meaning informed, ready, and with a clear vision). I created a logo, got letterhead and business cards printed up, opened a business bank account, including a checkbook with large business sized checks. I was in business, all right!

There was only one problem. I knew how to spend money, but not how to earn it. I knew plenty about video technology, including light, optics, sound, electronics, and even batteries. But what I didn't have was any connection to the industry. I didn't know other video producers nor what markets they were serving. I was essentially a video artist who thought he could get paid to go out with his portapak and make black-and-white videotapes for people. I thought I was above making commercials for furniture stores, used car dealers, or the local dry cleaners. I didn't think I needed any experience serving as a crew member on someone else's productions.

Another issue was that I didn't have any kind of smooth transition. I literally didn't touch a computer for over two years, I was so done with it. I walked into a Radio Shack store in a local mall one day, and walked up to one of their computers on display. I wrote a six-line program in BASIC to draw a diagonal red line across the screen and walked out. That was it.

As a result, I slowly used up all my savings. At the end of the year, losing money, a roommate warned me that I hadn't "paid my dues." Until I figured it out, he recommended that I take a job that would just earn some money. I decided to drive a taxi. I got my license and drove a cab in my suburban town for about a year. There were really only two kinds of work doing that: Short trips, such as carrying a shopper and her groceries up the hill from the supermarket, or a longer trip to the airport. Nobody hailed a cab from the street and there was very little "stand" business (where someone walks up to a cab parked at the stand and asks for a ride), so there was a lot of downtime. I had to bring a paperback book or prepare to be bored while waiting for work to come in over the radio.

In the long run, I was not very well-suited for the job. No matter how well I did the work (open doors for passengers, stow their luggage in the trunk gently, drive efficiently, know the best routes), my income didn't increase one iota. There was only just so much work to be had, a fixed number of cabs and drivers to do that work, and that was that. I might get a slightly better tip based on my efforts, but most people just tipped the standard amount anyway.

At the end of the second year, as I had very little income, I thought I would owe no income taxes, and get a refund. But by April of 1982, when I filed, I discovered that I still owed self-employment tax (for Social Security and Medicare), and I didn't have enough money left in my bank account to pay it.

I was stuck! I was very nervous and distraught. What could I do? I didn't want to just ask my parents for money. They might have given me some, but just to tide me over. But tide me over to what, exactly? There was no future in that.

Fortunately, a new opportunity was about to open up.

Making a Living

Right around then, I received a phone call from a friend. He and his business partner needed someone who could write assembly language code for a Mostek 3870 microcontroller chip.[57] I could work for them as a freelance programmer and get paid by the hour. "Do you have any experience with that chip?" they asked. Yes, I did (I worked on one back at my full-time job). So, was I interested?

Well, yes, indeed! I started work right away.

They were developing a toy for children that would play simple tunes generated by the computer chip. Soon, however, that project was shelved as they got more work from Coleco to write code for game cartridges for their ColecoVision home video game console. I ended up participating in the first video/computer game industry explosion. This was the age of *Pac-Man*, *Space Invaders*, and hundreds of other games. On every street corner, in every pizza shop, there were game consoles the size of small refrigerators that ate quarters at an astounding rate. If you couldn't afford to stand at a console and feed it quarters, you bought the home version from Coleco, Atari, or Sega, and hooked it up to your TV set. It wasn't as good, but it was way cheaper.

That era was short-lived, however. By the time I started, the computer game industry had exploded! It had grown so big that its gross revenues were larger than all other forms of entertainment *combined!* But in two years, it all crashed just as hard. A few years later Coleco, Cabbage Patch Kids dolls and all, had gone bankrupt.[58]

Around 1982, I also started to get a little video work. A friend of mine introduced me to Dan Bricklin, co-founder of Software Arts. He hired me to record the monthly meetings of the Boston Computer Society, where new personal computer products were being introduced by various companies. I used his camera and VHS deck to record them for historical purposes. The sound wasn't very good from the microphone on the camera, and it was hard to get good images off the projection screen in the auditorium. During the audience Q&A, it was hard to pan the camera back and forth between the presenter and the audience. I kept thinking that we should shoot these meetings with two cameras, on 3/4"[59] and then edit the recordings into a single well-produced program.

Eventually we worked out a deal between Software Arts, the Boston Computer Society, and myself to start. We would start a video subscription service for corporate

---

[57] A single chip 8-bit computer of the day. It was based on the Fairchild F8 family.

[58] See: https://en.wikipedia.org/wiki/Golden_age_of_arcade_video_games

[59] Otherwise known as "Sony U-Matic" – a much better quality videotape medium, typically recorded on more professional equipment with better sound, professional microphone connectors, etc.

subscribers, who would receive a recording of the meeting each month. Software Arts would donate the funds to make it all happen.

The first meeting I recorded this way was in late 1983. For one camera "roll," I owned my own portable 3/4" recorder, but now I had to rent another one, along with two color cameras, and hire an assistant, each time there was a meeting. By January of 1984, I decided to purchase a high-quality three-tube color camera (the Sony DXC M3), which cost me $10,000.

The high point of all this was when Steve Jobs presented the very first Macintosh computer to the BCS at the end of January 1984, and I was able to get a good recording of the event.[60] It was very difficult to get the folks at Apple to give me some of the images and video they had presented at the event, so that I could include them in the edited program (They had not permitted me to record off their screens with my camera). Eventually, I had to give up and leave some of those sections out.

Soon, however, everything changed. First, I began to run into trouble: The job of editing took more time than I had expected. I started to get further and further behind schedule. I was shooting the next program before the previous one was edited. The subscriptions were not selling well, and finally, Software Arts itself shut down and sold all its technology to Lotus Development Corp. The funding they provided stopped. The last BCS meeting we shot this way was in June of 1984. Although I was glad to still have my good video camera, the income I was hoping to make with it had now dried up. It was very difficult to go out to find similar work.

---

[60] I saved the recordings for the next 30 years and eventually turned them all over to the Computer History Museum in California. They were able to obtain some funding and, along with Dan and Jonathan Rotenberg, former president of the BCS, we were able to locate many of the materials missing from the original edit I had done.

Emotional Growth

Sometime around 1983, my group house needed another roommate. I went to a meeting hosted by New Community Projects (part of a nonprofit called Project Place) down in Boston. They had monthly meetings where people looking for a group to live with would go to meet people already living in an apartment or house who were looking for new roommates.

There were two women there, also looking for a roommate. They were describing their situation, and as they did, they were laughing and having a great time. Something about their spirit appealed to me, so I took down the phone number for one of them and called her sometime later. I ended up starting a relationship with her soon after. After awhile, she invited me to an evening introduction to Reevaluation Co-counseling, something she had been doing for awhile. It sounded interesting, so I took her up on it.

During the exercises, I didn't think much of it, but near the end, just as I was supposed to end a practice session, someone asked me a trivia question intended to help me focus on the present. I think they asked me to spell "Massachusetts" or something. I started to answer, but instead I started laughing. I had no idea why. But I laughed so hard I couldn't stop! There I was, lying on the floor (where I had positioned myself at the start of the session), with a few others sitting close to me, laughing almost to exhaustion! The evening was supposed to be over but I just couldn't stop! Finally, I was able to calm down and take some deep breaths. So I just lay there, with others surrounding me as we wrapped up. Eventually, I got up and went home, but not before I signed up for the series of classes they offered. Clearly, something was going on inside me and that fit of laughter had started to provide me with some kind of release.

I soon learned that this organization, known as RC for short, had been started by an atheist, so the whole program was strictly atheistic. That suited me just fine at the time. If someone had mentioned "God" to me around then, I probably would have just walked away.

My romantic relationship with her came to a close eventually, but we have remained friends ever since.

Days of Darkness

In the summer of 1984, another romantic relationship I was in ended in a sudden and particularly difficult breakup, soon after the BCS video series ended. I found myself with no relationship partner and a sudden drop in income. I ended up going back to software engineering work. I started working freelance at CSE, the very same company where I had worked in the late 1970s. They put me on a project that had run into trouble and fortunately, I was able to determine how to get it back on track.

Later, in 1985, when that project was over, I took an assignment at another company. They needed to finish testing the software in a cockpit instrument designed to monitor the jet engine in an aircraft. The plane for which it was designed had already been in production and was in the air, but the testing documents had never been finished, so the government contract wasn't complete. It was some of the most boring and pointless work I ever remember doing. I had terrible trouble concentrating, sitting at a desk in front of a computer that was, by then, considered obsolete.

In July of that year, I came home one evening and one of my roommates informed me that the woman who had broken up with me the year before had just committed suicide. I was devastated. This was the weekend of Live Aid, the giant international fundraising concert. I just sat in my room all weekend watching it on TV. Later, I attended the memorial service for her. I learned that she was determined to be "successful" and had very carefully planned her own death. I was depressed but didn't know what to do besides keep working and hope I'd get over it after time passed.

Earlier in the year, I had started a new relationship with another woman, but by the summer I began to realize that it was not going to last. Although we initially seemed to have plenty in common, I realized that I could not reach a level of communication and emotional intimacy that I found essential in a relationship. That August, she left town for her annual vacation overseas. Her roommate also left on vacation around the same time, leaving someone she had recently met to house-sit and care for their cat.

I became attracted to the woman doing the house-sitting. At the time, I was conflicted and uncertain. I had not officially broken up with my existing partner who was away, but I started dating the house-sitter anyway. In spite of my inner conflict (or, perhaps because of it), I ended up having sex with her. She insisted that she was not fertile and that birth control was not necessary. She even said, "Well, if you don't believe me you can go to the drugstore and buy a condom." She said this while I was standing right there in the bedroom, partly undressed. I said, "Okay, okay, I believe you," and acquiesced.[61]

---

[61] This being the mid 1980s, AIDS was still thought to be a disease mostly of gay men, so many people used the pill, the diaphragm, or IUDs for birth control and frequently omitted condoms. If anyone did develop a sexually transmitted infection (STI), antibiotics were typically used to fight it off.

Very soon, some serious conflicts erupted between us. After one particularly rancorous argument, she stated that she loved arguing, and by the way, didn't I also enjoy it? I said no, certainly not. After that, we quickly parted. We had only been together for about three weeks.

I felt guilty, embarrassed, and confused, and wished I had not done what I did. I was relieved that it had ended quickly, but I felt terrible that I had "cheated" on my original partner, who was due back at the end of her vacation.

When she returned, I told her right away about what I had done and admitted that I had "broken" our relationship. She joked about how the house sitter had "taken everything but the cat" but I knew that she felt hurt as well. I apologized profusely, and we agreed that our relationship was over.

After about a month and a half or so, I got a call from the woman who had been the house sitter. She requested a meeting in person, so I met her after hours at her place of work, as she requested. She was alone when I walked in. She announced that she was pregnant.

I was taken completely off-guard by this. I did not know what to think or say, so I was probably not that coherent. I found myself with various conflicting feelings. On the one hand I felt some sense of joy that I might be a father. On the other hand, I barely knew this woman and our breakup had been terrible. Now she seemed to be acting so sweetly. She said that I could have as much or as little involvement in raising the child as I wanted. She even took me to the birthing center near a local hospital, where she expected to deliver the baby.

But within a week or so, however, the truth came out. She defined "as much involvement as I wanted" never to include any custody. This was going to be *her* baby and she meant to make all the final decisions about raising it. On the other hand, "as little involvement as I wanted" meant that whatever else I did, I would always be expected to provide full financial support.

Now, I was truly distraught and terrified. I felt defrauded and powerless. I had no idea how to handle this! What choices did I have? There was no way I wanted to try to raise a child with someone so controlling. After thinking it over for another few days, I called her back and asked her to have an abortion. Her response was to call me cruel, a murderer, and so on. In short, she flatly refused, claiming that I was unwilling to fulfill my obligations, as she saw them. The conversation was certainly every bit as rancorous as the ones we had had during our brief affair.

I was terribly upset. I sought counseling. I went to an attorney. I talked to my friends. Then, one night while talking to a friend, she asked me, "Well, how do you know it's yours?" Somehow I had just believed that it was. In those days, there was no DNA testing, and anyway, the woman was still pregnant; even blood tests were not typically done until after birth.

So, for the next few months, I did not try to contact the woman and she did not contact me. The winter holidays came and went. Then, one day in March, I got a call from her. She requested a meeting in a local restaurant. I showed up and she gave me a proposal. She would have a statement drawn up whereby I would agree never to seek custody or visitation, and she would agree never to seek support, if I would give her the sum of $5000 outright.[62]

Something didn't seem right about this. I realized that I needed an expert to advise me; no ordinary lawyer would do. So I looked up the best attorney I could find who specialized in laws related to child support and custody. His fee was $150 per hour at the time, a very high rate back then. But I only needed an hour or two, so I went to see him.

He explained that such an agreement would have no force of law. The rights for support and visitation ultimately belong to the child; the parents cannot sign them away. I would just be giving her the money outright, for nothing. If she ended up on public assistance and named me as the father, the state would come after me for child support payments anyway. If I didn't pay, I'd end up in court and perhaps even serve jail time. Meanwhile, joint custody was usually only awarded if the two parents were getting along well enough to negotiate care of the child. If they were not, then the court would typically award custody to the mother unless she could be shown to be neglectful or incompetent.

By this time, she had moved multiple times, left no forwarding address, kept an unlisted phone number and told me to call her at work during the daytime, when I had made a decision. I ended up having to call her while I was at work. I remember standing at a wall phone in the computer lab talking with her, as I had no desk or office. It was the only place with even a small amount of privacy – the mini-computers there made plenty of white noise.

Finally, at one point during the call, she said, "Well, clearly you don't care about this child, you're only interested in your money." For some reason, in a moment of lucidity, I blurted out, "No, *you're* the one only interested in money. You're the one who wanted me to just give you money and never see the child!" Within minutes the call was over. I was relieved that I had finally found a way to stand up for myself, but otherwise, I felt strangely numb.

I would not hear from her again for another nine years.

---

[62] Nearly $11,000 in 2017 dollars.

At the Bottom

By December 1986, I felt more and more stress in my life as the Christmas holidays approached. I planned to drive to New Jersey, where my parents and siblings lived. But trying to shop for gifts and get ready seemed especially difficult. I remember packing my car while feeling poorly prepared, as if what I had with me was bound to be disappointing. I was running late.

Finally, I drove off and headed west on the Mass Pike. After about an hour of driving, I was particularly stressed out, conflicted, and depressed. I pulled into a service area and used a pay phone to call my parents' house. My father answered. I told him I was feeling upset and I wasn't sure I was coming after all. He listened to me on the phone but he didn't know what to tell me or how to help. He said I would be welcome, of course, as always, and he hoped to see me, but he did not pressure me.

After I hung up, I got back on the highway, but a short while later, I exited onto Route 20. I started to drive back east, but soon I just pulled over and stopped at the side of the road. I couldn't go back to my house in Massachusetts. This was Christmas, after all. There was nothing there, except perhaps one roommate who didn't celebrate the holiday.

I was trapped in indecision, my mind twisting back and forth from one dismal option to the other. I didn't see any way out of my dilemma. I tried to make myself just drive to New Jersey and have Christmas with my family. I turned around, but I didn't get far. I stopped again. I turned around again and stopped yet again. I felt as if I would be stuck on the side of that road, in the middle of nowhere in central Massachusetts, forever.

I felt as if I were unable to move forward with my life as a whole. There I was, with my hands on the steering wheel of my car, wondering if I should just get back on the highway and steer in front of a large truck, get run over and crushed, and end everything. I sat there pondering this. After a while, I began to realize that that plan wouldn't work anyway. I would probably chicken out at the last minute, the truck would veer across the highway, flip over and crush other cars instead. I would still be alive and be arrested as the cause of a horrendously tragic accident.

I sat there, imagining the horror. There I was, unable to drive anywhere, feeling perhaps the worst I could ever remember feeling. I screamed out loud inside my car. I yelled at everything I could think of that was causing me stress or anyone who had hurt me or taken advantage of me. I pounded the seat next to me with my fist. I burst into tears and cried my eyes out. I sobbed and sobbed.

Eventually, I decided I could not drive to New Jersey. And I couldn't just sit there in my car. So, I started the engine and got back on the highway to drive back to my house in Massachusetts.

When I got home, I walked in and found my roommate Matthew sitting at the dining room table. He saw me come in but he did not look at all surprised at my arrival. I said, "Well, I didn't go to New Jersey." He said, "I know. I've been expecting you." I was dumbfounded. How did he know? He told me that my mother had called him.

It turned out that after my father got off the phone with me, my mother had asked who it was. He said, "It was Glenn. He's not sure he's coming." She asked, "Well how did he sound?" My father said, "Well, not too good." But my mother didn't feel right about that, so she pressed my father to explain further. "How bad did he sound, really?" she asked. My father replied, "Yeah, I guess he sounded pretty bad." So, she had called my house and Matthew had answered. She told him that she was very worried about me and would he please keep an eye out for me if I showed up back there. He agreed.

Matthew was perhaps the best friend I had in the world at that time. I sat down and we just talked, although I don't remember about what exactly. It was just nice to know that even though I wasn't going to show up for Christmas, it was my well-being that concerned my mother the most. The gifts could be exchanged some other time.

§ § §

A few days later, another roommate of ours returned and reported that when he visited his family, they had had a huge, bitter argument. Later on, someone told me that she knew of a woman who got onto a plane to fly home for Christmas. Suddenly, as they were just about to close the door and leave the gate, she got up, pulled her carry-on bag down from the overhead, and said, "I changed my mind, I'm not going!" and walked off the plane. I've always been curious as to what the planets were doing right around that time.

A Great Loss

In my group house, we had a slow turnover of roommates. Each time someone moved out, we would run ads for new roommates in the local newspapers. We'd schedule interviews in the evenings and on weekends. If we liked someone enough after the first interview, we'd invite them back a second time, perhaps for dinner or another group activity, before deciding whether to invite them to move in.

In 1987, my roommate Matthew moved out to get married. So we ran ads and found someone else to take his place.

One afternoon in 1989 the phone rang. It was my friend Russell. He told me that he had bad news. Matthew had been killed in a car accident. His wife, who had been driving, had minor injuries and was taken to the hospital, so she was going to be okay. The car, a Chevrolet Citation, had had a catastrophic electrical failure the night before, while they had been driving up to a folk dance festival in New Hampshire. The entire electrical system had gone dead, causing the engine to quit, and all the lights to go dark at once.

They were in the left travel lane, with the car losing speed rapidly, so she could not head for the shoulder at the right. She pulled to the left, but there was not much shoulder there. There were no overhead lights on that section of the highway, so they were now stopped in complete darkness. Another vehicle, traveling at full speed, struck them from behind and flipped over. Matthew died instantly in the impact.

Russell apologized for not having time to stay on the phone with me because he had to call a number of other people. I thanked him for telling me and said goodbye.

I sat down on the couch in the living room. There was a mad collision of thoughts in my mind right then. First, this just couldn't be! Matthew just died? There must be some kind of misunderstanding! Then simultaneously, I realized that Russell, although a guy with a great sense of humor, would never joke about something this serious. Just from his tone of voice, I knew he was telling the truth.

I must have sat on that couch for twenty minutes, with both thoughts continuing to collide in my mind. It *can't* be true, but it *must* be true. I had never had such a powerful sense of denial in my entire life. I just sat there, unable to move or do anything else, while my brain unsuccessfully tried to reconcile the two thoughts.

Eventually, I got up. I realized that I had a grave responsibility. Matthew had many interests, and by virtue of an announcement on a local college radio station, everyone in the folk music community had heard the news by now. But Matthew had many friends who were not part of the folk music community. Most of them were people he had met through me. So I had to start making phone calls just like the call Russell had made to me.

One by one, I had to tell people what had happened and wait for their expression of shock before eventually saying goodbye and going on to the next call. We were planning a memorial service at a nearby church, so I had to give people the specifics on that as well.

For two weeks, I was consumed by these two things, calling people and helping to plan for the memorial service. I did not cry or even sense my great sadness during this time. I just had to focus on the tasks at hand. Finally, the day came for the memorial service, and I was in charge of some volunteers who were recording it all on video (as many folk musicians were performing in his memory).

The next day, I drove up to Lawrence, where Matthew had helped produce a Labor Day folk music festival for the previous few years. Some people had planned a smaller memorial service for him there. I didn't have any role in helping to plan that one, so I could just go and be there.

I remember standing up, as we all got up to sing "Lord of the Dance." Suddenly, I was in tears. They ran down my face. I could hardly see the notes or words on the page I was holding. I just sobbed and sobbed, as quietly as I could, while standing there with everyone singing. All the emotions and feelings that I might have had during the previous two weeks, things that I had pushed aside during all that work, just came pouring out of me.

Over time, I have adjusted to the fact that he is really gone. I still have video recordings of him in my tape library. I'm not sure how I'll feel when I take them out to convert them to digital form.[63]

---

[63] He produced a series of folk music programs at our local cable TV studio. I plan to digitize a few segments so that they can be cablecast now, over 25 years later.

The Spirit

After spending a few years in co-counseling,[64] I began to think that the process seemed rather ... well, inefficient.

The theory was that you identify some hurt that you endured in your life, where you didn't have the opportunity to "discharge" (physically express) the emotions that resulted. For example, if you felt deep grief but someone or something else kept you from crying (which would have been the appropriate response), then you reacted by holding in your tears. In counseling sessions, we would review that time in the past, get back in touch with the grief, let the tears flow, sob, and finish the discharge process that had been interrupted back then. That would free us up from being "restimulated"[65] by similar circumstances in the present day; our ability to think creatively would be restored in that particular area of life.

In practice, this all seemed to take many, many hours of sessions. At one point, I was struck with the question: Isn't there anything else I can be doing to help get through this process in slightly less time? Or with slightly less effort? I just felt as if I was slogging along and my life would be over before I had "cleared up" all the old emotions that were holding me back. I'd have one foot in the grave while declaring, suddenly, "I'm free!" Then, boom, my funeral.

To be honest, the people who headed RC claimed that their practice was not a substitute for therapy or other treatment by professionals. But what occurred to me was not that. Instead, I asked myself if there wasn't some kind of spiritual work I could be doing to supplement the counseling process. Although I had spurned anything to do with spirituality when I had started RC, I now seemed ready to explore the possibility.

Around that time, I was having therapy sessions with a private social worker. One day, she suggested that I might benefit from some kind of group therapy. She hosted a group herself, but it was too far away. So she suggested that I try a twelve-step group meeting instead. She gave me a list of five group meetings to try. Four were Al-Anon and one was Codependents Anonymous (CoDA). I took the list and realized that, as there was no alcohol abuse in my family, I'd feel out of place in an Al-Anon meeting. But co-dependency was another story. Perhaps that was more like it.

So, I started going to meetings. Although the spirituality seemed vague at first, I began to get a sense that I could get a bit of what I found lacking in RC. After awhile, I attended fewer and fewer co-counseling events and sessions and began to attend CoDA meetings out in Concord on a regular basis. Soon, the meetings there grew so large that they started more meetings on other nights of the week. At one point at

---

[64] Reevaluation Co-counseling, often referred to as "RC."

[65] Some would refer to this as "triggered."

least six or seven of us realized that we were all driving out there from the same town where I lived, so we started a new meeting, right in our town.

This turned out to be the heyday of twelve-Step groups all across the nation. From the late 1980s through into the early 1990s, millions of people attended twelve-step groups related to addictions and issues of all kinds, from work, to debt, to food, to drugs, to sex, to love, to gambling, and of course alcohol. There were even skits on *Saturday Night Live* making fun of the whole movement.

In the process, I learned a lot about how some of my patterns in life were parallel to other addictions. For me it was helping others while neglecting myself. Sure, it's good to be altruistic in life, to an extent. But if you go overboard, you may end up neglecting your own needs while you're pouring your heart out for everyone else. After all, I realized that if my own life went to ruin, I wouldn't have any capacity left to help others. Life seems to be about balance, rather than extremes.

I heard a number of interesting sayings in the process. One was, "The sex addict comes on, the love addict hangs on, and the relationship addict moves on." Another was "Your opinion of me is none of *my* business!" That was a good one. Sure, we all care about what others think of us, to an extent. That's normal. But if you're running your life primarily for the approval of other people, or out of a constant fear that they might become angry with you, then it's not really your life anymore.

I slowly began to understand how deeply ingrained my tendency to please others had become. However, I remained uncertain as to how to change that. The meetings helped, but progress seemed slow.

Seeking

"In the beginning, ..."
the good book starts.

But I am not
heaven and earth,
just one person.

To create me
did not take all that.
And yet
I am not so simple
as a planet.

I knew they loved me
and yet they failed me also,
when I was too small
to know what hit me.

Tiny and helpless
I needed everything,
but I had to take
only what was given.

Now, when I ask for love
how much failure
will I also get
in the bargain?

The Universe is
so big,
it has everything,
I'm told.

I will leave my fear
as far back behind me
as I can
while I put one foot
in front of the other.

The Inventor Gene

The very first computer I bought for myself was an Apple Macintosh 512K, back in the spring of 1985. I took it upon myself to learn how to write software for it. I signed up as a developer and obtained a copy of *Inside Macintosh*.[66]

For some time, I had a number of ideas on how to improve the process of video editing with the help of a computer. My ideas still involved videotape, because computers at the time didn't have the capacity to store digital video. Instead, my idea was to use a personal computer to control video machines with software.

Although what I envisioned was certainly creative when it came to technology and design, I was a bit optimistic about achieving my goals. My business plan was rather short-sighted, now that I look back. I was so proud of my ideas that I was afraid they might be stolen by others, so I ended up trying to do everything myself. I had heard that the key to entrepreneurship was not how much money you had, but how much you could borrow. So, by the late 1980s, I was living and working mostly on borrowed money.

I borrowed money from family members and from credit cards. I hired a business consultant to advise me. Finally, we showed a very primitive prototype to some others under a non-disclosure agreement, but I only got a lukewarm response.

I decided to cut back a little on my ambitions. I had figured out how to control an industrial VCR directly from the computer, so why not start with something simpler? I would make software to do logging instead, where only one VCR is needed. Logging is the process preliminary to editing, whereby someone runs through a tape and takes notes on which takes or scenes seem best. They could use it to transcribe dialogue, which would be especially useful for interviews, where the subject might say anything (rather than speak lines in a prepared script).

I remember visiting my parents' house at one point. I was sitting alone in the guest room on the edge of the bed, late at night, after they had gone to sleep. I remember thinking that if I didn't have this project to focus on, I didn't have much else in the world to live for. It was as if the project was keeping me alive.

Eventually, after a Herculean effort, including writing an entire user manual, I was ready to sell my product. I had 100 copies ready to go.[67] I rented a booth at Mac World Expo when it was here in the Boston area. I hired friends to help me staff the booth and demonstrate the product.

---

[66] I had the "phonebook" edition, as it was printed on newsprint and resembled a telephone directory.

[67] Each one consisted of a box with a ring binder, all the pages of the user manual inserted, a diskette with the software recorded on it with a label affixed, and even a warranty postcard to mail back to me (with a stamp for postage), marked with a serial number so I could keep track.

At the show, we got a ton of inquiries, but only one customer actually bought the product.[68] After the show was over, I started calling all the people who had given us their contact information. I also had contacts from inquiries in a video magazine where I had run a press release.

In those days, long-distance calls still cost extra for each call made, depending on the distance involved. Within two weeks I had run up close to $300 in long-distance phone bills, and not a single sale to show for it! Mostly nobody answered the phone or ever returned calls. Well, my product only cost $300! I had only sold four copies. I was $50,000 in debt. Friends of mine involved with the computer business told me, "Didn't you know? For every 100 leads, you might get one sale if you're lucky." For some reason, I had never expected the ratio to be that small! Less than 1% ?!??

So, I just stopped. I couldn't borrow any more money and I was exhausted from all the effort (including hauling all the equipment needed to demonstrate the product at the trade show, and then back out again when it was over).

I felt like an idiot when it came to real marketing. I had seduced myself with my own dream of a great product! I had even used my product on my own video productions. One of my customers said it had been invaluable for their documentary. But those turned out to be the exceptions.

In the past, when I had told friends of mine what I was doing, they almost always said, "Wow, that's a great idea!" But as it turned out, only rather expensive VCRs had the two-way remote control features needed for my software to work. Very few of my friends were really in my target market, which was video producers and editors working on documentaries.

What my friends *didn't* say was, "... and when it's ready, I want to buy one!" Instead they said, "I'm sure someone will buy it." But they were just reacting to the idea. They had no concept of my actual target market. Years later, I realized that if people are enthusiastic about a product idea but don't want to buy one, it's not a good sign.

I was fortunate that my family forgave me some of what I owed, but I still owed about $30,000 to the credit card banks and to friends who had helped box up the product and help me staff my trade show booth.

I was demoralized, but my focus turned to trying to stay afloat financially. Around that time, I was fortunate to get some video production work documenting the construction of the Minuteman Trail, here in the suburbs of Boston. I did a little bit of database consulting now and then. But this was barely enough to live on. I started getting threatening letters from the credit card banks. I remember waiting days or weeks for checks to come in the mail, after which I would carefully figure out what I could pay to whom. I remember putting off buying groceries because there were only a few dollars left in my account.

---

[68] Soon after the show, I sold two more copies through personal contacts.

My Own Two Feet

Back in the mid-1980s, I had joined the Boston Computer Society. By the late 1980s, they had grown to become the largest computer user group in the country. The monthly magazine for Macintosh computer users had over 10,000 subscribers alone. In the first few pages, there was a list of members who volunteered to help other members, along with their phone numbers. They called it the "help lines." Our names were grouped by topic or kind of software. If a member had a question, they could look up a help line volunteer by category, then call and ask their question.

I listed myself under Word, Excel, FileMaker, and Beginners. By the early 1990s, I was getting up to two calls per day, answering questions for other members. Then, one day, an interesting thing happened. Someone called me about FileMaker. They admitted that continuing to design their own database was taking too much time away from their core business. So, instead of asking a question, they wanted to know if I knew of a consultant they could hire to work on their database for them.

I hesitated for a moment. Then I said, "Well, *I'm* a consultant." They replied, "Good. What is your rate?" I paused again. I had no idea! I blurted out, "Fifty dollars an hour." They didn't miss a beat, "Okay, when can you come in?" they asked. I opened my appointment book and we scheduled a time. After I hung up the phone, I mused that they had agreed to my rate awfully fast. Perhaps I should have asked for a higher amount? Oh, well, it was going to be my first paid assignment, so I would have to figure out how to set my rates for other clients, later on.

For a few years, I got similar work here and there. Over time, it started to build up slowly. I remember distinctly how I felt in the summer of 1993. I was still quite broke, still trying to pay off my credit card debt. I kept thinking that perhaps work would begin to pick up after Labor Day. Suddenly, in the second week in August, I started getting more calls. After I had answered a few, I reviewed my schedule book. Three out of the five days the following week were now booked. Wow!

Starting that summer, work in FileMaker became a steady source of self-employment income for me. For the next few years, I worked diligently, kept my living expenses low (I was still living in a group house, sharing the rent), and paid off all the money I had borrowed. My father even loaned me enough money to pay off some credit cards, so that I could pay him back at a much more reasonable interest rate.

By the mid-1990s, after finally paying off my loans, I had accumulated a modest amount of savings for the first time in almost a decade. I began to wonder if I would live in the same group house forever (it had been twenty years already!). I started to investigate co-housing. I found a local group that included a few friends of mine. They were planning to build a co-housing village but were struggling to find suitable land. I attended numerous planning meetings as land was finally located. It was a huge struggle for the group, as most neighborhoods in the area fought against increasing housing density. Eventually, I selected a unit and became a full member, putting up half a down payment.

At the same time, the twelve-step movement was shrinking. The CoDA meeting in my own town dwindled until the few of us remaining finally decided close it. When people asked me if I belonged to a religion, I joked that I attended "The Church of the *Boston Sunday Globe*," which meant that we had the newspaper delivered and I sat around in my bathrobe on Sunday mornings reading it.

Around the same time, a friend of mine in co-counseling would call every six months or so and invite me to join her ongoing class. Eventually, I decided to go and became a regular participant again, at least for awhile. Still, I kept wondering about spirituality. Twelve-step meetings were good, but where could I find a spiritual community that wasn't centered around a problem? I considered various religions. Should I convert to Catholicism? Judaism? Perhaps become a Buddhist? Nothing seemed to fit.

I started a few relationships during those years, but each one eventually fizzled. Occasionally, when I was at a party or with a group of people, someone would ask who had children. At first, I would think, "Well, not me." But then I would realize that I didn't really know, so I raised my hand halfway. I was left with an uneasy feeling in my stomach.

Every time I thought about it, I felt stuck. The woman who had gotten pregnant had been so nasty to me, I couldn't figure out what good it would do if I tried to find her. She had left no way to contact her. Was I really the father? Or, was all her bluster merely a ruse to swindle money from me? What if she decided to take out a restraining order against me, just because I tried to look her up? My life would be ruined, even though I intended no harm. Men with restraining orders against them are usually assumed to be guilty by the public, without any due process! I could easily end up with no work, evicted by my landlord, and so on.

What if it turned out that I was indeed the father (which I suspected), but she got the authorities to force me to pay, yet somehow kept me from seeing the child? I had heard horror stories on both sides. Men who paid nothing, even though they had plenty of money, but other men who had to pay an excessive amount of support and were left nearly in poverty. There were even men who were ordered to pay for children fathered by another man! The mother told them that they were the father (instead) and they had volunteered some support. I saw the legal world as a risky and dangerous one for most men. My mind was riddled with questions that I was afraid to even try to answer.

Knowing what I know by now, staying frozen in inaction was not the best thing, but at the time, I felt powerless and vulnerable. I was so uncertain of the possible outcome, I failed to do anything.

Family Matters

By 1996, some big changes occurred. First, I got a call from the woman who had been pregnant ten years earlier. All she said was that she wanted me to take a private DNA test and start paying child support. She said she would call me back four days later to get my answer. She gave no phone number, so I couldn't call her back.

I went back to the same attorney I had seen years ago. By now he was a partner in a prestigious law firm in downtown Boston. He said it was almost unheard of that someone would come back for child support after almost a decade! He told me that if I was proved to be the father, I would have almost no rights, whereas the mother could demand all sorts of things. He drew a line down the middle of the paper and listed them all on one side. On the other side, for me, there was only the right to visitation.

When the mother called back, I said I would take the test, but only if supervised through the courts, as I had never heard of a private DNA test and I didn't trust her. After she said goodbye, I expected that I would soon hear about where to go for the test. Instead, nothing happened. An entire year went by.

One day, while sitting in my living room, I looked out the window and saw a bright red SUV drive up to the curb right in front of my house. Instinctively, I got up, walked outside, and said hello to the driver through the open window of his car. He asked, "Are you Glenn C. Koenig?" I said, "Yes I am." He said, "I have to give this to you," and handed me a summons with instructions to report for a DNA test.

§ § §

Meanwhile, after yet another relationship had ended, I was left single again. I was quite sad. I remember standing in the shower one day, with the water pouring down all over my body, wondering if I would ever find a compatible partner. What could I do? My mind was empty. I remember reflecting on the concept of a "higher power" from my twelve-step meetings. So, right there, I admitted that I was powerless and needed help. I could feel every muscle in my body relax when I thought that. My attitude was: whatever help I received would be welcome. A few days later, a calm feeling came over me. The sense I got was that things would be okay, but that it might take awhile. So I accepted that, and stopped worrying about it so much.

One day, my friend Mark called and invited me to dinner at the house of a woman who was a friend of his. He said he thought I would really like her. It was a Wednesday night and I had a computer user group meeting, so I thanked him and said maybe some other time. He called again a few times over the next few months. Always for dinner on a Wednesday, but I always seemed to be busy that night.

Finally, in the middle of February, he happened to call when I was available, so I went over and had dinner with him, his friend and her teenage daughter. We had a great time, so they invited me to come for dinner again, the following Wednesday and I agreed. Their place was only about one mile from my house, so it was easy to just drop over. This became a weekly ritual, and over time, I spent more and more time there.

§ § §

Meanwhile, that summer, after receiving the summons, I had the DNA test. The results showed that I was indeed the father of a boy. It turned out that he and his mother lived in a neighboring state. The court instituted temporary orders, so I had to start paying child support right away, almost $1000 per month. I was shocked at how much it was, but soon I learned that Massachusetts had the highest child support rates in the nation. The mother had submitted a form showing that her income was below poverty level.

So now there were two families in my life, so to speak. My son, age eleven, whom I had never met, who was living with his mother, and a woman and her daughter, now fourteen, who lived nearby. To keep from getting confused as to who is who, I'll refer to one woman as my son's mother and the other one as my wife (because we later married).

By the end of 1997, I was spending every night with my future wife, sleeping over, and returning to my house the next morning after breakfast to shower, change clothes, and get ready for my day. I had never done this before. All my past relationships had been "sleep together on weekends only" arrangements. And here I was, practically living there full-time!

The following year, I decided to leave my group house, where I had been living for twenty-three years and move in with them. It took all summer to pack and move, as I hadn't realized how much stuff I had accumulated over all that time! Some of it was video equipment and a videotape library, so I rented an office in the center of town for all that, put some other things in storage, and sold or gave away the rest.

As my future wife was a member of the Unitarian Universalist church down the block, I started going to church with her on Sunday mornings. After awhile, I realized that this was a good answer to my previous question of where I would find spirituality that wasn't centered around a problem. Here, I could develop my own sense of spirituality without someone dictating it to me. Soon, I signed the book and became a member.

After moving in, we started to adjust to life as a family of three. I became a stepparent and quickly began to understand the challenges of living with a teenage daughter! We had fun, but disagreements and struggles too. One evening, her daughter had stomped upstairs and slammed the door after she and I had had an open disagreement about something. Later, lying in bed, I wondered out loud why I seemed to so easily drawn into conflict. I felt foolish and embarrassed that I had ended up arguing. Was I being a bad parent? My wife replied that her daughter wouldn't argue with me unless she trusted me. Otherwise, she would have just kept to herself. Don't worry, she said, I was doing just fine as a parent. I felt a little better, at least.

Meanwhile, the legal process had gotten to the point where I could see my son for the first time. His mother insisted on a supervised visit, as if I were some kind of dangerous criminal. I was hurt by that, but I accepted the arrangements because I had no choice. My future wife gave me a ride there and waited at a restaurant nearby while I went in. As soon as I sat down, my son's first question to me was, "Why did you abandon me?" At first, I was struck dumb. I started to say that I hadn't gone anywhere – I had lived at the same address for over twenty years. But as soon as the words came out of my mouth, I realized that such defensive talk was inappropriate. He had been told that I had abandoned him and no argument I could make was going to help now.

On the way back home, I thought it over. From his perspective, I had abandoned him. I started to realize how badly he must have felt to think that his own father didn't want him. How tragic! I began to realize that, even though his mother had run away from me, it was now my job to make sure that he would never feel that way again, if I could help it. I admit that I haven't always done a perfect job of that, but I was dealing with a lot of feelings that were unfamiliar to me.

As his mother and I met to negotiate a settlement for what they call "permanent orders," I remember feeling a level of intense rage and grief that surprised me. Where were all these strong feelings coming from? I started to understand why child custody battles easily become so rancorous between parents. The feelings just rise up inside you unexpectedly when it comes to your own children. There was certainly nothing quite like it in other parts of my life!

Finally, after a few meetings with my attorney to work out the legal language, the day came to have a "four-way" – a meeting where the mother, each of our attorneys, and I would sit down to work out a final written agreement. We each brought our version of the document to start with. We met in a conference room at my attorney's offices and worked our way through all the provisions until we reached the part about visitation. My version said I would get to visit my son every two weeks.

Her version had no schedule for visitation at all. The mother was emphatic; nobody would ever compel her son to visit anybody if he didn't want to, period! My attorney asked, perhaps monthly visits instead? Nope. The mother promised to fight me in court until the child was eighteen if that's what it took. Even her own attorney tried to explain that some schedule of visits was customary. It made no difference.

Finally, I realized what I wanted to do. This woman meant what she said. She would fight me in court for years, run up terrible legal bills, and I would likely not get to see my son until he was eighteen, if ever. Not only would this be a waste of time and money for me, but what would my son think? Without my input, what would his mother tell him? The risk was that she would just focus on the court battle and vilify me in his eyes. He might end up feeling as if I was abandoning him all over again.

124

So, I motioned to my attorney to leave the room with me for a few minutes, go down the hall to her private office, shut the door, and talk it over. My feelings had changed from confrontation to calm. I knew what I wanted to do. I asked her, what if we just agree to their version? She looked surprised. Was I sure I wanted to agree to pay support without any guarantee of visitation whatsoever? I said that's what I now realized I needed to do. I was willing to give up everything on the chance that, with the legal battle over, things would be better, even if I didn't get to see him right away. She said okay, if that's what I wanted.

So we went back into the conference room and I agreed to sign. The meeting was over in a few minutes. As we were all going down the stairs to the parking lot, the mother remarked to me in a dispassionate manner, "I'll call you in a few weeks and we can set up a visit." Just like that.

Sure enough, she called a few weeks later and the three of us (she, my son, and I) met for lunch at a restaurant in a town about halfway between us. It was as if nothing had ever happened. My son seemed happy to see me. We ate and talked and said goodbye when we each left to go home. Other visits soon followed.

§ § §

After I had been living with my future wife for awhile, she brought up the idea of getting married. I discussed it with her but I remained uncertain. We talked about it now and then, but I still hadn't made up my mind. At one point, I had a logistical question. If we decided to get married who should be first to tell her daughter? Right away she said, "Oh, I think you should ask her permission!" We both laughed, but it made sense in a funny way.

Then one night in November, my friend Mark came over to join us again for dinner. After eating, the four of us sat there talking and laughing awhile. For some reason, right in the middle of all that, it suddenly struck me that I was ready to marry her. After Mark left and my future wife had gone to bed, I found her daughter, still in the living room, also about to go up to bed. I asked her to wait because I had a question.

She sat down and I said, "I'm thinking of marrying your mother, but I wanted to know if that was okay with you." There was a pause, then she gave me a wry smile. "You mean I have power?" she asked. I said, "Well, yes, I'm asking you." She said, "Okay, I guess so." There was another pause, then she asked, "Can I go to bed now? I have to get up early for school in morning." Still, somehow, I knew she was glad this was going to happen.

As my future wife had already gone to bed, I opened the bedroom door and sat on the edge of the bed next to her. I told her I had asked her daughter's permission to marry her and she had said yes. I went on, "So, will you marry me?" My now fiancé reached up, pulled me down on top of the covers next to her and hugged me. Then she said yes.

We threw ourselves into planning our wedding. We were married outdoors the next May and had our reception in the social hall of our church. We had three rings made, so that each of the three of us could wear one. After all, I was, in effect, marrying a family, not just a partner.

Soon after that, the co-housing project I had joined asked for the second half of my down payment to complete the land deal and eventually start construction. But by then my stepdaughter was in the middle of her junior year of high school and moving there would have forced her to change school systems, just as she was getting ready to apply to colleges. Not only that, but the townhouse unit I had signed up for would have been a bit small for the three of us.

After thinking things over, I decided to back out of the co-housing project. I had to take the risk and hope that they would eventually build it and sell my unit to somebody else. Otherwise, I would lose my initial investment. Fortunately, they worked out their problems with the neighborhood, built the village, and refunded my money a few years later.

Prophecy

By the late 1990s, as I approached the age of 50, I began to reflect on where life was going, not only for me, but for society as a whole. I remembered people asking me, "But what's a reality?" back in the mid-1970s.

What I had called "a reality" was really a time not only of optimism, but of progressive social change. What had been happening after the mid-1970s was kind of a "valley of fatigue." We had pushed so hard for change in the late 1960s and early 1970s, we had become somewhat burned out, it seemed. But it was clear to me that it wouldn't last. We would eventually have to come back to finish what we started.

I began work on a lecture about my vision of the future. Around that time, there were a lot of headlines about what was called the "Y2K" problem. That was shorthand for the "Year Two Thousand." Since many early computers only used two digits for the year (assuming that the prefix was always going to be "19"), few people knew what we'd face when the year went from "99" to "00." Any software that depended on such dates might produce comically (or tragically) wrong results. Calculations of people's age, for instance, might come out negative. After age 49, I'd suddenly become "-50," right? Whoops!

But that wasn't why I decided to write. What interested me was how different life seemed to be when compared to our predictions for the future, made in the 1950s and early 1960s when I was a child. Back then, we were all excited about high technology. Rockets and space flight, computers and electronics, robots, fancier appliances, and whole automated factories were all supposedly coming. We would enjoy a life of unparalleled luxury, with practically any product produced cheaply and in unlimited supply! In the cartoon series, *The Jetsons*, the old family model of *The Honeymooners*, and later *The Flintstones*, was updated to show a "space age" future, with personal aircraft to replace cars, a robot as a nanny/housemaid, and even a talking dog.[69]

What really happened instead was already evident by the first Earth Day, in 1970. The byproducts of the industrial revolution – litter, pollution, and deforestation, for examples – were all on the rise. We became aware that population growth was out of control; we were rapidly messing up the very planet on which we lived. Beyond that, our human institutions were faltering. War, political and economic turmoil, social unrest – all these things took over the headlines more and more. All that shiny technology of the future we envisioned back in the 1950s had a downside that was getting pretty scary.

The Y2K problem looked as if it would be the crowning glory of technology going awry. Would power plants shut down, plunging us into darkness? Would water

---

[69] Interestingly, the nuclear family structure and male/female roles remained largely unchanged in these fictional worlds.

treatment systems suddenly halt, dumping sewage out into rivers and lakes? Would traffic signals all go dark, leading to a massive gridlock?

Fortunately, we had enough lead time for armies of software engineers to review all the critical systems. New Year's Day 2000 came and went without much more than a blip. We all breathed a sigh of relief. At least for a few moments. But the big problems were still there and seemed to be getting worse.

By the summer of 2001, I remember experiencing an increasing sense of dread. I had no idea exactly why, I just felt kind of ill the entire time. I was still working on my lecture text in September when terrorists attacked the World Trade Center in New York.

I knew it was a tragedy of death and destruction, but my first reaction was strangely one of relief. I thought, "So *this* is what I had been dreading all summer long!" The USA had become an imperialist power in the world, through actions by both our government and by major corporations based here. After the collapse of the Soviet Union, I had started to consider the idea that a world with only one superpower was inherently unstable. Now, it seemed, that something had come along to shock us.

Sadly, this shock did not seem to provoke us to enter a time of self-reflection regarding our impact on the rest of the world. Instead, it seemed to elevate our level of fear and stimulate an even greater desire for control and security.

Finally, by the spring of 2004, I completed preparations and presented my remarks in front of a live audience. I had a video recording made of the whole thing, including a question and answer period. By today's TED Talk standards, my 40-minute talk now seems a bit slow and plodding. But I think I got my main points across.

Before I go any further, I would like to explain a few things. First, I'm going to depart from my life story for the next few pages and delve into the content of the talk I gave that spring. Second, I want to explain why I think what I said then is pertinent to the theme of this book now.

Back then, I described how we were entering a period of very rapid and significant change in culture, worldwide. I predicted that there would be a major shift in the balance of power between men and women. However, I didn't fully realize that we would eventually challenge the entire gender binary model, nor did I yet see how I would come to express that in my personal life.

In addition, I clearly understood that rapid change can be stressful. However, in the decade or so since then, I've observed that more and more people are reacting to that stress by increasingly blaming other people, rather than looking at the bigger picture. I think blame is mostly a tragic waste of energy. Instead, I believe that we're all in this together and that demonstrating love for each other is the only way to go.

So, let me start by saying a few things about change.

Change

One thing about change, whether it be within us, or in the world around us, is that it's good to have a balance. Too little or too much can both be difficult.

If changes come slowly, a little at a time, then life stays more familiar from day to day. This familiarity can give us a sense of security, knowing that we can depend on ourselves and the people around us to act in familiar, well-known ways. However, taken to the extreme, if almost nothing ever changes, life can get pretty boring!

On the other hand, if changes come rapidly, then boredom is likely to give way to more excitement. However, there is more work to do to adapt to what's changing. The less familiar things become, the less secure we may feel. Life poses more risks, leaves us facing more uncertainty, and less dependability. All this can get rather upsetting!

Regardless of the rate of change, we are typically faced with two jobs: One is to learn how to adapt to whatever is new, and the other is to let go of what we are leaving behind. Both these things take time: time to go through the learning curve for what's new, and time to grieve the loss of what we have had to give up; what is now gone.

I believe that we are living through a time of very rapid and dramatic change, when compared to the last few hundred years, and perhaps even the next few hundred years. There are many predictors of this, including interpretations of the ancient Mayan calendar, Christian Bible passages, various types of astrology, and a variety of other predictions and prophesies.

Yet, it is difficult to quantify the rate of change in culture and society when compared to something like the speed of a car or how fast the temperature rises on a sunny day. Even with better measures of cultural factors, there is still little to go on when it comes to changes that span hundreds or even thousands of years.

So I will say a few things about what I think is going on, but I cannot offer much proof or scientific evidence; what follows is largely my own subjective observations and conclusions.

As I see it, we here on earth are making a transition from one 2000-year period to another. I think we're right in the middle of this transition, right now, roughly during my lifetime. I have drawn a graph to represent this, shown on the next page.

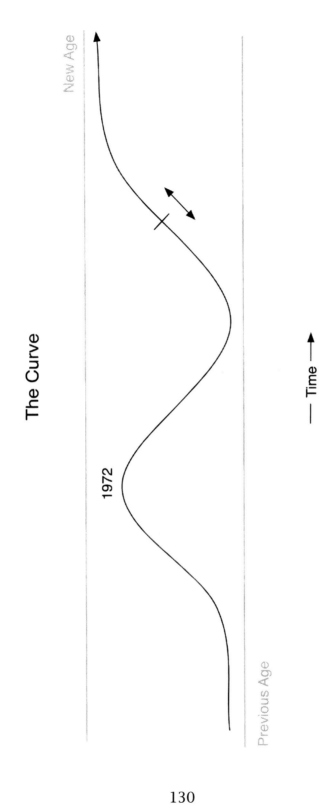

The Curve

The curve on the previous page has to do with my belief and experience of a gigantic shift in culture, worldwide, as we make a transition from one 2000-year era to the next. Some people think we're actually transitioning from a 12,000-year era to another 12,000-year era, but let's leave that as a topic for another time. Others might call my "Previous Age" the "Christian Era," or the "Piscean Age," and my "New Age," the "Aquarian Age." But what you call these two periods of time is up to you.

This curve shows a period of time approximately covering my lifetime, from the end of World War II, shortly before I was born, to sometime around 2050 or so (when I'll be 100, if I get that far). It's meant to show the progress of what I call a "progressive shift" through the 1960s, up until a peak around 1972.

What happened, in my opinion, was a surge of energy leading up to that time that was rapid, chaotic, messy, and unnerving. But such intense energy could not be sustained. We were shocked as major public figures (Dr. Martin Luther King, Jr., John and Robert Kennedy, and others) were assassinated. Well-known music artists (Jimi Hendrix, Janis Joplin, Jim Morrison, etc.) died unexpectedly within a few years of each other.

By 1972, it seemed to me that the social unrest phase had given way to what I called "the age of optimism"[70] Some of us saw a future where we would clean up the planet, grow organic food, develop solar energy, and live more gently on the land. President Jimmy Carter even put solar panels on the roof of the White House in the mid 1970s.

But by the 1980s, President Ronald Reagan had those solar panels taken down as we entered a period of decline, recession, and materialism widely known as the "Reagan-Bush era." It was a time of the feminist backlash, a resurgence in the great imbalance of wealth, known as trickle-down economics, where not much actually trickled down. We went on to experience the housing bubble and subsequent crash in the 1980s, and the dot-com bubble and crash in the late 1990s.

In my own life, I witnessed all this happening around me. In the mid-1980s, I went to an introductory seminar on how to make big money in real estate. The speaker told us that if we signed up for the full weekend, they would teach us the principle of OPM. That stood for "Other People's Money." They were going to teach us how to go into debt up to our eyeballs, buy small apartment buildings, make minor improvements, and then flip (resell) them for a profit. When it was over, I walked out to my car with a feeling of unease in my stomach, knowing that this was headed for disaster. Places to live couldn't keep getting more and more expensive when our wages weren't going up nearly as fast. Sure enough, by 1989, the big real estate crash had come.

---

[70] My use of the word "age" was intentionally inappropriate. After all, most people would hardly call a period of barely five years an "age."

However, by the time we reached the late 1990s, I sensed that things had already started to change for the better. When I finally gave my talk in 2004, I was fully convinced that progressive social change was gathering steam. In 2000, most of my friends were all upset that George Bush had "stolen" the presidential election. The margin of victory was so close that election officials in Florida were squinting at punch card ballots, trying to count the last few that were in question. Eventually the Supreme Court called it and gave the victory to President Bush.

But to me, the story wasn't about classic government corruption and who won or how they won. The story was how close it was! To me, this election was symbolic of how progressive or "new age" interests were neck and neck with the regressive interests of the previous age. That's why I placed a small hash mark and double arrow at that point in the curve in the diagram. That's meant to show that we were right at the breakeven point.

We live in times of not only rapid change, but of fundamental change. What's changing goes down to the very roots of society, culture, and civilization itself. I see these changes as inevitable. As I will point out later,[71] I don't think it's possible to look too far into the past and predict the future. That's because the changes I'm talking about are so revolutionary that we have few, if any, parallels in recorded history to draw from.

Specifically, we are moving from a world organized around hierarchies, centralized control, and uniformity, to one characterized by networks, decentralized control, and individual choice. Along with this, I believe that we are moving from a world dominated by men, masculine priorities, and power, to one where there is a much better balance between men and women, between the masculine and the feminine.

To symbolize these changes, I created two simple diagrams. The first represents the shift from hierarchy to network:

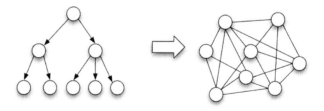

[71] See "Fashion Trumps Everything," page 141.

The second one represents a transformation of the relationship between masculine and feminine:

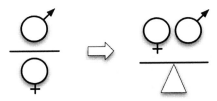

Some evidence for this involves the evolution of the internet as a gigantic worldwide artwork. As art, it is not only a tool for us to use, it represents our aspirations by modeling a new kind of society based on a level playing field (which is why the "net neutrality" struggle has been so vital). The current revolution in gender identity and sexual orientation or affiliation is more evidence of our leaving behind the dominance of masculine power and priority over the feminine.

What we've had might be called the "man at the top" form of organization, or what I call the "Father Knows Best" culture. Many of us put our faith in the father figure, depending on him to guide us, see more than we could see, take care of our problems, and manage institutions properly. At the same time, many flaws in this system are now coming to light, such as corruption, oppression, and war.

In the process that we are now undergoing, every hierarchically organized institution that was based on male domination is crumbling, losing its power and effectiveness. The government, the military, the institutions of medicine, education, religion, business, journalism ("the media") and non-profits – pretty much *every societal institution* is shifting from one organizing set of principles to the other. Here are some of the other aspects of culture that are changing:

- from uniformity to diversity (from one-size-fits-all to individual choice)
- from centralized to decentralized
- from linear to simultaneous communication (e.g. from books to social media)
- from static to kinetic expression (e.g. from paintings on a wall to videos online)
- from violent confrontation to a "live and let live" world of negotiation and collaboration
- from exploitation of nature, to living in harmony with the natural world
- from external "carrot and stick" motivation to intuitive and heart-centered

Now, before I go on, I want to clarify that my use of the terms "progressive" and "regressive" do not necessarily line up nicely with people who consider themselves Democrats versus Republicans, liberals versus conservatives (or anarchists), or spiritual (or atheistic) versus religious. Rather, I use these two terms represent desires that we all have, at times. Progressive generally means looking forward to changes and new ways of thinking, relating, and organizing ourselves. Regressive means looking more to the past, to history, to a proven track record, and desiring more continuity, with more reliance on previously established ways that are familiar.

After all, there has been a certain sense of comfort, knowing that the man at the top in our "Father Knows Best" culture was taking care of things. What happens if he is suddenly missing? Or if he is discredited after we find that he has abused his power, or even committed a crime? Where do we turn? What if the evening news comes on and there is nobody at the desk to tell us what is going on?

It's easier to see that traditional institutions are failing than to find evidence of new ways succeeding, *especially* if you still depend on traditional institutions of journalism and academia for your news and perspective. Many people may naturally end up upset, afraid, or perhaps even in a panic. Look at it this way: If everything you've known while growing up seems to be falling apart, and you don't see anything new to replace these things, what can you expect? The very decline of civilization itself, perhaps? That might seem quite scary indeed!

Well, it's no wonder, if you look at it that way, you might struggle to repair or reform or just prop up the old institutions. Sadly, this will not work, in my opinion. In fact, I see this as perhaps the *biggest mistake we can make.* But fear is a strong motivation, and vision is sometimes hard to come by. The familiar is sometimes very desirable over the less familiar or the stark unknown. We are a society built on having answers, rather than being comfortable with questions that we cannot yet answer.

For example, there are people who refer to themselves as "liberal" who think the US government should still take charge and make changes for the better. Or that if they apply enough pressure on big corporations, they can force them to "do the right thing" for society, rather than ride roughshod over people and the natural world around us. They are often "knocking on the doors" of Congress, trying to get legislation passed to implement these goals.

Perhaps some of this effort is worthy. But over time, I'm firmly convinced that trying to instill more power in our central government will become more and more difficult. Not only that, the power that central government already has will become less and less effective, over time. Eventually, knocking harder on the doors of Congress will do little more than bruise your knuckles. Yet, at the same time, the temptation to keep trying is very strong, *if* one cannot see any alternatives.

On the other hand, people who call themselves "conservatives," who believe that we should have less government so that the "private sector" can manage itself, will also find that big non-government entities will fare little better. The bigger that businesses get, the more levels of hierarchy they typically establish. That makes it all the more difficult to manage their entire enterprise. It also makes it more likely that they will lose focus on their original purpose and devolve to adopting a mission of self-preservation.[72]

I certainly don't blame people for not being able to see alternatives. I also don't blame people for feeling some panic. After all, as I see it, we have no direct experience for

[72] See "Size Matters," page 137.

going through such a deep transition, one that only happens once every 2000 years or so. Humankind has lived through so many generations since "Year 1" (of the Christian Era or Common Era) that it's nearly impossible for anyone to have any memory of what such a transition might be like, nor how to act when it comes along. And if you happen to think that there have been twelve such cycles over the last 25,000 years, each one different from the last, then it's even *more* difficult to think that anyone would know what to do now, based on past evidence.

Now, I imagine that you might be somewhat (or perhaps deeply) skeptical that anyone would know or be able to predict that we're going through such a deeply profound transition, worldwide. What evidence is there? How could anyone know this? Is there any scientific theory to back this up?

As I describe in the following essays, "Fashion Trumps Everything," and "What Is Science?" no one can necessarily "know" what we're going through ahead of time. I think I have better than a 50-50 chance of being correct in my predictions, but clearly, I cannot predict everything.

Regardless, I have a distinct feeling that this is how things are going. And, as I look around me today, I see particular changes going on that seem to be significant.[73] Of course, people tend to look for evidence to support their existing opinions or predetermined conclusions, so perhaps I'm doing some of that. I'm only human. I am probably not immune to such a tendency, so perhaps that is partly what I am doing here.

I'm not writing this book to convince you that my vision is correct in all aspects. Rather, I'm asking you to open your mind and consider for yourself what is happening. Keep an eye on cultural shifts and draw your own conclusions. Critique what I've said here. Pose questions for which you don't *necessarily* expect an answer right away. I invite you to stay curious and observant as much as you can. If you do just that much, my purpose in writing this here will at least be partly fulfilled.

---

[73] I talk about this in more detail in "Steering a Course" later on.

Border Crossing

In the darkness of winter
I can barely see
what has happened
this past year, to me!

One life was stolen
and replaced by another
while I was busy fighting
my agents of change.

When the sun came up
my room looked the same
But outside my door
the world was now strange.

People are still using
all the same words
but now they are using them
to speak a new language.

What is this place?
Where is my guidebook?
I have no passport
back to the land before!

I want to live
in the New Age
Yet I am still afraid
to leave the old one
behind.

Size Matters

It pains me when I hear people discussing politics, culture, or even business, without including scale or size as a significant factor. We can discuss democracy versus dictatorship, free market versus state control, capitalism, socialism, communism, or anarchism, but if we're not also talking about how many people are involved in any particular case, then we're missing a very significant factor!

So, why would the number of people involved make any difference to the success of a particular organizing theory? It all comes down to how we communicate with each other and reach decisions. I can think of many examples where actual quantities are critical to how we live, work, and learn.

Consider, for a moment, a half-hour meeting. If there are three people present, then each one will have, on average, 10 minutes to talk and 20 minutes to listen to the other two. If there are 30 people in such a meeting, then each person will only have, on average, just one minute to talk, and 29 minutes to listen to others. But what if there are 300 people in the same half-hour meeting? If the time is divided up equally, then theoretically, each person will be able to talk for only 6 seconds! You get to say your name and job title, and then ... time's up! Clearly, a meeting with 300 people (for half an hour) can't work anything like the one that includes only 3, or even 30 people!

If you start a meeting, and then more people slowly join in, it can be very difficult to decide when to change the rules of who gets to speak and for how long. It's natural to stick with the methods that have "always worked in the past" until one day you wake up to realize that those methods are not working anymore at all. All along, it seemed as if "just a few more people" wouldn't matter that much. But enough more, and it matters a lot![74]

I chose my example of a meeting with three people for a reason. When the United States was formed and the first census was taken, in 1790, our population was about three million. There were even fewer voters, proportionally, as women and slaves could not vote. By that time, we had set up Congress, the Executive Branch, the courts, and the entire set of institutions as set forth in the Constitution. So far, so good.

But today, we have over 300 million people in the US, about 100 times as many! Yet, many of us expect our form of government to function just as well under these conditions. Just by the numbers alone, I contend that it's just about impossible! Add to this the explosion in means of communication (the telegraph didn't even come into common use until long after 1790) and the rapid rise in today's data storage capacity, to name just two things, and life today is beyond any concept the framers of the US Constitution may have had.

---

[74] For more detail on this phenomenon, see the book *The Tipping Point*, by Malcolm Gladwell

In 1911, Congress voted to keep itself at 435 members. If there were any more members, then managing debate would be too unwieldy. Well, that was over 100 years ago! Meanwhile, the population didn't stop growing. By now (2017), each representative represents over half a million voters! Or nearly three quarters of a million people, if you count those who cannot yet vote.

This is not just a "larger number" of people, when compared to the few thousand voters per representative in Congress in 1790. It's a completely different ball game, with totally different rules, regardless of what it says in the Constitution. Sure, you can carry a cute little copy of the Constitution around in your pocket, for what good it will do you.

Don't get me wrong. The Constitution is a great document. The government it spells out has been one of the most effective ever seen on the planet. But everything has its limits. The problem is, we are expecting it to be just as effective today as it was back in 1790. There is no way that that can be true anymore. As much as we might wish that it would still work, as much as we continue to (virtually) go pound on the doors of Congress to tell them to take some action or adopt some policy, the very structure of our system has already broken down under the strain of so many people, and so much technological change. One result is our recent "do nothing" Congress, stuck in gridlock.

The problem, I say, is *in our expectations*, not the Constitution itself. I have often said that if the founding fathers got into a time machine and were suddenly transported to today, to observe our central government as it operates now, they would exclaim, "Why haven't you changed it? We gave you the power of amendment, and you haven't used it to solve your problems! Your amendments, while sensible at face value, haven't really adapted government to what's going on now!"

I know activists who are still working to go back to something that used to work. Conservatives talk about term limits and liberals gather signatures to "get big money out of politics." I predict that not only will these efforts fail, they would not actually fix anything in the first place. That's because the people who are elected are, for the most part, not bad people. I contend that they are usually *good* people, just trying to work in a system that's worn out and overburdened. You can't get money out of politics because it takes mammoth amounts of money to communicate with the 500,000 voters you're trying to represent! And term limits only give priority to inexperience. Unless the lobbyists and corporate donors also have term limits (and that's not happening), the playing field would tip even further in their favor.

Meanwhile, we're trying to reach traditional legislative compromises in a nation that is more and more diverse every day. No wonder there is so much rancor! Recently, I looked at a number of studies of Congress over the past four decades. Based on representatives' actual voting records, they show that the number of moderate members has steadily declined over that entire time, until by now it has just about reached zero.[75] I'm sorry, but if you think you can apply some kind of quick fix, or elect different people, to bring back the "good old days" of legislative compromise, I say you're sadly mistaken.

I have seen messages and posts from friends of mine as to how the people of Iceland threw all the corrupt bankers out of their country and revolutionized their entire economy. Wonderful! They ask, "Why don't we do that here?" I say there's a very good reason: Iceland has about half the population of even our least populous state,[76] and a small fraction of the population of even our largest cities. Compared to Iceland, the US is a very large and diverse country! There is no way all 325 million of us will get together and agree on such a revolution.

But that's just government. The same principle applies to today's giant businesses, nonprofit organizations, and religious institutions, as well. Many of them are also Too Big To Manage and Too Complex To Comprehend. How often have we heard a manager in a large corporation claim that they "didn't know what was going on" until some major failure occurred, after which it all comes to light. Sure, they could be lying, but it's just as likely that they cannot keep track of what all their people are doing, buried deep within the very organization they're supposed to be managing.

Throughout millions of years of evolution, we human beings have become best adapted to face-to-face communication and working together in small groups. An institution the size of the federal government or even most state governments cannot work on such a level. The more diverse our country becomes, the harder it becomes for such a large number of people to agree on anything. It's just human nature.

The more people we have who are trying to participate, the less we are able to know each other as individuals. Instead, we see each other more and more in terms of statistics and percentages. Terms like "the voters" or "people on the East Coast" conjure up images of faceless masses. It becomes easier and easier to make blanket assumptions about "people" without actually knowing them or what really concerns them, deep down.

For example, the classic thinking in the insurance industry is that the bigger the group, the lower the risk. The whole idea is to share the risk of loss so that no one person has to face an insurmountable burden. Instead the risk is spread out among many people, so if one person meets misfortune, then the impact on everyone who has contributed to help out is bearable or even miniscule. That's the theory, anyway.

But in practice, the larger the group of people who are participating, the more the side effects of what I call the "impersonal factor" occur. If I am part of a giant pool of participants, I'm less likely to have any feelings for the others as real people. Even the

---

[75] See: www.smartceo.com/iq-the-political-polar-express/ for a discussion and diagrams.

[76] As of this writing, Wyoming has just under 600,000 people whereas Iceland has a little over 300,000. There are more people living in Aurora, Colorado than in all of Iceland.

people administering the insurance system can't deal with participants as unique individuals anymore. Understanding and compassion for each other gives way to statistical analysis, rules, procedures, and bureaucracy, all of which ignore our individuality and instead focus on our uniformity. The more diverse the population becomes, the more poorly such a system can serve them all properly.

From the point of view of the individual, taking unfair advantage of the system becomes easier and easier to rationalize or justify. After all, if I cheat by taking more benefits from the system than I'm entitled, who cares? The other millions of people involved will barely notice, right? Their premiums might go up by one cent, if that. Our sense of responsibility to a community sharing the risk is all but lost.

So what's to be done? How can all this be fixed? The answer lies not in trying to fix "it" but to shift our attention to an entirely new way to arrange ourselves and accomplish what we have traditionally expected government or large institutions to do. Instead, we are seeing changes being initiated by much smaller groups of people, who then set an example for others, who learn of their actions through networks. They, in turn, adapt the changes for themselves, giving things their own "local flavor" as necessary. I believe this is the way we are headed. Our previous ways of communicating through a hierarchy and "going through channels" to get anything done are rapidly fading.

For example, when it came to same-sex marriage rights, the federal government was way behind the states, not leading them. The same can be said for the use of hemp (*Cannabis sativa*) as a recreational drug. The states are leading the change. When it comes to many other changes, such as shifting to renewable energy, it's the cities and towns that are proving to be even more adaptable. Often, their ability to make needed changes is only hampered by policy at the state and federal levels. The fervor over testing in education is another example.

When a system is in trouble, it's tempting to blame the individuals working within it, rather than look at the system itself. It's also tempting to try to restore everything to its former glory, rather than admit that times have changed and face a future of unknowns.

Now we have an opportunity to shift our focus away from blame and instead direct our energies to rediscovering the true humanity of each other. I firmly believe that the vast majority of people are doing their best, given the circumstances. We don't have to live by labels, such as "red state" or "blue state" and let it go at that. One good way to melt the barriers those labels represent is to work at the personal level. I encourage you to take the risk, gather your courage, and get to know someone who at first seems unlike you, whether it be about politics, race, religion, or gender identity.

I see plenty of signs of people stepping up right now, so you don't have to start from scratch. Look for the opportunities that already exist and find a way to participate.

Fashion Trumps Everything!

When you think "fashion," you might imagine runway shows in Paris or New York, or giant magazines on the tables at salons featuring makeup, jewelry, and clothing.

But I use the term to mean what's "in fashion" in a much larger context. I'm like that. I often take many steps back to take a look at the bigger picture.

Here, I'm referring to everything we feel like doing, whether it's what we wear, what movies we watch, music we listen to, what foods we eat or what products we buy, what research gets funded, which party gets elected, and whether a war is popular or not. Yes, even war can be "in fashion" in a way. Sometimes what's in fashion crosses boundary lines between cultural aspects. Features of military clothing are worked into designs for civilian clothing, for example.

Many people I know blame government or major corporations for dictating what the public will do. They cite these institutions' desire to concentrate power or increase profits as the motive. But I contend that it doesn't necessarily work that way. Instead, I see the public as usually having the final say in the long run.

Why do people do what they do? No one can really tell you. Oh, there is plenty of research into human behavior, but in the long run no one can predict what goes viral. Why did "Valley Girl Speak" infuse the language here in the US, and around the world? No one really knows. What makes something "cool?" The answer is likely, "I don't know, I just felt like it."

Language itself is probably one of the best examples, as no one (not even the French government[77]) can really dictate how it evolves. We do have dictionaries and book editors and so on, but they are typically following changes in language, not leading them. Language is very much an egalitarian or decentralized exercise, where all the power ultimately lies with the public.

I contend that what's "in fashion" trumps art, science, commerce - practically everything we do. How can fashion trump science? Well, what we have discovered through scientific investigation depends on what we wanted to find out about in the first place. We fund research into things we're interested in, the things we're most curious about, or the things we are motivated to prove. If we're not all that interested in something, then we won't spend as much money, or put in the effort, and that area of knowledge will end up being weak.

Of course, it all depends on who "we" are. The process of making decisions by large numbers of people is incredibly complex. The classic three branches of government

---

[77] The French government frequently issues edicts, which are often ineffective, in an attempt to keep the French language from changing. For more, see the Wikipedia article "Language policy in France."

they still teach in civics class are just the beginning; it's way, way more complex than that!

Ultimately, we still don't know how our own brains really work. We make decisions based on a mixture of logic and facts along with plenty of intuition, hunches, and gut feelings. Where do these things come from? It's still largely a mystery.

What is Science?

OK, look:
Science is not astronomy.
Science is not computers.
Science is not geeky people.
Science is not creepy crawly things.
Science is not fossils.
Science is not equations on a blackboard.
Science is not a subject in school that you were no good at.

Science is none of these things!

Science is not a thing or a thought or a fact or a subject. It is a method! Science is a way of discovering and learning. Science is a human process. Science is always flawed because humans are always flawed. Science is a grand process of guessing, then looking for some evidence to tell how good your guesses are. Science is our process of amassing "knowledge" (if you want to call it that) about ourselves and the world around us. But look out! The word "knowledge" seems to imply facts that are solid, known, fixed, and complete. But it turns out that most of our knowledge is no more than guesses that we are "pretty sure" are good ones. That's all.

I'm not saying we know nothing. But I am saying we don't know everything. I contend that we know very little, actually! It seems easy for us, as humans, to think "Oh, we know so much by now!" Sure, we do. But with all that knowledge, it somehow becomes hard to remember that today's facts might easily become tomorrow's obsolete theories. Many of today's truths will end up just that way!

And there's nothing wrong with that happening. What we thought yesterday turns out to be "wrong" (in some way, at least) because we "now know" that something else is "true" instead. This goes on all the time in scientific work.

Science is nothing more than we human beings dreaming up a reason why things are the way they are, and then going about trying to test these dreams to see if we are "right" about what we were dreaming up. We use our senses and we extend our senses using instruments we've devised to help us. If we can't sense something with our own senses, and we haven't yet devised any instrument to sense that thing, then we are likely to miss its existence completely.

When I say "fashion trumps science," what I mean by that is that we dream up, then test all sorts of things, but it's all based on our whims and desires. What would you like to research today? Oh, I don't know, let's investigate this phenomenon or that phenomenon, or something else! Why? Because somewhere along the line, we feel like doing that. Sometimes, our motives seem clear. We want to cure cancer. People are suffering and dying with it, so let's see if we can stop that from happening. We want people to be happier and live better lives.

Well okay, fine. Let's do that. But just remember that we humans are the ones who decide what to work on for a whole host of reasons, some more obvious than others. We appropriate funds, hire researchers, acquire equipment and materials, travel, use computers to do analysis, and so on. It's easy to get lost in the details. It's easy to forget, sometimes, why we decided to do all this. And it's easy to forget what we're missing, what we are neglecting to study. We forget to check our limiting assumptions at the door, so we fail to approach our questions and tests with a truly open mind.

All of this is natural human behavior. Don't get me wrong. There is nothing inherently bad about this. I'm only saying all this because I'm asking you to step back from it all and look at the big picture. Look at what we were so sure about 50 years ago. Ponder what we might "know" 50 years from now, as hard as it might be to imagine. How ignorant does our "knowledge" of 50 years ago appear to be, based on what we have learned since then? How will what we "know" *today* look to people 50 or 100 years from now? Ignorant? Short-sighted? Totally misguided?

Frequently, I hear people say, "there's no evidence that x is true" (such as climate change, or harm in eating genetically modified foods, or astrology, or whatever). Perhaps that is a true statement! There might be no evidence, *that we know of, ... at this point in time!* We might have no evidence *that our current research has been able to discover.* Fair enough. But often such statements are uttered with an air of fact as if we are somehow infallible at this moment in time. As if what we "know" today is somehow complete and perfectly researched. Well, that is truly absurd!

I guess human hubris (excess pride or self-confidence) will always be a part of human nature. We like to think of ourselves as smart, accomplished, or clever. We want something worthwhile to show for all our work and investment, to be in control of the facts, in control of the world around us. Alas, sometimes such hubris is just as dangerous as *not* being in control, of being ignorant, of going off half-cocked to apply our "knowledge" somehow. That's all because we are never completely in control. We never have all the facts. We are always somewhat ignorant. We are just doing our best, with the best knowledge and understanding we have been able to come up with *so far.*

Life is more about an unfolding process rather than fixed knowledge. Life is a dance between what seems known and what seems yet unknown. Science is a series of questions, theories, evidence, and then more questions. If we think of it only as a series of facts and fancy technology, then we are missing most of what science really is.

Look at it this way: *You* are a scientist. Everyone acts as a scientist, pretty much every day. You have experiences and you try to make some sense out of it all. You have some aha moments, and some "what the f—k??!?" moments. Tomorrow, you might look back at today and think, "that makes sense now." Or you might look back and say, "I guess I was wrong about that." We all do this, pretty much all the time, as we go through life.

Is there such a thing as climate change? Well, the best evidence we have today is that there is. Are we humans causing it? It seems very likely. Shall we take some action, therefore? Well, yes, I think that might be a prudent choice. After all, why be reckless? If it's even somewhat likely that we are, in fact, damaging the atmosphere and our biosphere as a result, is it worth the risk to do nothing about it? We only have one planet. There is no spare planet in case we ruin this one. So, I'm for erring on the side of caution myself. I call myself a "conservative" on this because to me, that means I want to conserve the planet and nature, as much as we can, rather than run roughshod over it and risk killing off so much that we humans will die along with it.

Of course, in that example, taking action will have an impact on our way of life. Some people fear that they'll lose their jobs as a result. Coal miners. Oil company workers. Cattle ranchers. Entire industries may have to change.

Admittedly, change can be difficult. Yet jobs are always in flux, being created or eliminated for a whole host of reasons. I can't help that and neither can anyone else, really. We just do our best. There's no reason to stop trying. Just because we're acting out of ignorance part of the time is no reason not to strive to do our best, whenever possible.

If anything, it is up to us to take care of each other, somehow. Sure, we're capable of individual action. But at the same time, we're all connected, whether you think of that spiritually, or not. For example, you didn't make all the products on the supermarket shelves, someone else did. When you select one to buy, you're acting as an individual in that moment, perhaps, but in the long run, you are intimately connected with everything that was done to put that product on that shelf for you to grab, buy, and take home with you.[78]

So, if we're all connected, then I suggest we think of finding ways to help and support each other. We typically do this if a tornado comes through our village. We pitch in and help people find their family members, find their precious objects left behind, give them shelter if they have no place to sleep, start to clean up the next day, rebuild eventually, and so on. We can use this same spirit to help each other find new work when old work or jobs become unnecessary.

---

[78] Not to mention where it or its remnants go when you're done with it. Reduce, Reuse, Repair, Recycle, Rot (compost), or Refuse. We can never really throw anything away because there is no such place as "away." Everything ends up somewhere and someone or some thing (in nature) has to live with it.

I Start Asking

Sometime around February of 2001, I finally had the courage to begin researching my own sexuality and gender identity. Before then, I remember thinking that I didn't expect my local library to have much of anything on sex or paraphilia. Finally, with the internet at hand, I decided it was time to explore.

Late one evening, after my wife had gone to bed, I sat down and opened a search engine. I was nervous. I had never really reached out to find out what was out there. I took a deep breath, typed in the words "plastic pants," and hit return. One by one, I started reading the articles that came up. I discovered a whole host of websites related to infantilism, age play, and so on. I realized that what I had identified for myself was merely a tiny corner of a whole world of related activities and interests. Soon, my searches branched out into other areas. I discovered more and more of the literally thousands of things people do that are connected to sexuality in one way or another.

In the process, I realized that I had a variety of reactions to each thing I encountered. After awhile, I developed a four-level scale to describe my reactions. Eventually, while discussing these levels with a friend, she suggested a fifth level. So here they are:

1. Ick! Ewww! I find this disgusting, repulsive, frightening, gross.
2. Huh? I don't get it. Why would people find this erotic?
3. Okay, I get it. It's not me, but I can understand why someone would like this.
4. Well, I never thought of that! … but I hope *somebody talks me into it!*[79]
5. Wow! I'm turned on just thinking about this! I'd like to try it. (Or, I already do this!)

Now, I realize that many people are perfectly happy with "ordinary" heterosexual sex between cisgendered people, so this list might seem irrelevant to you. But it was clear right away that I was a lot more complicated than that! I won't go into all the details about what I discovered, as that's not the point of this book. (Perhaps a topic for my next book?) The point is, I remembered that I had a fantasy for which I did not find a name, at the time. That was, imagining that my body was transformed into a woman's body.[80]

I also encountered articles about how sexuality is connected with spirituality, rather than being the antithesis of it. I was fascinated. Through a connection with a friend, I discovered a group called the Boston Area Sexuality Spirituality Network, (BASSN), started by Linda Marks.[81] As soon as I found out about it, I started going to their monthly meetings. In less than a year, I joined the "core group," the small group that planned upcoming meetings, and managed our website and finances.

---

[79] This is the one that was added later.

[80] I later learned that one term for this is anatomic autogynephilia.

[81] The group was active during the 2000s but has since dissolved.

Among the people of the core group, an entire new world opened up to me. People used terms or mentioned groups with which I had little or no familiarity, such as Tantra, Dark Odyssey, Sterling Institute, Human Awareness Institute, and Family Tree. At first, I felt as I did when I first got to Goddard College; I was the neophyte among the more advanced.

Then sometime in 2003, I received a party invitation. A group of roommates who lived in a nearby town was throwing a party in February to help chase away the winter blahs. They typically had themes for their parties, and the theme this time was "glam." Guests were invited to come in whatever they thought glam meant to them.

Something inside me clicked. I decided to go to the party and wear something glamorous. In my head, I pictured what I would have on: A silver lamé top with long sleeves and a boat neck, white linen pants, silver shoes or slippers, and silver nail polish on my fingers and toes. I knew that silver or gold lamé tops weren't in current fashion, so I went to the Garment District, a consignment loft in Cambridge, to search for something used. My wife was a little uncertain as to how she felt about all this, but she agreed to come with me.

When I got there, I climbed to the top of the stairs and looked out over the entire floor. To the right were racks of men's clothes and to the left were the women's. At that moment, I realized that I had given myself complete permission to buy anything from either side of the aisle for the first time in my life. At that moment, I felt like the happiest man on the planet!

I found some white polyester pants that fit and some silver strap sandals with Lucite heels (for $6!). My wife told me, "You're going to last about five minutes in those shoes." When I asked why, she said the pressure of the tiny straps would dig into my feet. I bought them anyway, because I didn't know if I would find anything else. Later on, I learned how to hike my feet back up a little so I could put most of my weight on the heels. That way, I could wear them for an hour or two.

I went home and tried on the pants. My wife took one look at me and said, "Well, you can't wear that underwear with those pants." I was wearing white men's briefs under them, which showed through the polyester fabric. Oops! So, I went off to buy some women's underpants in a color that would match my skin, since they don't make that color for men.

But there was no silver lamé top to be found. I must have gone to almost a dozen other stores and shops. Nothing. I learned that it had been in style too long ago and all the leftovers had already been either purchased or discarded. I returned home. As I stood in my living room, looking dejected, my wife piped up, "I bet they still make the fabric!"

Sure enough, a local fabric shop had bolts of lamé, in silver, gold, and other tints. We bought a pattern and took it all home. Despite having some doubt about why I wanted to do all this, my wife measured me, then cut and sewed what I wanted. I had no purse but she lent me an old one of hers. I also had no earrings, so she lent me an ear cuff. I thanked her profusely, for everything, and wore it all to the party.

At the party, I had a great time! At one point, I picked up my purse for a moment to get something and kept it on my shoulder. Soon, a woman asked me, "Oh, are you leaving already?" I said no, but why did she ask? She informed me that having my purse on my shoulder was a common sign that I was saying goodbye and preparing to depart. I started to realize that there was a whole language of clothing and fashion that I had yet to learn.

The following year, the same group held another party and decided that the theme would be "pantsless." You could show up in a tunic, a skirt, a dress, a robe, a sarong, or a kilt. Just no pants. My wife had some old clothes she didn't want, including a wool wrap skirt, which I tried on. The look on my face told her right away that it was too itchy to wear without a slip, so I had to go buy one of those as well.

I didn't want to wear panty hose under the skirt because I didn't think that would be in keeping with the theme of the party. I set off to find real stockings. First I would need a garter belt.[82] I ended up on the third floor of Macy's in the lingerie department. The saleswoman there was very nice when I asked about garter belts. She went up and down the aisles with me until we found them on a bottom rack, down below some bras. They didn't have a size label, so I had to guess what would fit. She told me I'd have to go down the first floor to the hosiery department to find stockings.

When I got down there, a much younger woman was at the counter. "I want to buy a pair of stockings," I said. "Well, you're in the right department," she said, motioning to the racks of panty hose lined up behind her. I said no, those were panty hose; where were the real stockings? She looked at me blankly. I tried to explain how each leg was separate. "I don't think we have any of those," she told me. I headed down the mall to Filene's and sure enough, they had real stockings. I bought a few pair.

Finally, I had everything, ... except my own purse. Rather than borrowing one from my wife again, I figured it was time to have one of my own. She advised me to try a local discount store. When I got there, I walked in and there was an entire section of purses and handbags to choose from. Right away, I saw a small black one with an adjustable strap, so I could either carry it on one shoulder or lengthen it and wear it bandolier-style (cross-body) if I wanted.

But perhaps there was something else that I would like better. I walked up and down through the section, looking at various purses. And each time I found something I thought I might like, I would go back to that first one and compare. I kept going back to that first one.

---

[82] I could have shopped for a girdle instead, but as I am tall and thin, I figured a garter belt would do.

148

Finally, I realized that that little black one was it. I took it off the shelf and started to walk all the way across to the registers on the far side of the sales floor. Suddenly, as I was walking, I felt a very special feeling inside me. This was totally unexpected. This purse was somehow much more than just another accessory. For some reason that I couldn't explain, my heart was happy. I paid for it and went home.

On the night of the party, I took awhile to get dressed. Gathering and pulling up stockings, and then attaching them to a garter belt takes practice, especially for the grippers in back, behind each thigh! My chapped hands kept snagging the sheer fabric of the slip and the stockings, so I tried applying hand lotion a few times in an attempt to prevent that.

Finally, when I finished getting dressed, I drove to the party and found a parking space a few blocks away. I stepped out of the car and began walking down the sidewalk. There I was, walking in below-freezing temperatures, on a cold February night, realizing that stockings, as thin as they were, did offer some warmth! The wool skirt was also surprisingly warm, as there was no wind to blow up under it. But the most remarkable sensation I experienced was that of the garter straps at the back of each of my thighs, stretching and retracting with each step I took. So this was how women used to walk in the winter, all the time.

I realized that I had been unintentionally giving myself a history lesson in women's clothing, at least in terms of what women had been wearing during my lifetime.

I had a great time at the party. People were dressed in all kinds of creative things, according to the theme. There was even a woman authorized to walk around with a mirror on the end of a stick, looking up under people's garments to assess how "pants free" they really were. As a result, I won a third-place ribbon, probably for my effort to avoid panty hose and wear real stockings.

While there, I remember talking with a few women about my experience in buying a purse. When I got to the part about the sudden feeling I had, they all started to nod in acknowledgement. "What was that all about?" I asked them. They explained that a purse is a very personal thing. You keep all your personal things in it. It's kind of a private space, and you have to keep it with you or keep your eye on it most of the time, whenever you have one with you, lest someone steal it or go through the contents without your permission.

Later, I reflected that I might do well to use the same rules that one might use for a child. Never leave it alone in a car. Don't let it out of your sight unless you're in an environment that you deem to be safe, and only with well trusted people present!

Some time after that party, one of the hosts of the party gave me a book, *My Gender Workbook* by Kate Bornstein. In the book, Kate poses many challenging questions about gender. I took quite some time pondering before penciling in my responses. I used pencil because, one of these days, I'm thinking I'll take it off the shelf and see how my answers may have changed over the years.

Shopping for Clothes

Over time, I've gotten quite an education in how to shop for women's clothes. Growing up as a boy in the 1950s and 1960s did not really prepare me for any of this, that's for sure!

When I used to go shopping for men's clothes, and it was anything but a suit, I would go into the store, pick out a few shirts or pairs of pants and try them on for size. Take pants, for example. There are shelves with dozens and dozens of pants, all in the same style, in a variety of sizes and a few limited colors (black, navy, hunter green, gray, or tan). It was often hard for me because I'm tall and skinny, and there was usually little or nothing there that would fit me. But if they had something in my size, it was a pretty simple process. I would check the price to see if I might want to buy more than one pair, then try them on in the changing room with one question in mind: Do they fit? If so, I would head for the registers and check out.

I remember shopping for a new sport jacket years ago. I walked into the men's department and asked, "Can you show me the one jacket you have in a 38 long, unless you sold it already?" The sales clerk went to take a look and returned to say, "Sorry, we must have sold it already." This happened about half the time. The other half of the time, I had to decide if I liked the style and color of the one jacket they still had in stock that had any chance of fitting me.

Shopping for women's clothes is a whole different experience. To me, it can be more fun, but on the other hand, it's way more time-consuming. There are racks and racks full of items to wear (much more than there is for men) in a variety of styles, fabrics, and colors, that can be overwhelming. So, I paw through the items, rack after rack, looking, looking, looking for something in my size that I like. Sometimes, I just have to walk back out of the store without buying anything, because, despite of all the items available, I can't find anything that appeals to me.

If I do find a few things I like, I head for the changing rooms. I remember one of the first times I went shopping for tops at a discount store. I picked out six different things that looked colorful and attractive, and then grabbed one more, a conservative ribbed turtleneck, on a whim. When I approached the saleswoman about trying them on, she motioned toward the other side of the store, to the men's section, because I wasn't allowed in the women's changing rooms.[83] So I traipsed over there to try them all on.

---

[83] That doesn't always happen. Since then, in some stores, ones devoted to women's clothing only, they have a woman standing there as a changing room monitor. Usually they're nice enough to show me to a room, close the door behind me and tell me to ask if the coast is clear before I emerge. Once, at a discount women's clothing "warehouse" store, I had to try on skirts in the handicapped bathroom because there was no men's changing room and I was told that the changing room for women was a large open communal one with no privacy.

Inside the changing cubicle with the door closed, I tried on each of the things I picked out. I put them on, one item at a time, then stood there, looking at myself in the mirror for a moment. Each time, my reaction was, "Hmmm ... Oh, well, I guess not," and then I would take that item off. I didn't like *any* of the six things when I finally saw myself in the mirror wearing them! Finally, when I tried on the conservative ribbed turtleneck, I really liked it! I took the other six tops back to the women's department. The woman on staff there said, "Thank you." I asked why she said that. She told me, "Well, you didn't drop any of them on the floor and you didn't try to re-rack them yourself." Then she added, "Now you know why it takes women so long to shop."

When I tell women about this process, they all nod in agreement. This is what women go through all the time when shopping for clothes. It looks good or even great on the rack, but once you try it on and look at yourself in the mirror something inside tells you, "Uh ... nope. Now that I see it on me, I just don't like how I look wearing this." Other times, you get that special feeling inside, "Yes, this is me; I want to wear this."

Nobody seems to know what the criteria are, exactly. You look at yourself and you just know. Either you like it or you don't. It's just an intuitive sense you get, pretty much right away, most of the time. If you have a friend with you, sometimes they'll think something looks good on you when you're not so sure. So it's not an absolute cut and dried process. But usually, if you say, "I don't like it," they'll nod and say, "Yeah, it's not for you."

The wonderful thing is, I have always been treated well by store personnel! Only once, when I asked about the sizes for panties (a wacky numbering system all its own, 5, 6, 7, 8, 9, etc.) did I have a woman tell me flat out, in a thick accent, "You should not buy that, it won't fit you properly!" I insisted that I needed something in beige, which was not available for men, but she wouldn't let up. She kept insisting, "It will not fit you properly!" I bought them anyway. Fortunately, I got the right size. I'm a 6.[84]

Aside from that one time, everyone else has been great! They've even helped me decide if something looked right on me if I ventured out of the changing room while wearing it and asked for an opinion.

Mostly, I shop at consignment shops and secondhand stores and once in awhile in a small clothing shop for a new item. Even there, the proprietors have always been very helpful! Flea market fundraisers for churches, libraries, and the like are the best. Not for getting assistance, but for the most clothes for the least money. I once walked out of a church sale with five different items for $23. But I did have to try things on in the men's bathroom.

---

[84] You might think that my genitals would not fit into women's underpants successfully, but I discovered that if the size is right, the fabrics are usually stretchy enough to wear without discomfort. In fact, as there is no fly to eventually sag, I never have to worry about "fall out" while wearing them. If I need to pee, I don't stand at a urinal. Instead I go into a stall, pull them down, and sit, just as a woman would.

As a Woman

Sometime in late 2005, after acquiring a few more items and getting dressed for a few parties, conventions, etc., I decided that I wanted to present completely as a woman.

For at least a few hours, I would be as much a woman as possible. This was an intimidating thought, but I began to get used to the idea. In early 2006, I decided to go to a "kink" convention[85] as a woman. My thinking was that people there would be accepting of just about any variation in gender presentation, so I would most likely feel safe enough.

Leading up to the time, for about two weeks, I set about shopping and preparing. I bought shaving cream and a razor in order to get the closest shave I could. I went shopping for a wig and eventually bought one. I had an eye exam and ordered a new pair of glasses. I bought a necklace, a bracelet, and a pair of panty hose. I ended up choosing rather conservative clothes, that ribbed turtleneck sweater from the discount store, and a long black skirt that came down to just below my knees. All in all, I spent around $500 doing this.

Finally, I had to get a bra. I decided to go to a store called Lady Grace because they were known for making sure women had the best fit, rather than the most outrageous styles or colors. I looked up their list of retail store locations and drove to one.

It was early evening as I entered the store and went up to the sales desk. The woman there told me that this was a brand-new branch store and it wasn't officially open just yet. It was fully stocked and I could buy things, but the register had no cash for making change; I would have to use a credit card.

I stood there for a moment in the brightly-lit store, surrounded by racks and racks full of bras and other lingerie. I said, "Well, I'm looking for a bra, and I need it to fit me." I continued, "I don't want something too big; I'm not trying for a drag queen look." (I motioned with my hands to indicate "boobs way out to here" in front of my chest.) "I want something that will look natural on my (tall, thin) body. Perhaps an A cup."

The woman did not look surprised in the least. Without missing a beat, in a matter-of-fact but gentle tone of voice, she said, "No, ... I think probably a B. I think I have just what you want." She headed off down an aisle lined with hundreds of bras and came back with a simple style, in a light purple color, with very slight padding.

---

[85] By kink, I mean a convention specifically for people involved in a variety of sexual and gender expressions. They have classes, seminars, and a sales floor featuring fetish clothing and other items. Most people attending understand what it's like to be interested in something that the rest of society does not understand, condone, or perhaps even want to know about. The one I attended was hosted by the New England Leather Alliance, an organization I hold in very high regard. See www.nelaonline.org.

"They're still painting the fitting rooms," she explained, in an apologetic tone. "So you'll have to try it on in the stockroom behind the counter; I hope that's okay." I said that would be fine. Then I asked about something to put inside the cups. They didn't have full breast prosthetics at the time, but she was able to offer me two kinds of enhancers, one pair made of foam and the other made of silicone gel. I chose the silicone ones because I wanted something with at least some weight, even though they wouldn't feel quite as heavy as real breast tissue on my chest.

She led me to the stockroom, just behind the counter, and explained that when she closed the door, I should put the bra on, then knock on the door when I was ready for her to come in so that she could help me adjust it. When I was ready, she came in and adjusted the straps carefully, asking me how it felt, and so on, pretty much as she would have for any woman. We worked at it a little until it felt just right.

It was such a tender moment for me. I felt so well-attended to and cared for! When was the last time anyone paid such close attention to me, and about something so personal? It was a rare experience.

When we were done, she went back out and closed the door. I took the bra off and put my regular clothes back on. After paying, I asked her how often someone came in for this kind of thing (a man coming in to buy a bra for himself). She replied, "Oh, it happens more often than you might think!"

I drove home with another warm happy feeling in my heart.

§ § §

At home, I tried everything on to make sure things fit and looked okay (colors worked well together, fit without wrinkles, etc.).

Finally, the day came. I shaved my face and legs, got everything ready, packed everything into a large bag and drove to the convention. When I registered, they asked if I wanted a name tag with a name other than my real name. I chose the name "Hope." I skimmed the booklet describing the policies, events, and workshops. One thing I noticed was the policy about restrooms. On the main floor of the hotel, in the convention area, there were two large restrooms, with traditional signs on the doors saying, "Men" and "Women." But now, those were covered over by temporary signs that said "Male identified persons" and "Female identified persons."

I entered the "Male identified" one and used the large handicap-accessible stall to change. I wasn't planning to stay overnight, so hadn't booked a room (the hotel rooms were fully booked anyway). That meant that this was the only place I thought I could do that.[86] Once I got everything on, including my wig, stockings, shoes, skirt, top,

---

[86] Later, I learned that there were also two gender-free bathrooms, which were single occupancy restrooms, where you could go in and lock the door behind you.

necklace, and other jewelry. I put my jeans and shirt back into the bag and stepped out into the hallway.

As I stood there, I realized that I was scared. What if someone saw me who already knew me as Glenn? How would they react? I hadn't told anyone that I was going to do this and I knew that friends of mine from BASSN were going to be there, staffing a table. The first one who saw me was Karl. He stopped for a moment and looked at me. Then he said in a low voice that was quite hesitant, "Glenn?" I said, "Well, yes, but I'm 'Hope' right now." Right away he offered his hand and said, "Pleased to meet you, Hope!"

I was immediately struck by two things.

One was that in spite of my expectations that all this would feel very erotic to me, that was not my reaction at all! In fact, I had no erotic stimulation whatsoever. Instead, my experience was more of a spiritual one. Everything I felt was in my heart, not down between my legs. It was as if I had found a part of me that was buried somehow and I was expressing my love for that part, bringing everything together for the first time.

The next thing I realized was that I barely had an identity. I felt like a brand-new person who had never existed before. I had no history. I hadn't grown up as a girl. I hadn't experienced life as female ever before. I was full of questions with few answers.

I approached the BASSN table and a woman who I knew welcomed me. I was going to give her a hug, but I stopped and asked, "How do women hug each other? Do you move slightly to the right or left so that your breasts fit between each other?"[87] They laughed politely. No, they said, you just hug gently and don't press too hard.

At one point, I had to pee. Okay, I thought, I'm going into the "Female identified restroom." I was scared again. Would I really be okay? I hesitated for a moment, then went in. There were about a dozen women in there, most of whom were engaged in conversation. A few were leaning in toward the mirror to fix their makeup.

The woman closest to me turned around and it was the very same friend I had first approached at the BASSN table. She said, "Oh, welcome!" and gave me another hug right there.

I went into a stall and learned for the first time (the hard way), not to pull panty hose all the way down to your ankles! It's a devil of a time to get them all the way back up again once you're done![88]

---

[87] The way gear teeth would mesh, right? Hey, that was the first thought that came to mind.

[88] For those who don't know, only pull them down to just above your knees.

When I came out of the stall, I took my lipstick out of my purse and opened it. I was surprised to discover that I had not turned it down all the way before putting the cap back on the last time I used it. The end, which used to have a nice point, was now all squished. I said something out loud about my disappointment and right away at least two other women responded, "That's okay, it's easy to forget. Here, take a bit of paper towel and reshape it a bit. After that, as you use it, eventually your lips will smooth it out again."

I was treated so well that I really felt as though I belonged there. I wasn't afraid anymore. I also realized that this is *not* what it's like in the men's room!

§ § §

At one point, while I was at the convention, I sat at a table in the atrium, eating lunch with a woman who was a friend of mine. She thought what I was doing was great and told me that a friend of hers should meet me. She knew he had just left the convention, so she called him on his cell phone. He was just getting on the highway to go home when he answered her call. She was so intent on having him meet me that she convinced him to get off at the next exit, turn around, and come back.

He came in, sat down at our table, and she introduced us to each other. He was wearing jeans and a nondescript shirt. He revealed to me that he also cross-dressed, something which she already knew. She told him, "See, you could come here!" - meaning that he could do what I was doing, here at the convention.

But he protested. He said his family might find out. "But," she argued, "there's no way they could know. Photographs and video are forbidden here. People agree to confidentiality when they arrive. Your family would never come here. You'd be safe!" But still he refused. "I couldn't risk it," he said. It turned out that his practice of dressing up was a complete secret from everyone in his daily life, his family, colleagues at work, everywhere, save for a few friends who knew. He kept his clothing in a secret box, hidden in his house. Once our conversation concluded, we said goodbye and he left to drive back home. I felt sorry for him. Here I was having such a great time exploring all this, whereas I imagined that he was cloistering himself in a bedroom at home with the shades drawn.

Sometime after the convention was over, I met at least two other men, one while shopping for shoes, and another at a bar in a restaurant. They had each taken extensive measures to present as women. Their routine was to make an excuse to their families, go out with their clothes and jewelry hidden in a bag, use a restroom somewhere to change, and enjoy life as a woman for awhile out on the town. They did everything - shave and apply makeup, wear a wig, bra, dress, jewelry, shoes with heels, and so on. Then, later, they reversed the entire process. They took it all off, scrubbed off all the makeup, and put their "man clothes" back on before returning home.

Eventually, I learned that most men who did this, or something similar, did so in complete secrecy, either confined to their own bedrooms while their families were away, or out somewhere where no one who knew them as men would see them. They had two different lives, completely separate from each other.

I knew that I could never do this, nor did I desire to. First of all, the strain of having to lie and cover up all the time would be a lot for me to maintain. I guess I could do it, but I already have enough stress in life without that. But more to the point, I never wanted to hide anything. I always wanted to be open, to be out (of the closet, as they say). My feminine side is part of my truth. It's something I wanted to share with other people from the very beginning.

I especially enjoy talking with women, openly discussing what I'm doing. Most of them seem eager to share experiences and stories of what it's like to live in this society as women. I get the sense that most women wish that more men would take an interest in what they go through as women. It seems sad to me that there are such barriers to communication in our culture at large.

Private Lives

I remember being in the car when my father would occasionally make remarks about women drivers. His comments were intended to be humorous. He didn't seem ever to be angry or upset about this. But somewhere, indirectly, the point was: Men were just better drivers than women. He cited something about men having better peripheral vision than women.

Later in life, I realized that you can just turn your head a little farther to compensate if that's the case. No big deal. Recently, I found some studies that suggest that women have better peripheral vision than men, but men are better at seeing objects at greater distances when looking straight ahead. Of course, these are just generalizations. In the long run, you can't really say who is likely to be a better driver.

§ § §

Recently, I have realized that there are a whole lot of things that men and women seldom discuss with one another. There are aspects of being male or female or living in this culture with our variety of attitudes and assumptions about each other that we just carry around with us and don't bring up. Sometimes, we just don't think of saying anything because what we're experiencing is just part of daily life. It's routine. Sometimes, we don't mention something because it would just be too much trouble to explain or we think the other person wouldn't be interested and stop listening. And sometimes, it's actually intimidating, frightening, or even terrifying to bring something up.

A woman approaches her locked car in a parking garage, and looks in the back window to make sure there's no predator hiding in the back seat before she opens the door and gets in. She shudders a little, imagining what it would be like to actually see someone in there. A man stops himself, unconsciously, from doing anything more than shaking hands with another man, because it's too scary to get any closer than that. People might think he's gay or a pervert or something. There could be violent consequences in both cases, but often we just live through the moment and move on.

I want a world where the woman feels safe, not because there are no predators out there, but because we've all "got her back" if anything happens. If she's attacked, we won't ask if she was wearing anything provocative, we'll just help her in any way we can. I want a world where the man can feel safe, not because there are no violent homophobes out there, but because we'll back him up if he's ridiculed or attacked just for hugging another man, without blaming him for doing so.

As I write this, as a man, I realize how my feelings are kicking up. I realize how much fear I still have about expressing affection with other men, even though I do it all the time these days. The homophobia is still going on inside me, I guess. It's ugly. I hate having it. But sometimes, it's just there.

Walking at Night

I'm on the bus.
It's late in the evening.
It's dark.
My hometown's streets are empty.

It's my stop. I get up.
And then,
a young woman gets up,
and steps out of the bus
ahead of me.

Just the two of us exit.
Nothing is said.
I do not know her
She does not know me.
As far as I know.

She walks ahead of me.
Her steps are quick.
She holds her head up,
her gaze is straight ahead.

One woman walking down the sidewalk.
One man (me) walking behind her.
At night.

There is only that one way
for me to get home.

I guess that she is afraid of me.
A man.
Walking behind her,
even some distance back.

But I would never do anything to harm her.
I wish I could do something to let her know that.
But if I speak,
she may flinch.
If I approach her,
or try to overtake her,
that could be worse.

I cross the street to the sidewalk on the other side,
even though it will add more steps for me later,

when I have to cross back to get home.

I walk faster,
so that she can see me.
Perhaps she will relax a little,
knowing that I'm not
following her on purpose.
I'm just trying to get home.

I hate this tension.
People afraid of me.

If I were a woman,
following another woman,
at night,
would it be like this?

If I were an African-American man,
following a woman,
at night,
would it be a lot worse?

I hear
that there are more attacks
on women
by friends and acquaintances
than by strangers,
even at night.

I wish I knew
how to help her feel safe.
Not just feel safe,
but *be* safe.

Perhaps,
on this one night
if we had at least talked a little,
if we had said just enough to know
that there was nothing to fear,
then our tension
would have been eased.

But we both
were perhaps
too afraid
to say anything.

The Big Question

Over the next few years, I added more women's clothes to my wardrobe and went to a few other places as a woman. I even went out to a Halloween party one year, in a "sexy nurse" costume I bought at a costume shop. I found white stockings and white soft-soled shoes and a blonde wig to wear with it. I shaved my legs, shaved my beard off, wore the right kind of wristwatch, and so on. I had a great time!

I also continued to wear various clothes and jewelry, but as a man, as I had done before. I stuck to places where I felt relatively safe to do all this, such as at parties where friends would accept what I was doing, at my UU church, at workshops, and at the convention where I had first presented as a woman. I remember sneaking back into my own house on one occasion, hoping that my neighbors wouldn't see me.

During this time, I thought a lot about where I really wanted to take myself with all this. Originally, I had imagined that transitioning was inevitable. But now I wondered.

Did I seek to have a life as a woman full-time? What would that mean? How did my experience compare with that of other people I had met who either split their lives between living as a woman and living as a man, or were trans - people who had changed everything so they could live as women, abandoning their former male selves as completely as possible?

A jumble of thoughts went through my head. Some of them were more practical or logical in nature, some stemmed more from pure feelings or intuition. Some of them seemed trivial and others of grave importance. I mentally placed myself in various situations I might encounter in life and tried to imagine what it would be like if I began living life as a trans woman.

What about my parents and siblings? What about my current marriage? What about my son and my stepdaughter? What about my work? What about future relationships (as it had started to seem that my marriage was not going to last)? What would my "sexual orientation" be? I think this was perhaps the most challenging set of questions for me. It seemed that I would have to make the most major changes in my life in the area of relationships, when compared to any other part of transitioning.

I did not seem to be attracted to men, so I would have to look to other women for romantic relationships. Would I be dating lesbians? Perhaps even some women who sought relationships with other women would shun me. How did I feel about that? I love women, including lesbian women, but also straight and bisexual women as well. Straight women whom I had considered as potential relationship partners (with me as a man) might no longer be interested in me.

I realized that the excitement and wonder of living as a woman might not turn out to be all that different in daily life, once I had lived that way for a few years. After all, most people who have a job have an ordinary daily routine. You get up in the morning, shower, get dressed, get things ready and go to work. Sure, as a man you might have to shave, choose a tie to wear, make sure your hair doesn't look like you just got out of bed, perhaps. As a woman, you have to choose clothes, jewelry, perhaps put on some makeup, fix your hair. The point is, even though these routines are different in the "gender binary" world, they were routines just the same. You do what you have to do to prepare for the day, every morning.[89]

I thought about my body. Some trans friends of mine remarked that they couldn't wait to get hormones or surgery or both, because they were so extremely uncomfortable with their original body. People born with a female body couldn't wait to have a double mastectomy, for example.

But I realized that I didn't hate my body. I looked at the prospect of hormones as okay, but surgery seemed like a big deal. It would be very expensive, risky, and painful for awhile. I'd want to have my beard removed by laser or electrolysis. I'm over six feet tall, so I'd end up becoming a very tall woman. As a man, my head was mostly bald. Would my hair come back in or would I have to wear a wig everywhere? Could I go to the beach, go swimming?

By the time I was considering all this, I was in my late fifties. Almost all women of that age have already gone through menopause. So, here I was, contemplating a transition to become a postmenopausal woman! I would be taking hormones that most women's bodies, at my age, were no longer secreting at such a level. Sure, some women chose to be on hormone therapy, but that wasn't the point.

And then there was my voice. I understood that surgery on vocal cords was very risky; I could lose my voice altogether. When presenting as a woman, I had tried to speak in a higher register, which seemed to take a concerted effort. I suppose that with more practice, it would start to become more natural to talk that way. But even though I tried, it was very easy to slip back into my male voice.

Throughout all this, I began to realize that one of my issues was that I wanted to be a woman in all aspects. But as a trans woman, I'd have to make many compromises and adjustments. I would have no ovaries, fallopian tubes, or uterus. My pelvis and hips would still be the original shape I was born with. I suppose I could get facial surgery, but what about my height or the size of my feet?

I started to think about the fantasy world I was in when experiencing my autogynephilia, as if someone could just magically change me completely over to having a natural female body. But in real life, that could not happen.

Then, ultimately there was another question. I noticed it when I went out as a woman. It's hard to describe, but I felt almost as if I were hiding inside of a façade somehow.

---

[89] Now, I know that women and men have to face different things as they travel to work and do their jobs. Things like sexist attitudes and unwanted attention can certainly be major factors in daily life.

While I appeared as a woman on the outside (which many people remarked seemed quite convincing), inside I still felt conflicted, somehow.

After ruminating on all this, I realized I had to look very deeply within myself and try to get in touch with what I really wanted in life. My autogynephilia fantasy was exciting and even compelling, but I started to wonder if it was better to just let myself have that as an erotic fantasy, and not try to live as female in my daily life. After all, I had already discovered that living as female was not erotic, but more of a matter of my heart. The question was, what was my heart really feeling?

The whole idea of my transitioning started to fall apart. It just didn't add up. Something was missing. Earlier, I had read a few books about gender identity (*My Gender Workbook* and *Am I a Woman?* being two of them), but I hadn't really connected with my own experience until I had gone out and experimented for myself.

So, if I wasn't trans, then what was I, exactly? It certainly didn't feel right to just give away all the clothes and go back to the life of a cis man.[90] So, now what?

I reflected on the fact that I could live with my voice and my body, just the way they were. But at the same time, I clearly had a strong feminine side as well. I love women, loved connecting with women, talking about, learning about, and sharing experiences with women living in today's world. This was still deep in my heart somehow.

Over time, I began to realize something. I could allow myself to be guided by the spiritual feeling I had felt when I first stepped out into that hallway as a woman (at the convention, years ago). The feeling that I was "hiding something" started to make more sense – showing up as a woman, I was expressing only my feminine side and hiding my masculine side! Living as a cis man at other times was just as inauthentic because that meant hiding my feminine side and only letting my masculine side show. The best thing to do would be to show both.

Somehow my clothes and jewelry were much more than just something to wear. I still felt something special and nice when I dressed that way. It seemed as if wearing traditional women's clothes and jewelry was a way for me to help connect myself to my inner feminine side. And at the same time, my outward appearance would signal to others that I was not just another cis man.

I decided to wear whatever I felt like wearing. I would keep my male body, but I would be different from most men, who dared not venture outside the confines of traditional male clothing and behavior.

Walking down the street, I would simply appear to be ... a man wearing a dress.

---

[90] "Cis" is short for cisgender – meaning "same gender," where one's gender identity matches the sex one was identified as having at birth. Essentially, the opposite of transgender.

The Power of Women

I have often wondered why prostitution is mostly one way. The women are selling and the men are buying. And why is it that images of women's bodies are used to sell things more often? We say, "sex sells," but isn't it usually images of young women in provocative poses that sell? Aren't these images doctored up to look even more "beautiful" than any real woman? Why in some cultures are women asked or required to cover their hair or even their entire bodies? Why is it hard for many men to avoid staring at a woman's cleavage while standing in front of her?

In my elementary school, in the sixth grade, we all had dance class after school, one afternoon a week. We were taught the waltz, the foxtrot, and swing dancing to some of the newer music of the time, such as the Bristol Stomp. Boys had to wear jackets and neckties to school that day, and girls had to wear nice dresses. After classes ended for the day, we assembled in the gymnasium, with girls sitting on one side and boys on the other. One time, when the dance teacher said, "You may now ask a partner for the first dance," four boys practically ran across the floor toward one girl. She was considered to be very pretty, with long blond hair. One of the boys stumbled and fell face down on the floor before he got to her. Ouch! Everybody noticed. He was fine, physically (he got right up again), but he was embarrassed. We were all embarrassed, I think. Nobody got up to help him and nobody said anything, at least publicly.

§ § §

As infants, we see ourselves as an integral part of our birth mother. She is essential to our world, the center of our universe, our home base. She holds us and keeps us warm, and feeds us with her own breast milk. This attachment is very strong, for without these things, we would literally die. Over time, we come to realize that we are separate human beings, able to walk around on our own and assert our own will. But the power of our mother to sustain our very lives while we feel the warm loving safety of her embrace is an experience we remember on a gut level for our entire lives.

Fast-forward to puberty. Reproductive instincts in heterosexual men stimulate pleasure centers in the brain when gazing at a woman who is fertile. This provokes very strong feelings. Without these feelings, the human race would have failed to propagate. Women's bodies send certain visual clues to indicate fertility. Breast cleavage is just one of them. Actually, the entire surface of a woman's body is involved. During her fertile years (after puberty, before menopause), hormones in her system stimulate the growth of subcutaneous fat. That's a thin fat layer just below the skin. This layer gives a smooth appearance to her entire body and acts to hide the texture of muscles, tendons, vessels and other bodily structures beneath. In addition, on average, women's bodies have less hair than men's bodies do. When menopause comes, the hormonal balance shifts, the subcutaneous fat layer dissipates, and wrinkles start to appear.

All these visual cues are powerful signals to the most primitive parts of men's brains.[91] The "thinking" pre-frontal cortex tends to take a back seat to the inner workings of the hypothalamus. Men don't need to think about it, they just want what they are seeing. Their eyes gravitate. The pleasure hormones in their brains increase. It's almost like an addictive response. You just want more.

When we enhance the images of women in advertising, we're really taking these visual cues to extremes. We make the skin even smoother-looking. We erase all excess hair and wrinkles. Even in real life, women are expected to shave their legs, or have hair plucked or waxed or bleached. Spaghetti-strap dresses and tank tops help expose smooth expanses of skin around the neck, shoulders and arms. A huge industry sells creams and other potions that are supposed to "erase" wrinkles, and give women a younger look. Women are hesitant to admit their age. All this is really about fertility.

So women have the power of nurturance, as our mothers, and women have the power of sexual attraction as adults.

The result of this power can be seen in the classic movie scene where a (male) police officer pulls a car over for speeding. He walks to the driver's window, but when he sees a woman at the wheel, and she winks at him and promises she will pay better attention to her driving, he melts and says "aw shucks" and walks back to the patrol car without a thought of writing a ticket. If it were a man instead, no such luck. He's more likely to be the recipient of a stern gaze and slapped with a fine.

Historically, we have expected women to use this power to their advantage. Flat tire? Just stand beside the car and look pretty and helpless and a nice man will show up and do all the dirty work for you, right? That was the culture I grew up with in the 1950s. It's even with us today. Recently a woman friend of mine was moving into a new apartment. She put out a request for helpers and at least a dozen men showed up to help. They were not all likely to become her romantic partners, but I doubt so many volunteers would have shown up if a man had asked for the same help instead.

The most extreme aspect of this is sex workers, members of "the world's oldest profession." The movies *Trading Places* and *Pretty Woman* are good examples of an idealized image of the "working girl" who supports herself by exchanging sexual services for cash.

My opinion is, many women don't fully realize how much power and influence they have, just as many "white folks" are oblivious to their own privilege in this society when compared to people of other races.

And yet, as is often the case with power, there is a dark side.

As a woman, if you want to get something done and romance is just not on the agenda at the moment, then all this attractive power can get in the way. Let's say

---

[91] Or the brains of many gay or bi women.

you're a woman at a meeting to work out a marketing plan, with a mix of women and men. You certainly don't want your body transmitting mind-numbing "rays" of sexual attraction to the men (or other women who might be influenced in a similar way), such that they will stop thinking rationally, right? How do you turn it off?

If you are considered "classically beautiful," what's going to happen as you go about your daily life? Whether you're dating or not, an inordinate number of men will fall all over themselves to "hit on" you. Some may approach you with respect, but others may approach in a bumbling or ignorant manner. Clearly, many are in a "look first, ask questions later" mode, when you might want the questions to come first. Even if you happen to be dating, who knows if any of them might be compatible partners?

And yet looking attractive is part of a good self image. It feels good to look good, to feel good about your body, to be well dressed, and walk confidently with your head up. I know, because I've done it.[92] But as a man, I've escaped much of the unwanted attention from other men that many women experience. I know about it because I've had conversations with hundreds of women and I've listened to their descriptions of what happens all too often when they are objectified and what it feels like.

Another part of the dark side is how society at large has reacted to this power. I think a few words sum it up: Fear, anger, and exploitation. First, fear, because someone without a particular power may tend to fear someone who has that power, even if they don't understand it or its nature. The powerless person may feel inferior or overwhelmed. Second, if you desire something but are told over and over again that you don't possess that same power *and* you can't get it from someone else, then what kind of feelings do you end up with? Yearning? Sadness? Resentment? Resignation?

And finally, exploitation, because if women are seen to have power, then others may find it tempting to take advantage of this power. We end up with the pimp, the porn director, the modeling and fashion industries, with their narrow (pun intended!) image of women to promote. Women are used as tools by others to provoke a desired result, to turn a profit, yet often kept underpaid so that their continued need for money can be used over and over again to trap them in these industries.

Now, clearly, I'm describing a gender-binary world here. I've ignored the reality of other gender identities to simplify my point. The truth is, we are starting to outgrow a gender binary past. It's an uncertain and inexact process. Our ways of looking at gender are changing very rapidly right now, so it's hard to keep up.

But in the long run, adapting to a pan-gender society has the potential to benefit all people, regardless of their sex or gender identity. We're trying to see each other as people first. Valuable human beings, all of us, who can approach each other with increasingly open minds, ready to ask good questions, hear the answers, and get to know one another as individuals.

---

[92] While presenting as a man, presenting as a woman, or as a gender non-conforming man.

Armpits

One way to bridge the gap between genders is to try doing some things that you don't normally do, just to experience it. Sure, this kind of thing has been made fun of in movies,[93] but I'm not suggesting you do any of these things to engage in humiliation, humorous or not. I have done them all and learned a few things in the process.

For example, if you have never done it, try shaving your armpits. At least once. If you don't know how, let someone who knows show you.[94] Then, dry off, put on deodorant, put your clothes on and go out. Wear long sleeves if you like. It doesn't matter if anyone can see that you did this.

Why?

For many reasons. To feel what it's like to do something that typically only women have done. To see how hard it is to shave there. To see what it feels like to shave there. To see what it feels like to walk around with just skin touching skin. To see what it feels like as it starts to grow back in. And, as I said, to build a connection between you and those who have done this, or still do this. A common bond of experience and perhaps understanding. It's just one little thing. You can do this!

Conversely, if you are used to shaving your armpits, then try letting the hair grow out, if you don't usually do that. I don't have to tell you how to do that!

§ § §

Recently, I found that you can buy bras for men. Of course anyone can buy a women's bra and put it on, and perhaps fill the cups with something if you don't have much in the way of breast tissue. But the bras I'm talking about are not made to be filled with anything. They have a very slight curve to fit a typical man's chest without having a cup size, per se.

So I bought one. One company markets them to "straight" couples so they can both have some lingerie to wear in the bedroom, perhaps as a fun prelude to sex. But I decided to see what it would be like to wear one all day. In fact, I tried wearing one all day, for a string of days, even an entire week.

I remember many years ago, a housemate of mine would come home from work, in her blouse and beige skirt (this was the 1980s) and trudge upstairs to put down her

---

[93] The film *What Women Want*, for example.

[94] When I do this, I use the pop-out trimmer on my electric razor to get as close as I can, then use shaving cream and a razor designed for the purpose, once I get into the shower. Otherwise, shaving long hair will just clog the razor, leaving it unable to shave anything further, and you'll be in there forever trying to rinse it out.

bag and keys, etc., muttering something like, "I've got to get this stuff off!" It was clear that she couldn't wait to take off that bra![95]

Sometimes, when she had more casual clothes on, she would come to me and ask, "Will you scratch my back?" She sat straddled on a chair, leaning over the chair back for support. She pulled up the back of her blouse to reveal the broad expanse of her back, with only the back of her bra interrupting the smooth curve of it. Either she or I would unhook it, allowing each of the two sides to snap back sideways out of the way. Then I would run my fingernails (such that I had any) up and down her back, according to her instructions. "Okay, a little higher, over a bit to the left, ... oh, oh, ok, ... good, ... yes, right there!" and, "Ohmygawd, yes!" Once she even sighed, emphatically, "There *is* a God ... and he *has fingernails!*"

So now I know a little of what it's like to wear a bra all day long. Including in hot weather. Sometimes I forget I have it on, but other times, such as when taking a deep breath, I realize it right away. I even got to the point where something seemed missing if I didn't put it on. Other days, I skip wearing it, and, as a man, there are no public consequences. There is nothing to sag and my nipples don't usually show.

Now, of course, my bra is not carrying any weight on my chest, so I haven't had the full experience that many women have, of wearing a D cup for instance, where the straps cut into your shoulders, the sides pull down, and so on. But I have had the experience of sitting in a cheap plastic stacking chair, leaning back, and experiencing the wonderful feeling (not!) as the hooks press through the fabric into my spine.

So, men, here's my invitation to you. Give it a try. Oh, and you'll learn how expensive bras are. They cost something like three to six times as much as a good pair of underpants. Don't say I didn't warn you.

§ § §

If you are a man but can't bring yourself to do either of those things, then perhaps try this: Always sit to pee. Now, I understand that for some men, with certain prostate issues, it might be too difficult to pee while sitting down. But except for that, wherever there is a toilet bowl, put the seat down and sit, rather than stand. At least for a month. As of a few years ago, I have almost completely changed over to sitting.

There are many advantages to this. The first of which is that the bathroom will stay much cleaner! Peeing from a standing position causes an awful lot of spray, no matter how good your aim is. That spray gets on the toilet, the walls, floor, radiator, and so on, then dries out and leaves that odor that men's rooms are famous for. But if you're sitting down, there will be very little spray, and none of that which does occur will escape the bowl. Another advantage is that you can't forget to put the seat back down (as you didn't have to put it up in the first place), so nobody will complain.

---

[95] And probably the panty hose she was likely wearing as well.

But of course, you will be experiencing what women have to face all the time. That gross bathroom at the gas station, for example. Or the one at the run-down diner. Women don't have a choice about this. They either have to sit (after taking time to clean the seat off) or hover over the bowl in a squat without actually contacting the seat (should be an Olympic sport!) or hold it in while searching for another bathroom.[96]

§ § §

Having done these things myself, I've had many conversations with women about them. Quite often, they open up about what it's like, describe things that I haven't yet experienced, or experienced the same way. Many seem happy to have a man, *any man*, make an effort to really listen and understand what it's like to live with these things.

Perhaps we've taught women that their bodies are not good enough, or that "nobody would want to hear about this." I think men have been taught to avoid intimate conversation, and discussion about feelings in general. This is changing, fortunately, so I'm all in favor of building more bridges between all genders. I think we can afford to support each other, even when we have different bodies or different gender identities.

Now, before I leave this topic, I want to reflect on one thing. As a man, a person born with a male body and having kept it all this time, there are limits to what I can experience just by shaving hair off my body, putting on a wig, makeup, a bra, clothes, and jewelry. That is, I will never actually experience menstrual flow, cramps, monthly headaches, what it's like to be pregnant, keep my pregnancy a secret in case I have a miscarriage, or wrestle with the question of whether to stay pregnant or not. Or, if deciding to have a child, deal with morning sickness, back aches, risk of diabetes, pressure on the bladder, or strangers patting my pregnant belly uninvited. Nor will I ever know what it's like to go into labor, deal with unexpected medical interventions, complete with the threat of having surgery (a C-section). I won't experience postpartum depression, or nursing a baby, with its pleasure and potential pain of sore chapped nipples. I won't have to decide where it's okay to breast feed, or have my breast milk start to leak at the sound of a crying infant nearby. I will have no experience of what it's like to watch a child grow up who started life inside my own body. And then, later on, menopause of course.

I just want to admit that what I've done, and all I've learned through what I've done and am doing now, is just a small part of the experience that many women go through in their lives. My hat's off to all the challenges of being a woman in today's world, whether you bear children or not, hold down a job, or have to walk down a street in the dark. I've learned a lot more than most men have, but let me be clear: I really don't know the half of it.

For one thing, I'm tall and thin, and have always been that way.

---

[96] Some women even wear disposables while traveling, just to avoid the whole issue.

168

Fat Girls

I listened to a program on the radio the other day. It featured stories from women who were considered fat. One young woman had graduated from college, but could not find work and never got a date. Men would talk to her, but never asked her out.

She went on a weight-loss program, lost over 100 pounds and was able to stay at her new weight with the help of medication. Soon she was hired, and men asked her out for dates. But, she wondered, how could she trust this new attention she was receiving? After all, she was essentially the same person inside, but she looked different on the outside, and that is what people seemed to be responding to.

I reflected on the fact that how people react to your weight, is for the most part, a cultural tradition, not an inbred or instinctive bias. After all, there are other parts of the world (outside the US) where ultra-thin women are seen as less desirable, rather than more.

The current tradition of "thin as desirable" was perhaps partly due to dress and fashion designers who liked the way their designs looked on tall thin women more than those with other builds. So, that's what appeared on the runway, in the catalogs, in magazine ads, and in shop windows.

But what I thought about afterward was all the girls and women who have been rejected over and over again, simply because they are bigger, rounder, or curvier, than the culturally ideal woman we compare them against. Somewhere my heart was touched. I could feel the pain almost as if it were mine. After all, I lived a life of isolation and rejection for a different - I was a boy who was skinny and not muscular. I was the one who got teased, abused on the playground, and never got a date. At least I was able to find work, eventually, but that's a different story.

Somehow, I never really bought into the skinny woman ideal. I *love* the women with curves, the big women (as my friends can attest!), especially those who have come to realize that there is nothing wrong with them. And what of those who are still in pain from all that rejection? I wish I could clone myself a thousand times, so I could go out and hug each and every one of them. Ask permission, of course, but if they said yes, just them a big, long hug. Of course one single hug isn't going to fix everything. But in my imagination (and in my experience), some women burst into tears, some squeal with delight as they hug me back, others just give a very deep sigh.

So I invite you to break through this invisible wall of isolation and rejection. Perhaps travel to somewhere in the world where women who have a nice round shape are respected, valued, loved, and desired. Soak up the culture there, if you can. Find the ultimate beauty of the big beautiful curvy woman, somewhere within you. And further, if you are someone who is attracted to women, start dating! Start falling in love! All the wonderful fat girls and the world around you will thank you for it!

Lying Awake

A woman lies awake
in the dark
a man lies sleeping
beside her

A woman lies awake
in the dark
as the world outside
is hurting

A man lies sleeping
next to her
dreaming about a
problem at work

A woman lies awake
in the dark
and although the world is
getting better,

she still lies awake.

Us and Them

Let's review. If you take a group of people, identified by some characteristic (sex, gender, affinity, race, ethnic group, or age) and you treat them badly, deny them opportunities, threaten them, inflict harm on them, and, most importantly, tell certain persistent lies about them and their rights and capabilities in life, then what happens?

What happens is that everyone, the people in that group, and people who are not in that group, come to believe these lies. The people in the group come to believe "I'm not as good," and other people come to believe that "they're not as good."

I have seen some research that shows that it's possible to set up a sense of "us versus them" in the minds of infants under the age of six months. These infants seemed to demonstrate an affinity for "their own kind" and an aversion to "those others." They were shown to come to the aid of their own kind and shun others, even if the others seem to be in trouble and in need of some help. Academics refer to this as "in group favoritism."

So perhaps we're struggling with a basic aspect of human nature here. Perhaps it has something to do with survival in some primitive way. Perhaps it's an outgrowth of our need to identify what's human and what's some other kind of animal, which might be a predator, and thus a risk to our lives. Maybe this tendency made the leap, during our evolution, to separating from other humans, who, in groups, might be some kind of threat. Clearly, tribal warfare has gone on for thousands, if not millions of years.

An example is what has happened with slavery, here in the US. Many people convinced themselves that dark-skinned people with African heritage were not even human. The legacy of this is that there are still remnants of this thinking being held today, here in this country. What's important to realize is that if you look at attitudes in other countries, even one of our two neighboring countries on this continent, attitudes are markedly different.

I'm not saying that everything is copacetic around the world, and that the US is the only place where this is happening. Clearly, there are groups struggling with this same dynamic in various parts of the world. It's just different groups, and different, but similar lies.

Another question is, are youth, otherwise known as "teenagers" (ages thirteen to eighteen years) actually an oppressed group? That is, despite not having "fully grown up," is it possible that society creates an oppressive environment for youth, that results in a self-fulfilling prophecy where the oppression causes many youth to "malfunction" as a result? Do adults then refer to these malfunctions as evidence that youth must remain oppressed?

Good questions. As I have worked with youth recently, I'll tell you what I think.

Youth

For a period of about eight years, I volunteered to work with youth (ages fourteen and up) who attended various Unitarian Universalist churches. Together we planned and hosted overnight retreats in various congregations here in New England. We've been very careful to follow the established "safe congregations" policies, so background checks were done on the adults involved and no youth and adult could ever be in a closed room with just each other. Also, the adults had to arrange to sleep in shifts so at least two would be awake at all times during the night.

In doing this work, I learned a lot. First and foremost, I've begun to realize that how teenagers act has a lot to do with the environment we place them in and the attitudes that both adults and youth hold about the capabilities of youth. I've seen all the same reports that you probably have seen, such as the brain doesn't fully mature until age twenty-five, teens have less impulse control than adults, and so on.

At the same time, I've observed youth as young as fourteen organize events even better than many adults do! I've sat in on elections for youth leaders. They nominate candidates (some of whom decline), nominees speak to the group about what kind of leader they would like to be, if elected. Then, the candidates leave the room, at which time everyone else discusses what they heard, the strong and weak points of each one, and finally take a vote (heads down, hands up, one nonvoting person taking the count).

I tell you, I have never heard more insightful, thoughtful, deep discussion anywhere else. Time and again, I am amazed at how carefully they each respectfully discuss the merits and consider how to vote.

Now, of course, these young people do not necessarily represent a full cross section of youth in the US today. They are mostly white, middle class, live with their parents, go to school, and attend church regularly. They typically live in neighborhoods where the streets are relatively safe. But I have seen enough to realize that it's very likely that youth anywhere could do the same, given the right circumstances. After all, they do live under many of the same pressures and face many of the same challenges as youth everywhere.

One of the keys to all this is what we have come to call "youth empowerment." Decades ago (in the 1960s and 1970s), that was taken by some people to mean that youth should run their own events without any adult involvement. As some people would put it, "things got out of hand," and support for that kind of arrangement was dropped.

These days, the way we practice youth empowerment is to set up an intergenerational group, where youth and a few adult volunteers work together to plan events and activities. This is not the adults doing the directing and youth obeying those directions, but instead the adults are asked to "hold the space" - i.e., to set a few ground rules, stay present and attentive, and provide a reference as youth take on the tasks involved. The youth decide everything about the event, including the overall theme, what workshops and activities will be held, who will lead them, and who will staff the registration table and collect the attendance fee. They also decide who will present the ground rules to everyone[97], what meals there will be, what food will be prepared, who will do the preparation, who is to do the shopping beforehand, manage sign-ups for performances at the talent show after dinner, design the entire structure and content of the worship service (late at night, by candlelight), including readings and other activities during it, who will be assigned to which small group during the event, and set up the schedule for the entire event.

During the event, if an adult notices something that seems troubling, their first task is to approach one of the elected youth leaders and describe the situation (as long as it's not a "call 911" type of emergency). Then they work together to resolve things, if need be. Typically, this is in the form of a question from the adult, such as, "I've noticed [situation], ... what's our plan for handling this?" There is no "us versus them" attitude between the adults and the youth. Everyone's goals are the same – a successful event where everyone gets something out of it, enjoys themselves, stays safe, goes home glad to have been there, and is excited about attending the next one.

As you might imagine, it saddens me when we get an email or a text a few days before one of our retreats, from a youth saying they won't be able to attend because they have too much homework. So, I did some research. What I've been able to determine, from various studies, is that most homework is a complete waste of time. For the primary grades, it has no effect on academic performance at all. Even for middle school and high school, it has very little benefit. Perhaps one hour per night would be plenty, even in high school.

Instead, I hear stories all the time of youth losing sleep, unable to finish all their work, having to turn down opportunities for other activities, and so on. The pressure to attend college is intense, even if a young person is uncertain of why they should even go to college, or what they should major in, at least at age eighteen. I also hear about bullying, depression, suicide rates, and so on. Suicide is the second-highest cause of death, for people ages fifteen to twenty-four nationwide.[98]

With all this going on, I have to wonder: Why do we treat young people this way? They deserve better. Much better.

---

[97] The rules are few and straightforward – no violence, no drugs, no weapons, no exclusive behavior, no sexualized behavior, no leaving church property, no physical contact without consent, etc. Everyone knows that if any of this happens, the church hosting the event may decline to host them in the future. If someone breaks the rules, a group is formed to review what happened and decide the consequences – typically the individual is sent home, and may be banned from attending one or more such events in the future. In all the years I've been involved, there has only been one such incident.

[98] See www.worldlifeexpectancy.com/usa-cause-of-death-by-age-and-gender

Parents

If you are a parent, I'd like to hand it to you – it's a demanding job! I spent a few years as an active stepfather of my wife's daughter and found it very challenging! Life with children is filled with unexpected events and situations that need constant attention and decisions. One's own emotions are likely to come up. There is no way anyone does it perfectly. Instead, it's a messy, inexact process.

So why do we so often do it in relative isolation? We have single-family houses or apartments, with just one or two parents and their children in each one. Often parents have minimal interaction with other parents or other adults who might be able to pitch in. I happen to think that it does take a village to raise a child. We just have a different definition of village today, compared to what we might have had a few centuries or millennia ago.

Our "village" starts with life within the family household, but the amount of time spent at home is likely dwarfed by time spent elsewhere. More of the time, parents are working, children are in school, involved in an after-school activity, doing something online, or just hanging out, perhaps at the local mall. Often, there are no adults who really know them, for them to hang out with.

So we, as a society, have taken the difficult job of parenting, and made it harder by drawing family members away from each other, drawing families away from other families, and by leaving parents with little support to carry on as parents. Oh, we say how important parenting is, and we speak of "family values" all the time, in public. However, our actual support for parents, economically, socially, and with dedicated resources, pales in comparison to many other places around the world.

The thing is, you can't measure the value of raising children by looking at the Gross Domestic Product (GDP), the Dow Jones Industrial Average, or any other financial measure. Those things measure the success of the economy in one aspect: How much money something makes. So where is our index of family support and success? I don't know of one.

Parents are constantly faced with new challenges that didn't seem to exist when they were children themselves. With TV, computers, and mobile devices, there's the question of how much screen time is appropriate. Protecting children from predators is a lot more complex than simply a question of "don't take candy from strangers," now that there's email, texting, internet porn, and numerous other routes through which rogue adults might try to take advantage of children.

Now, we add the challenge of gender identity. What do we do if our child is born intersex?[99] What do we say to doctors who want to perform sex assignment surgery? Or, if a child seems normal, how do we handle the situation where a child who we

---

[99] About 1 in 100 births, all told. So this challenge is not new. See: www.isna.org/faq/frequency

thought was a boy feels more like a girl instead? Or the other way around? Or a child who seems to be going in a more gender neutral direction?

The *last* thing I want to do is just heap some advice on you and leave it at that. After all, what good is someone telling you what to do, if they don't really understand your individual family situation? What you probably need is less pressure, not more. That's my guess.

I can think of a few things. One is a message I have for everyone, for both parents *and* people who are not parents (or people who are parents whose children are grown and now out on their own). That is: Please help find a way to build mutual support networks, to help alleviate some of the pressure parents live with today. You could call this "building a new village" if you like. I have no specific idea to present here. There must be thousands of different ways. All I can do is invite you to get creative and come up with ideas that work for you and the people in your community. If you are already doing this, then I thank you.

One of the basic challenges parents typically face is how to let go. When our children are infants, they are relatively helpless, so we learn to run their lives for them, for the most part. But as they grow, soon enough, our challenge is to change our approach from control, to management, to facilitation, to support. We are faced with asking them to trust us, at the beginning, and with asking ourselves to trust them, later on, so that within about eighteen to twenty years, the transition is mostly complete. For our children and for us, this can be an emotionally difficult set of changes to make. Time has a way of creeping up on us, leaving us behind in the process. It's easy to keep applying techniques that are no longer age-appropriate as our children grow and need to make more of their own choices, and experience the results for themselves.

Maintaining and demonstrating our love for them throughout this process is so important, yet seems to be so challenging at times. By now, there are many books and other resources out there to help guide us. But I think we could benefit from more collaboration, between parents and other adults, to feel loved by each other, and receive more support when difficult challenges come along.

The other message I have is also for everyone. We are all mentors for all children today. The information age has given children access to witness more adult behavior than ever before. In a sense, we are all serving as parents, in different ways, even if we don't have children of our own. We never know when what we do, how we act, or what we say, might be observed by a child or youth who will take our behavior as a model for their own.

If we think of the world this way, then it is up to all of us to live by our best standards, not just for ourselves, and not just for other adults, but for the generations who are following us. It is up to us to be as loving, as kind, and as thoughtful as possible in everything we do. If children represent more and more diversity these days (such as in gender expression), then I say it is up to all of us to demonstrate acceptance of that diversity as much as we can.

Educational Change

Recently, I learned of the plight of a high school student from a friend. The student had been home sick enough times during the school year that she had reached the limit of unexcused sick days. She was frustrated by her own frequent (but as yet undiagnosed) minor illnesses, yet she could not always get a note from a doctor. Any more unexcused absences, she was told, and she'd have to repeat the entire tenth grade over again the following year.

I was practically speechless. Here was a student who actually liked school and did well enough to get good grades. The idea that she would be punished by having to sit through the same classes all over again for an entire school year seemed absurd. Yet that was the policy and the school officials were sticking to it!

I had an idea. Why not let the student audit her classes, an option that is typically available to many college students? She could attend school as much as possible until age eighteen, then take a GED exam and have a diploma after all. But the school system does not offer that option. The only options are to show up as required or be left back a grade.

Oh, I can hear the excuses already. She might "get behind" or not be able to "cover all the material" in the curriculum. If they allow her to do this, would other students want to do the same thing? The entire system might be thrown into chaos! Anyway, we have truancy (compulsory attendance) laws. How would we enforce them then?

Are you kidding me? Really? It's been fifty years since I was in public school. In all that time, there have been numerous reform efforts, billions of dollars spent, new educational theories, revised teaching materials, and all kinds of new technology. And here we are with the same old bureaucratic tyranny over young people. As far as I'm concerned, it's not just sad, *it's criminal!*

It's time for a revolution. A real revolution! It's time to turn the entire thing upside down. It's time to let young people take the reins, with just enough guidance and support from us adults. After all, it is the *young people themselves* who know best what the future will require. We adults are fools to think we have better answers than they do. Hey, I'm in my 60s already. I grew up in the age of vacuum tube radios, dial telephones, and computers that filled entire rooms. The world has changed radically since then. Our education system has not.

I have no business telling any youth today what they should be studying. Neither do you. Until we as a culture can admit that, we're lost. Until we can learn to trust our young people as we support and care for them, we're hypocrites. So let's throw out our addiction to control through the use of coercion, shame, and humiliation. Let's start over. Let's give every young person the support, love, and encouragement they need to grow their own creativity, develop their own passions, and build their own resilience in the face of discouraging life events. We can do this! Starting now.

The Glass Ceiling

I have often said, "Look out if you manage to break through the glass ceiling! Once you get up there, you might find that nobody's home."

The glass ceiling is a metaphor, of course. There was once a real glass ceiling, in certain Post Office buildings, from what I understand. Managers stood on a floor with glass panels, to look down at workers on the floor below, to observe how well they were doing their jobs. To the workers, looking up, this was the glass ceiling. This was long before computers, surveillance cameras, and other electronic technology.

Of course, women could not go up there and serve as managers without workers below being able to look up under their skirts! So they were not allowed.

Today, the glass ceiling is a metaphor for the invisible barrier that prevents women from being promoted into the most senior management positions in business and industry because of a sexist bias. The theory has been that women just cannot handle the responsibilities and challenges that such jobs involve. The result is, the percentage of women in such jobs is much lower than it is in "lower level" jobs today.

But, what did I mean when I said "... you might find that nobody's home?" That's my way of saying that I don't believe that being at the top of a hierarchy is a good place to be anymore. I don't think one can bring about effective change in organizations and in society as a whole from such a position. Of course, we're in the midst of change, so there may still be some good that can be done there, but I think it's fading fast.

However, if progress isn't being made by people in positions at the top, where is the power to do that now? I think it is by engaging in collaboration rather than by being commanded from above by a small number of people running things, who are supposedly wiser and of better temperament that the rest of us.

Back one summer when I was at Dance Camp,[100] I was having a conversation with Daniel Trenner. He has taught various styles of dance and has put a lot of thought into what it means to lead and follow in partner dancing. It turns out that it's a lot more of a collaboration that it might appear to the casual observer. It might seem that the man "takes the lead" and controls the movements of the woman throughout the dance.

The truth is, both people must know how to move smoothly with each other to compose the result that we see. In fact, both people are leading and following, in a way, all at the same time. It is the dance itself that is the true leader of them both.

---

[100] Hosted by Dance New England, (DNE). See www.dne.org

Just as everyone making a movie is working in service to the story, not to each other.[101]

But Daniel went on to discuss something very fundamental about how we regard gender and empowerment in society right now. After we talked, I really got to thinking about the bigger picture in a new way.

I reflected on how women dressed in the business world in the 1980s. They often wore business suits made of thick fabrics in muted colors (such as dusty rose), consisting of a short jacket with a mid-length skirt in place of pants, a light beige blouse, and a matching scarf around the neck, instead of a necktie.

What struck me about that style of dress was that it seemed to be an adaptation of what men were wearing to work, carefully designed to be limited in style and color, as if such muted clothing was essential to gain power as one climbed up the corporate ladder.

In other words, "women's liberation" meant emulating the exercise of power and responsibility in the same way that men had been doing. Women were trying to fit themselves into the same rectangles in the corporate organizational chart that men had fit themselves into, for decades, even centuries.

The idea was that if women could occupy the positions of power previously only held by men, and paid the same salaries as men, then they would be liberated. Liberated from being restricted to the so-called "pink collar" jobs: teacher, librarian, nurse, stenographer, telephone operator, waitress, or receptionist.

But, in a way, this meant that the traditional ways, originally created by men, were still dictating how women could fit in and ultimately, gain power. The structure wouldn't change that much, just the people occupying the job slots within it. In other words, women were learning how to play the masculine role, to express their masculine side.

That's fine, but what about the feminine side? Somehow that seemed to get lost in the process. We have been extolling the virtues of everyone emphasizing the masculine side of ourselves, while ignoring what it means to be feminine. In a way, we have been continuing the very patriarchy that many of us were so upset with in the first place.

So, what does it mean to be feminine? Perhaps the underlying issue is what feminine has come to mean while patriarchy has been the guiding principle in society. We have equated the feminine, perhaps, with, vanity, hysteria, weakness, and lack of intelligence. In the past, women were expected to go clothes shopping, waste time putting on makeup, gossiping with each other, or doing work that didn't demand

---

[101] Well, if they're doing a good job of it, that is.

much responsibility or mental acuity.[102] As long as we succumb to such images, of course we are left wondering why anyone would want to express their feminine side!

But femininity is powerful as well, just in a different way. I think of images from "new age" art, where women are sometimes depicted as goddesses, ... most definitely female, but at the same time with their heads up, eyes in a soft but steady gaze, looking out at the world, confident, centered, and wise.

So now I think we're working on a new more positive image of the feminine. Let's consider the art of being receptive as just as important as providing or giving. After all, if there is no one to receive, what good is a gift? Is not listening as important as speaking? Are not the heart and feelings just as important as the mind and thoughts? Don't intuition and creativity play just as important role in life as do logic and facts? We expect women to nurture children, but in truth, don't we *all* need nurturing?

Indeed, what of nurturing? I understand that men die sooner, on average, whereas women live longer. Why is this? Researchers are investigating chromosomes, cell structure, etc., but I have a different question: Have we not trained the nurturance out of men?

So, perhaps women's liberation and men's liberation are really about the same thing. Essentially, "men's liberation also liberates women." By that I mean that most men have missed out on the virtues of the feminine. We have raised boys stripped of their feminine aspects. We have socialized men to engage in ruthless competition, to fight each other in wars, to go down with the ship while the women and children are saved. As we have devalued the feminine, we have left men to live in fear of being too feminine lest they be ostracized by other men and women alike.

Although the title of this book is *a man wearing a dress*, the clothing that I wear is really symbolic of my quest to embody both my feminine and masculine qualities in life. The fact that dresses are associated with women and femininity is part of the point, yes. But being free to wear whatever I want opens me up to being and feeling whatever I want, on the inside. Sure, I have chosen to wear bright colors, to allow myself to feel as soft and snuggly as I want, or to get that dance-like feeling when wearing a skirt. But, I'm also learning how to be liberated enough to let my gentle, nurturing, sensitive, intuitive side come out as much as I want.

Make no mistake about it, things are changing. More men are finding their feminine sides in various ways and are starting to stand up as proud of what they are doing. I see more young men and young women working together in collaborative teams in the workplace, in new organizations and new businesses where hierarchy is fading. I see more fathers actively caring for their young children. I see more people coming out as gender fluid or androgynous or queer and expressing sides of themselves beyond the cultural expectations placed on them, based on their birth sex.

---

[102] Apparently, child rearing and homemaking were also not deemed to be significant challenges under patriarchy!

And, at the same time, there is much yet to do. For men and women, and people of *all* gender identities, liberation involves letting go of false assumptions and fear. We are each challenged to reach out and own something for ourselves that we had been taught didn't belong to us.

So, put on a skirt or not, the point is to dance, to feel, find that balance between control and nurture.

The Softness

Years ago, I remember being worried about which of my parents would die first. I asked myself, which one would survive better without the other? I knew my mother would be very sad without my father, but she would carry on, I thought. But my father would be lost without my mother, it seemed to me at the time. They had been married for over sixty years by then, but she still cooked the meals they both ate, and made the beds they both slept in. More importantly, she was there to hear his complaints about many things in life. True, in later years, she had found more of her own voice and had become less afraid of being in conflict with him.

Now, I'm not saying he was ignorant of her needs as well. He was often kind and active in keeping other aspects of the household running. But there was something missing that worried me. His ability to nurture himself, to connect with others on a deep emotional level, rather than at a conversationally competitive level.

I never got to see what he would have done, as he experienced a number of strokes and eventually died first.[103]

I think the classic issue with men attempting to comfort themselves is this: Our perception is that if we are being comforted, even by ourselves, then we are somehow weak or needy. It's as if good self-care is a contradiction to good self-confidence and responsibility in life.

So let's dispel that notion right now. If anything, getting off your own back (the constant self-criticism, downplaying your feelings, etc.) is very likely to improve your health, your strength, and your capabilities in the world. Of course, this goes for everyone, all across the entire gender spectrum.

Instead, please give yourself permission to feel tender and loving toward yourself, if you can. I say permission because I know how hard this can be. It took me years (decades, really), to reach the point where I wasn't embarrassed to admit that I'm a good person, overall, and that I deserve to treat myself well and be gentle with myself, as often as possible.

After all, I'm the one person I'm going to spend my entire life with! In the long run, I'm my own constant companion. I might as well have a good relationship with ... me!

---

[103] My mother is still living as I write this in 2017.

Little by Little

Back in 2003, I started carrying a purse full-time. At first, it was just the little black leather one. On occasion, I wore nail polish, but I typically wore a very faint color, so people wouldn't notice unless I told them. When I went to work for clients, I wore traditional men's clothes. In the summer, I wore polo shirts in bright colors, and matching socks to go with them. I wore light-colored slacks and perhaps a modest bracelet. When I didn't need to be dressed for business, I wore jeans or shorts and T-shirts or long-sleeved men's shirts. That was it.

I limited all my experiments in dressing in women's clothing (that eventually resulted in my presenting as a woman, a few years later), to places I felt safe, such as workshops or conventions where I knew the crowd was very open to a diversity of gender expression. After all, there were plenty of stories of trans people who were living out in society being shunned, or even attacked. I didn't feel especially fearful, but I was certainly timid and cautious.

I only went out on the street a few times while presenting as a woman. One time, it was just outside the hotel where I was attending another kink convention. I walked down the street alone in the morning (with my 2-inch heels making a "clock, clock, clock" sound on the pavement – I was so happy!) to eat breakfast in a restaurant. I remember feeling very self-conscious, sitting at my table, alone, eating slowly. Would people know? Probably, but how could I actually tell? The waiter was pleasant and gave no indication that anything was out of the ordinary. Later, I went out to have lunch with some others from the convention in a shopping mall food court. I knew we were drawing attention, but then it didn't matter so much. After all, other people there knew the convention was going on, so we expected to be stared at.

But for some reason, through all that, I stayed relatively confident. I walked with my head up, my shoulders relaxed, and with a normal (not worried) expression on my face. I liked what I was doing. I felt good about myself. Somehow, that took precedence over my fears.

It took a few years for me to go through the process of understanding that I didn't seem to be trans, as I have explained earlier.[104] As I came to understand the balance of masculine and feminine within me, I relaxed a little more. I kept expanding my wardrobe. I decided to get my ears pierced, so I could wear earrings. But most importantly, I took more risks by going out to new places in the clothes I was acquiring.

I started going to services at my UU church more often in clothes that I enjoyed wearing. I went to an art museum. I started going to Dance Camp each summer. I was often nervous, but each time I tried something, I felt more and more confident.

---

[104] See "The Big Question," back on page 160.

I remember one time, just a few years ago, when I decided to go to a storytelling event (where I planned to tell a story of my own). It was June, so I wore a light blue sequined top over white pants and white flip-flops, with a white purse. I had trimmed my beard (mostly white by now), to be very short. I took the bus and then the subway down to Central Square in Cambridge. I remember sitting on the train, feeling rather nervous.

After I came up the escalator, I started walking down a tree-lined street toward my destination. Suddenly, a couple walking the other way stopped directly in front of me. The woman remarked how much she liked my outfit. I smiled, said, "Thank you," and then continued. Then, a few moments later, it happened again! This time, the man was the one in the couple who remarked on how nicely dressed I was. Again, I smiled and thanked them.

As I continued, I felt lighter, happier, less nervous, and much more confident. I went to the storytelling, listened to the other stories, got up to tell mine, and received applause. Afterward, even more people remarked on how much they liked what I was wearing and how I looked.

This wasn't the first time I had ventured out, but it sticks in my mind as a turning point. I started to realize two things. One, I was getting pretty good at putting together "a look" for myself. Two, I really didn't have that much to worry about after all.

Over the next year or so, I continued to acquire more clothes and jewelry. Over time, I stored more and more of my men's clothes in the guest room closet as I filled my bedroom closet with the dresses, skirts, and tops that I was buying and wearing more and more often. I searched for shops for tall women but found none in my area, so I had to order from catalogs or the internet. It didn't matter for skirts or tops so much, but the waistline on dresses (that have a waistline) for average height women were a problem.

I kept expanding the places where I would wear what I wanted. Each time I decided to push past my previous boundaries, I was a little nervous. I would stand in my bedroom, about to get dressed and ask myself, "Am I really going to do this?" Somewhere, I found the courage to go ahead. I took the bus into Boston to visit a museum. I liked how I felt as I went around dressed as I wanted, so I kept going. I went to the bank, the post office, and the grocery store.

Although people are frequently very supportive of me, I also realized that some people can't help but stare at me as I walk out in public. Often, I just notice this out the corner of my eye. At first, I was tempted to turn around and look back at them, but I now realize that if I do that, they are likely to feel ashamed for staring and avert their gaze. After all, it's common for us to admonish children for staring, so we learn this kind of shame from a very early age.

My whole attitude about this has shifted. I actually *want* people to feel free to stare at me as much as they want! I want them to thoroughly "drink in" what they are seeing. I know I look unusual and it's natural to stare at something that seems out of the ordinary.

I want to give people an opportunity to really see me, and perhaps even find a shift in attitude taking place within themselves. What is at first new and strange can become just a little familiar and perhaps even accepted. To me, this is one way we adjust to changes in culture.

I imagine that I'm helping others who are also experimenting with going out in public. In a sense, I'm an agent for public adjustment to diversity. I'm just one person, of course. My impact is minimal, compared to those who are famous or receive a lot of publicity.

§ § §

I had breakfast last year with a few women who had met to discuss feminist issues. One had been living in a country near Afghanistan for about a year and had just returned a few months ago. She told me about how different it was where she had been. She said that if I had showed up on the street, even just wearing earrings on both ears (but otherwise in men's clothes), I would likely be attacked by an angry mob and perhaps even be killed, right on the spot.

I reflected that even here, in the US, there are places where I might be shunned or ridiculed or even attacked if I showed up wearing a dress. So I consider myself fortunate that I live in an area where people are largely tolerant and even welcoming to people with gender expressions different from their own.[105]

Clearly, we all have a ways to go. As I write this, there are still political struggles in some states regarding the fair treatment of transgender people. Same-sex marriage rights are still very new in many places. We are going through an intense process of changing our attitudes, assumptions, and sense of what can be "normal" and good.

Some people say we are fighting against hate. I don't see it that way. In fact, I don't think anyone can actually fight hate. As I've said before, change can be upsetting. Often, people are afraid when something or someone new comes along that seems to contradict or conflict with what they grew up believing. This is hard stuff! It takes time and plenty of listening, courage, support, and understanding from us all to move forward.

---

[105] In fact, I have never been harassed or bothered in any way. On the contrary, I have gotten compliments almost every time I go out.

Social Media

Everything social
takes place
within a medium

I like the kind
where you actually
get to hug someone

You can hug this book
or even your computer
if you like
but it's not the same

I now know about
more parties
museum openings
poetry readings
workshops
meetups
than I ever have before

I get to choose
my social medium
every hour
of every day

I am so tempted
to do everything
to exhaustion

Going?
Not going?
Not going.

But why?
Are you sick?
Have a conflict?
Need to work?

No.
I'm just trying
to finish
writing my book.

Prohibition

I don't think it makes sense to consider the political struggle over abortion rights in isolation. I see this struggle as part of a much larger disagreement. When I look at the struggle over access to birth control, abortions, marriage rights, and even equal pay for equal work (regardless of gender), I see a theme that I think should be identified and discussed more openly.

This theme might be expressed like this: Sex is only for a husband and wife who are legally married and are trying to have children. And if the wife becomes pregnant, it is her duty to devote everything to child care, while at the same time, she submits to her husband as the ultimate authority over the family as a whole.

Further, if a woman is raped, then she is partly at fault for allowing it to happen and if she becomes pregnant, but has no husband, then it is the role of society to assume authority over her, and compel her to deliver a child and raise it (or submit the child up for adoption, instead).

Let's stop for a moment. How did you feel after reading that?

Now, I understand that there are religious traditions that hold many of these statements as a standard. Certainly, if anyone wants to join such a religion and adhere to these standards, that is their prerogative. Or perhaps someone might choose to remain in such a religion and live by these standards or act to change them within that religion.

But there are laws in the US (and elsewhere) that are designed to apply and enforce these standards, or certain parts of them, on everyone, even those who do not belong to such religions or who otherwise disagree with them. As you may have guessed by now, I am strongly opposed to such laws.

You see, I believe that law is essentially an agreement made by a society as a whole. If an agreement is widespread, such as the idea that murder is wrong, then such laws are likely to be accepted and enforced in society in a fair manner (note, I said "likely to be").

But if a group of people make laws that attempt to force or bully other people, especially a majority of people, to conform to certain standards which are not widely agreed upon, then there is likely to be great trouble. More people with strong feelings counter to the law will violate it. There probably won't be enough people or resources to enforce it, and thus enforcement will be selective or arbitrary. Widespread violation of the law may become so great that the law is defied openly, and attempts to enforce it could easily spur great social unrest.

We tried this with the Eighteenth Amendment to the Constitution, here in the United States, and the results were so disastrous that it became the only amendment in our history to be repealed in its entirety, thirteen years later. Since then, the laws prohibiting taking cannabis (marijuana) as a drug have resulted in similar disastrous consequences (the rise of an international black market run by violent cartels).

These prohibitions (against alcohol and drugs) appear to be based on practical concerns, on the surface. However, they also represent the desires of a minority of people to control or assault other people with whom they disagree, resent, fear, or hate. The making of such laws is an egregious error, in my opinion.

So now we have prohibition of sexual activity! That's how I refer to the collection of laws, regulations, and policies that attempt to deny access to birth control, abortion, same-sex marriage, and even equal opportunities for women.

Make no mistake about it. I think such laws and regulations are wrong and I would like to see them eliminated as much as possible.

Now, I don't want to imply that sexual activity is of little value, is cheap, or should be engaged in without thought or consideration. And I don't think asking people to only have sex if they are married and want to have children is wrong, either. As long as we are just *asking* and not requiring.

I believe that laws against abortions and birth control are often enacted by people who are trying to bully other people. I see these laws as largely a failure, and they are causing great harm to a great many people.

As insufficient as it might seem, alcohol advertising today carries a statement that says, "Please drink responsibly." So, why not a similar statement, such as "Please engage in sex responsibly?" You may think I'm foolish to think this would make any difference. After all, people can have sex without buying a product with a label (as they would have to with alcohol) so there's really nowhere to put a warning label.[106]

Perhaps the statement "Please engage in sex responsibly" might be good for a start. We have already seen that people are going to have sex and even abortions as a matter of course in life. So, how can we encourage everyone to act with love as they do so? I know, I know, ... some people will ask me, "How can you talk about love and abortion at the same time?" I do so because I love the woman who finds herself pregnant (and the man who is the potential father) first! No matter what. I'm a Universalist, after all.

I love these two people because I think expressing my love to them, no matter who they are and what they did is the only way, ultimately, for me to support them in making the best decision they can about what to do. The world is an imperfect place. I cannot say how to solve all problems. But at least, please let's start with love.

---

[106] Perhaps you could get an abdominal tattoo that says "not for contact without express consent."

Abortion Rights for Men

There are people in the US who want to restrict a man's right to an abortion.

Wait a minute. What? After all, men can't get pregnant.[107]

So, why would I say this?

Because every pregnancy, if carried to term, will result in a child with both a mother and a father, biologically, and legally.[108] There is much talk and much written that refers to abortion as a "women's" issue. Well, I say that it's really an "everybody's" issue. Restrict or outlaw abortions and you prevent a family from deciding for themselves whether they want to raise a child. The mother *and* the father - their rights *together* are being restricted.

I'm not trying to say that the burden of pregnancy, birth, and breastfeeding is shared equally. Of course not. Human reproduction is quite lopsided. But I think we would do well to step back and look at the big picture. We're talking about potentially creating *a new human being* and that is much, much bigger than just "a pregnancy."

So, men, think about this: If the woman you're with becomes pregnant, you're automatically part of the process, whether you expected to be or not. If a baby is ultimately delivered, you will have a permanent, *lifelong relationship* with that new human being, just as the mother will, regardless of whether either of you pitch in to help raise it. You *will* be a father. You will always be a father, even if you never see your child (or are prevented from doing so) even if you don't or can't serve in the role of an active father; even if you outlive your child.

Do you get my drift? This is big! People who want to restrict abortion rights are restricting your rights as a man, as well as those of your female partner. They are saying, in effect, that you should be forced by the government to bear the emotional, legal, and financial burden of parenthood, even if you don't want to.

If you think that's wrong, then I urge you to make your opinion known. Please don't just leave this struggle for the women to deal with, without you.

I can't change biology. You can't force your partner to have an abortion or force her to deliver a child. And, alas, she *can* force you to become a father or prevent you from becoming one, at least with her as the mother, if she becomes pregnant. Hopefully, things don't come to that point. But while she's pregnant, it's her body, and during that time, she has the ultimate decision over what happens to it. Once your sperm has

---

[107] With the exception of some trans men, but that's not my point here.

[108] Of course, sperm donors, who father by anonymous artificial insemination, are in a separate legal category.

left your body and entered hers, you lose control. All you have left is negotiation. That's the burden you bear in this lopsided affair of human reproduction.

That's why a pre-sex discussion is so very important. Sure, you want to know if either of you have any communicable STIs[109] before starting. But the very next, very important topic on the table has to be, what if you are both fertile and she gets pregnant? What is the agreement between you? Are you ready to trust each other fully with your answers? Are you prepared to work closely together if it becomes necessary to make such a decision?

People have said to me, "All that talk will spoil the moment." No, I assure you that it won't.[110] The moment will be back soon enough (and might even be that much better) if you take the time for this talk, first. And just think of how much more things will be "spoiled" if you get started with each other, "in the moment," and it turns out that you have very different ideas about what to do later on if she becomes pregnant and things get complicated.

It happened to me, and I *don't* recommend it.

---

[109] Sexually Transmitted Infections, formerly known as sexually transmitted diseases or STDs

[110] If it does spoil the moment, then perhaps "the moment" was on shaky ground in the first place!

The Three Faces of Homophobia

Back when I was growing up, the term homophobia didn't exist yet, but the fear was out there. As I got older, I became aware that some religious traditions claimed that anything other than heterosexual sex was a sin. Psychology professionals had classified homosexuality as a mental disorder.[111] Later on, I heard that people who came out as gay often lost their jobs, were kicked out of the military, had trouble finding housing, and so on. Even worse, laws prohibiting a variety of sexual acts have been used to arrest, convict, and incarcerate the people who engaged in them.

Somehow, while I was growing up, any discussion of homosexuality was all about the men. Gay men were reviled and abhorred. Gay women were seldom, if ever, mentioned.[112] I considered myself a normal person, entirely separate from the gay community. It took decades before I began to consider that aspects of my own sexuality might be reviled by others. I was so secretive about my fetishes – they were such a separate part of my life – that it just didn't occur to me.

After Stonewall, and the first pride marches in the early 1970s, I slowly began to see all this as yet another struggle against oppression, joining the other public struggles against racial discrimination, sexism, and the war. Straight folks were in the role of the oppressors and gay people were the oppressed. It seemed to be just that simple.

So, this is what I refer to as the first face of homophobia: Oppression, discrimination, and even violent attack.

However, the entire liberation movement began to have an impact on me. As a few people I knew began to come out, my sense of separation began to dissolve. Rather than breed contempt, familiarity seemed to give me a sense of understanding and connection.

As I began to listen, I started to understand how one has to come out to oneself before coming out to others. How must it feel to find something within yourself that society has labeled as sick or sinful? This is what I'll call the second face of homophobia – the internal fear of one's own true nature and coming to terms with that. It would take many more years before I had to face this myself, when I began to question my gender identity, as I've described before.

I'll use myself as an example. Let's say I'm a man who seems to have a sexual affinity[113] for women (traditionally known as straight or heterosexual). What if I start

---

[111] See the *DSM 2*, for example.

[112] Neither were other gender or sexual identities. Terms such as bisexuality, gender reassignment, and others were seldom heard or didn't even exist yet.

[113] Affinity is another term for orientation. Alas, our language to describe such terms seems to be expanding and changing constantly, now that we seem to be in a gender identity revolution.

to question myself by asking, "Am I actually gay?" Since society has judged gay people to be inferior to straight people, that could mean that I'm at risk of joining the ranks of an inferior group. I could be falling down into a world where I would become one of the oppressed! I could lose *my* job, be kicked out of *my* house or apartment, or even attacked. Even worse, I risk reviling myself for who I am, just as I have been socialized to revile or abhor gay people in general.

Every person who asks themselves the question, "Am I gay?" faces this prospect. If the answer is, "Yes, that is who I truly am," then I'm faced with many questions and challenges, the most important of which is, "What about my own self-esteem? My self-worth? My value as a human being?" This is seldom an easy process. These are questions or thoughts that one may wish to hide from, to remain in denial of, or "stay in the closet" to oneself, so to speak.

So, this is the second face of homophobia. The fear of one's own true nature.

But what if the answer is, "I don't know," or, "I can't bear to think about it," or maybe simply, "That's just not me"? Regardless of which way I answer this question, there is still the fear that I might be *perceived* as gay by others. If people think I'm gay, then I could be vulnerable to the same discrimination and attack! Not only that, what if gay people were to start coming on to me?[114]

I refer to this as the third face of homophobia. Fear that others will assume me to be gay, or will treat me as gay, even if it turns out that that's not really my affinity.

As a result of this fear, many men subconsciously live with a whole set of rules that they abide by in order to restrict their own behavior. Just as with sexism, and the fear that you won't be perceived as a "real man," this fear adds another factor – that you won't be perceived as a real *straight* man. This fear is one of the main reasons that men often remain isolated from each other. The rules are:

· Don't show too much physical affection toward other men.
· Don't hug other men, but if you do, don't hug for more than a brief moment.
· While hugging, grunt or slap the other man on the back to give it a macho feel.
· Perhaps just avoid hugs altogether; go for a high five or a fist bump instead.
· Don't look each other in the eye for too long.
· Don't talk too much about your inner feelings or fears.
· Refer to women as sexual objects to help solidify your affinity in the eyes of others.

If you break these rules too often, not only might you risk losing your status as being enough of a man,[115] but you might be perceived as trying to get "too close" or signal a

---

[114] Except for sexual predators, this turns out to be largely a non-issue. Most of us, gay or straight or otherwise, generally seek willing partners. After all, approaching someone who is likely to recoil from us is something most of us naturally avoid.

[115] See my discussion of sexism in "Lost Men," the next essay following this one.

desire to form a relationship that's too intimate. These rules form part of what I call the "straightjacket" that most men walk around in.

Someone once told me that, compared to other places around the world, this issue, the third face of homophobia, was much more pronounced here in the US than elsewhere. For some reason, men in France, for example, can frequently hug other men and yet not confuse that with romantic or sexual affinity. In parts of India, I'm told, it's acceptable for men to walk down the street holding hands without any problem. Somehow, our culture here in the US has evolved to focus on this fear, sometimes to the point of a violent reaction (attack on the person perceived as gay).

Women in our culture have much more social permission to be affectionate with each other, so it's a little easier to avoid the risk of being identified as gay, although it is still there.

§ § §

By now, I've gone through the process of questioning my own sexual affinity, feeling some of the fear, struggling with self-doubt, and so on. Over the last decade or so, I was presented with some opportunities to try a few things out. In a carefully organized exercise at a retreat, I disrobed and faced the prospect of hugging other men in the room who were also naked. I had never done that before, and I was nervous. Would our penises actually touch? Yikes! But after a few hugs, I realized that it was no big deal.

Some time after that, I tried deep kissing another man (on a dare, at a party). The result? I found that it was quite similar to deep kissing a woman, except for some beard stubble around the edges. Another time, a gay man and I both undressed and I allowed him to gently handle my penis in an effort to get me aroused. The result? I realized that a person's hands don't really have any gender; it's all in how someone uses them. To some of you reading this, your response might be, "Well duh!" But for me, it was an aha moment. Later on, I realized that my mental image of the gender of the person to whom the hands belonged was likely the most important factor in my arousal.

After taking some time to reflect deeply on all this, I realized that although I could do these things with men, my heart was just not in it. It seems that the primitive part of my brain that energizes my sexuality just has no desire for it. I could let a man turn me on, physically, sexually, but I did not feel at all motivated to seek it out again.

After these experiences and my reflections on them, most of my fear subsided. I have since become more comfortable around men, regardless of their affinity. I have become more settled and relaxed in my own identity and at peace with my affinity toward women.

Lost Men

After growing up in an all-white suburb, raised by politically conservative parents, it wasn't until my adulthood that I really started to learn about oppression in the world. I think perhaps this was true of a lot of people who grew up in similar situations.

I'm white, male, tall, raised Protestant, born into a middle class family with a couple of modest generation-skipping trust funds, just for good measure. I'm supposedly dripping with privilege. And indeed there are things I've been able to do that have been difficult or impossible for others to do, through no fault of their own. We always had food on the table, a roof over our heads, a car or two in the garage, and time to play in the yard.

So, yes, physical conditions were generally good. But at the same time, I experienced plenty of emotional pain. I've been in men's groups with men of similar backgrounds. More than once, men have asked themselves essentially the same question, "If I'm supposed to be in the privileged class, how come I feel so rotten inside?"

This remains a mystery as long as we think of the world as having oppressors (the bad people who hurt others) and the victims of oppression (the good people getting hurt). What I've come to learn is that sexism and oppression are really a set of cultural norms – a set of rules that most people don't think about – that dictate how everyone "should" behave toward each other.

These cultural norms act to deny the true humanity of people in both groups, both the oppressors and the oppressed. Those men felt rotten inside because they were brought up to conform to the ideal of the privileged white male wielding power in society. To comply, they had to suppress their true feelings and go along with doing things they ultimately felt guilty about or ashamed of, deep within.

What has it meant to "be a man?" It has meant that you had to stay physically and emotionally in control. For one thing, you had to be ready to get violent at any moment, in order to defend yourself and those close to you ("your" woman, your children, and your clan). It meant that you were supposed to suppress any emotions that would get in the way of using violence. There could be no fear, no grief, no tender feelings, no guilt, no vulnerability, and no empathy for the others against whom you were defending yourself or whom you were attacking. Often, there could be no time for open joy, frivolity, or silliness, because that might mean that you were letting your guard down, and thus vulnerable to defeat.

Even when there was no adversary to fight, being a man also meant always being in competition with other men to gain more power and control. Without the glass ceiling that trapped women, you were expected to work your way to the top. If you didn't keep advancing in rank or position, you were seen as something of a loser by others, as not being "man enough" to take on more responsibility and control.

For men who did reach the top, it took a lot of effort to stay there. Even if one was quite benign in intent, there were always other men trying to "climb the corporate ladder" to the level you had reached, so if you wanted to maintain your position, you had to make an effort to do so.

Along with all that control comes great responsibility. The more power you attain, the more your decisions have an impact on many people. In the military, your mistakes get other people killed. Outside the military, your mistakes can have almost as much impact, leaving people impoverished, sick, or fighting with each other.

All this effort to control one's emotions, climb to the top of the hierarchy, constantly be ready for a struggle or a fight, and take responsibility or control over the lives of others left many men with a great level of stress. Just as I pointed out that women trying to reach the top might find out that "nobody's home,"[116] the phrase that applied to men in the past was, "It's lonely at the top." Sure, you had great power, control, and prestige, perhaps. But you might have had little or no companionship or any good way to seek solace for what weighed on you. As your expressions of grief, fear, or empathy were denied, the stress and tension from all this could easily build up.

What were the avenues for men to let off steam? They are legendary. The quick-fix feel-good addictions and indulgences: sex and drugs (typically smoking and alcohol, the legal ones) and perhaps violent outbursts (which is really an addiction of another order). Men, desperate to relieve their stress and pain, in privileged positions, sought out sex more for relief than to build a relationship. Either you got sex at home, in marriage, you got it in the role of endless bachelorhood, or if you were more desperate, you paid for it, or you abused others to get it.[117]

Of course, I'm generalizing here. Men come in all different shapes and sizes and temperaments, just as women do. Some men are generous and caring while others may be egotistical, sociopathic, or narcissistic. The more remorseless and aggressive a man might be, the better his chances for getting to the top. With such men highly visible to the rest of society, it's easy to see how men in general got a bad name even though those at the top were only a tiny minority of men in general.

Meanwhile, some men found themselves in a job that seemed to fit them and didn't desire to climb any further up in the hierarchy. Other men felt trapped in jobs that left them drained at the end of the work day, or worse. Attitudes about race or class or ethnic group certainly played a part in all this.

---

[116] See: "The Glass Ceiling," page 177.

[117] Since patriarchy has taught everyone that women and children are inferior to men, some men taken that to mean that forcing someone else to submit to unwanted sex is acceptable.

When feminism became active again, in the 1960s,[118] more women started to openly express their anger - an emotion that they had often been told in the past was forbidden to them. Previously, the general attitude in society was that it was "not ladylike," to express anger, and if you did, you could be labeled bossy or a bitch and shunned by men and other women alike. Instead, women were traditionally only permitted to express grief (crying), fear, and joy openly, but anger was off limits. So, after decades of struggle, women stepped up, more and more, to express their anger openly. Thus we saw the books, the speeches, the marches, and the demonstrations that were typical of the women's movement in the 1960s and 1970s.

Since men were seen as oppressors, many women saw men as "the enemy" and vented their anger directly at men. Meanwhile, many men, already feeling badly about themselves inside, felt even worse than before. There was a sense that just being male made you bad in the first place. Some women theorized that our testosterone levels were to blame. Well, as a man, what could you do about that? Our hormones are a built-in feature. Sure, I think hormones play some role in our lives, yes. But saying testosterone makes men bad is like saying the estrogen makes women unfit for work outside the home. Neither is true.

As women have started to gain power in society, they have begun to break through the glass ceiling and take on more and more positions of power, authority, and control traditionally held by men. However, men have been taught that those positions belonged to them; there was nothing else for them to do. Working outside the home and getting to the top was the mission given to men by society, a major goal in life. Without that, where were we? Men began to feel more and more lost.

So why has men's liberation lagged so far behind the liberation of women? And why is the liberation of women taking so long, now that we recognize how women have been oppressed? I cannot pretend to know the whole answer to these questions. But I do have some idea.

Because men have been seen to have had all the power and control in society, marching in the streets or holding demonstrations for men's rights seems inappropriate and pointless. Men also need to be liberated, but from what, exactly?

The answer is actually pretty clear - to be liberated from the conditioning that told us that constant work and exertion of control were all we were good for. To accept that tenderness, feelings, and complex emotions are part of being human, not just for women! We have found ourselves limited by the design of institutions, laws, and cultural traditions that limit men just as women have been limited.

Sexism taught us that women were inferior. The message was clear: women were less important and less capable than men. So as a man, if you believed this, then why would you do anything to associate yourself with women? That would be a step down, from power and authority, into inferiority and subservience. So, as a result, men have

[118] See the Wikipedia article on Second Wave Feminism.

distanced themselves from "women's ways" for fear that they would be heading down a slippery slope of losing their very manhood. Better to wear the straightjacket of restricted behavior that has been expected of men to avoid suspicion.

Meanwhile, women have been told they can never look pretty or thin enough, that they have to project themselves as always nice or sexy in order to be accepted in society and by men. They were told they were not strong enough, physically or emotionally, to handle the challenges of the working world. At the same time, men have been told they are more likely to be slobs, socially inept, or down right mean, aggressive, and careless.

In each case, there have been women and men who accepted these stereotypes and have adopted them for themselves. But others have ended up feeling incompatible with all this. It's easy to feel excluded and hopeless if you don't see any way to change things. One of our greatest fears is to be shunned, and if it seems that we have to conform in order to connect with others, then we're stuck with an unpleasant bargain, unable to be true to ourselves.

But still, why has women's liberation already started while men's liberation still lags behind? I think it has to do with women's original mandate to be attentive to relationships, whereas men have been taught to either work alone or work on a team with set expectations as to one's role. This attentiveness gave women a leg up when connecting with other women to discuss how gender stereotypes were limiting them and often ruining their lives.

Meanwhile, men, thinking that they were the ones in power, were fooled into thinking that they had everything to lose if they contemplated change. The fear of losing one's manhood (because of sexism or homophobia[119]) runs deep because it challenges our very worth as a person. If you are not a "real man" then what are you? A boy? A wimp? There seems to be no end to the derogatory terms for men who cannot manage to measure up or conform.

The tragic irony of the status of men might be summed up by this question: "What happened to mens' liberation?" Answer: "The men just have to 'be a man' and tough it out." The term misogyny[120] is familiar to most people, but the word misandry is almost unknown, because our contempt for men has increased yet remained largely unrecognized or discussed publicly. Images of men as fools or idiots or worse have become acceptable in popular culture, yet we seem to tolerate them without stopping to recognize them for what they are: Sexism that's just as hurtful as when it is aimed at women. Why do we allow this? Perhaps because we still think men should just stand there and take it? Or perhaps that men are still somehow seen as the enemy of the good (as represented by women), and therefore deserve the ridicule.

---

[119] See "The Three Faces of Homophobia," page 190.

[120] Dislike of or contempt for women.

Even worse, many men are directly abused, emotionally, physically, or sexually, by women or other men and somehow we still don't seem to take it as seriously as when a woman or a child is the victim. Just as we know that many rapes of women go unreported, so do many rapes or other abuse of men also remain a tragic secret. The same factors are in play - fear of shame, of not being believed, of retaliation for speaking up, of inaction (or overreaction) by authorities, and so on.

§ § §

So, what happens now? Are we stuck here with no place to go? I believe that we are starting to make progress. The key, I think, is to recognize that sexism, patriarchy, and homophobia are often serious challenges for everyone. Fear can be a very deep and compelling emotion!

We have the opportunity to teach ourselves that men are whole human beings who don't have to prove that they are men any more than women have to prove that they are women. Toughness and physical strength are options for anyone, but not requirements.

Growing into adulthood means meeting many of the same challenges, no matter what sex or gender you are. Access to the expression of a full range of human emotions is everyone's right, and is an integral part of our mental and physical health, both as individuals and as a society as a whole.

Words

My words snuck out
past the guards
I had stationed
at the portal of my mind

Once on the loose,
they were soon arrested
and held in secret
to testify against me

Alone in the courtroom
I could give no defense
A thousand judges
sat at the bench

The trial will never end
Yet I knew the verdict
would be guilty,
as soon as it had begun

The term of my sentence
is indefinite
There is no possibility
of parole

The bars of my cell
are invisible
I am free to walk around
trapped in public shame

Tragedy

This is difficult to write about. It may be difficult to read, as well. I'm sorry. But I think there is something very, very important to learn, here. But if you just can't do it, I won't blame you.

Recently, I went to a program about domestic violence in my town. While there, I remembered a story in the local newspaper from a few years ago. A man killed his wife and two children and then killed himself. I remember the paper included a photo of the woman and the two children. But not the man. He was not shown in the photo with them, and not even in a separate photo by himself. I was angry, at first. Yes, I understood how a photo of all four of them might be too painful for many members of the public to see. But, to me, this man was one of the four victims. He died too.

I tried to imagine what kind of awful mental state he was in, that led him to do this. At the meeting, I asked about his suicide. Someone answered that he probably took his own life after killing the others, because he realized that he couldn't face being sent to jail for the rest of his life. I said I didn't believe that. That analysis would presume that he was thinking logically at the time. I seriously doubt that anyone who would do something like this would be thinking logically much at all. Something else is going on, and if we don't seek to better understand it, then we're not going to do a very good job of helping to prevent it from happening again. The threat of jail time is just not going to do any good.

There was certainly a clue: The story in the newspaper told of how this same man, a few years earlier, had called his wife and threatened to commit suicide. After a search, he was later found on a nearby road by police, and taken to a hospital. It also mentioned that there was a family dispute the week before the tragedy.

This kind of story, of domestic violence reaching the ultimate tragic end, is very familiar by now. Someone (not always a man) tries to control their partner through various means. We hear that the most dangerous time of all is when the partner tries to leave the relationship, perhaps to seek shelter elsewhere or get a restraining order.

When we concentrate on the victim and how sorry we feel for that person (whatever age or gender), I think we're avoiding thinking about the other person, what we've come to call the perpetrator or the abuser because it's too easy to fall into classic "good versus bad" thinking. We feel for the victim, but somehow block out of our minds what's going on inside the mind of the person who commits the abuse. It's as if there's a wall that keeps us from seeing his or her motivation. We just don't want to "go there."

We're all familiar with the story: Someone hits their partner and then says they are sorry and won't do it again. Why? Why apologize? Just to keep control? Just to keep the partner close by, instead of running away? But that doesn't really say why, to me.

To me, that behavior is just a symptom of something much deeper. What feelings lie beneath this appearance of logic?

What if we look at it from a different perspective, instead? Somewhere deep inside, the abuser feels worthless and ashamed about themselves. They might seem powerful at first glance, but in fact they are likely terrified of being abandoned! They have a desperate need to feel love, but can find no love within themselves. They feel like a horrible person. So, they depend on their partner to supply that love.

Their loving partner often senses that this despair lies within, and desperately wants to fix them somehow. Their desire is to "bring them back to life" so that they can have a bona fide loving human being as a partner again. In their codependent minds, they keep hoping that if they shower their abusive partner with enough love, the abuse will stop. Perhaps they tried this with their own parents when they were children. Their parents kept malfunctioning as parents and they, as children, wanted desperately to fix them so that they could get back to having a normal childhood. It didn't work, but they kept hoping that it would, so they kept trying.

In the mind of the abuser, to have that source of external love supplied by their partner withdrawn is so horrible a thought, that they desperately try to do anything possible to keep control, to keep their partner from ever leaving. So, they resort to a pattern of control and manipulation. When they get especially upset and desperate, they end up resorting to acts of violence. And it seems to work. At least for a while. Perhaps for years. As long as the partner doesn't actually leave and still says they love them. The cycle of violence, apology, and temporary resolve often repeats and repeats.[121]

When the partner does try to leave, that dramatically increases this feeling of desperation, perhaps to an unimaginable sense of panic and terror within. What will happen when the partner is gone? Life will be unbearable without him or her around anymore. This sense of panic and terror distorts the thinking of the person who will be left alone beyond any logic that the rest of us might understand. They are enraged that their partner would leave them like this, and at the same time, scared to death that it will actually happen. This rage and desperation floods their mind. The "logic" of this is actually not that hard to see, really. Their thought is, "I will kill you because you are hurting me almost beyond comprehension, by abandoning me. And I will kill myself because I cannot imagine any life without you, either because you abandoned me or you are now dead."

It makes plenty of sense when you look at it that way. So, no, I don't think it has much to do with a fear of going to jail.

---

[121] If you are someone who has experienced anything like this, do me a favor: Go talk with someone about it. I know, I know, ... there are people out there who will regard you as some kind of mean horrible criminal, just for bringing this up. If that's the case, I implore you to find someone else who will actually listen to you, and help.

So, what's missing here? Love is what's missing. Real love all around. The abuser is caught in a classic dilemma – when they need love the very most, they appear to everyone else as most *un*lovable. Their very desperation and violent behavior puts off everyone around them. The way everyone else treats them reinforces their own idea that they are inherently unlovable and a bad person.

Perhaps without realizing it, we sense that they are self-loathing and we are afraid of getting dragged down in their vortex of depression, despair, and suicidal thoughts. We want to get away from them and not think about it. Perhaps their presence reminds us of our own times when we wondered what our purpose in life was and came up empty. We push them away because we are actually perhaps a little bit just like them, in a way. We don't ever want to admit anything like that for ourselves.

So, what do we do about this? How can we find a pathway out of this horrible, stuck place? I probably should write a whole book about how. But at the moment, please consider the following.

1. Isolation is a big factor. We have somehow lost our way when it comes to our sense of community, whether it be a close circle of friends, neighborhood, village, or town. A new car, nice apartment, and plenty of television to watch or computer games to play often makes it worse, not better. But we keep selling ourselves these things anyway. So, our (huge) task is to rebuild community somehow. I can't tell you how to do that here, but there are plenty of resources out there to investigate. Please try.

2. Find a "third way" to respond. Right now, either everything is hidden within your home, or the police come to take you away as a criminal. If your neighbor suspects there is critical trouble, what are their options? These two extremes, do nothing or call the police (and potentially witness the destruction of the family either way), are woefully insufficient. Where is the real "help squad" - people who don't just pay a visit to the house when there is a call about trouble, but people who hang in there to help understand what's going on and how to help everyone involved get through it and change it? Oh, is such a service too expensive? We can't budget for this? Well, we budget a whole lot more than this to train and arm our military. Billions of dollars. Somehow we have to find a way to divert at least a little of that vast budget to a cause like this. And if you think that most abusers will never change, I submit to you that it's possible to find ways, if we keep working on it.[122]

3. Recognize that the most egregious examples of domestic violence are like the canary in the coal mine, warning us of what's going wrong in society as a whole. These incidents are a bright flashing warning light that many more people are suffering in silence. People who would never hit anyone. People for whom the police will never be called. People who need help but cannot bring themselves to go out and find it. People who are ashamed to admit to anyone how they feel inside. Where are our services to reach out and identify and help people who feel stuck in this private tragic life? What if there was a shelter for this, just as there are shelters for those who

---

[122] See: www.emergedv.com

are trying to escape an abusive relationship? After all, perhaps to such people, they *are*, in fact, stuck in an abusive relationship, and the abuser is our materialistic culture itself! Perhaps this all goes back to the loss of community I mentioned previously.

4. *You* fill in the blank. Come on! I'm not the authority on all the possible solutions. I'm just one man, who happens to be wearing a dress. Please! Get curious, get creative, and collaborate with others on this. What we have here is a situation with threads that run through our entire culture. If we work on this, I bet a whole lot of other "problems" will shift as well.

Speaking of problems ...

The Ugly

When it comes to public policy, there are many areas where our ability to take action and solve problems often seem to fall short, somehow. Here's a list of some of the things that typically aren't handled well by governments, other institutions, and society in general:

garbage
sewage
toxic waste
debt
addictions
hunger
homelessness
isolation
abandonment
mental illness
disabilities
bullying
bigotry
sexual abuse
violence
slavery
crime
prisons
war
injuries
disease
pain
death
the unknown

We might ask ourselves, "Why doesn't somebody do something about (insert any of these things here) …?" The answer is pretty clear. Most of us find most of these things either frightening or repulsive. It's scary. It smells bad. It's terrifying! It's embarrassing to talk about. Many of them represent threats to our very survival, if not a reasonable life. Of course we want to have little or nothing to do with them!

When we experience fear or revulsion, those emotions often get in the way of clear thinking about how to proceed. We want to avoid those feelings, so we typically want to avoid contact with, or even think about most of what's on this list, whenever possible. Let somebody else take care of it! That way it will be "out of sight, out of mind."

If nobody wants to have anything to do with something, then someone, somewhere will take up the slack if it's worth their while. Why has organized crime become famous for being connected with addictions, gambling, debt, even garbage collection? Because power steps in to fill a vacuum.

Well, you know what? I don't blame you! This is hard stuff! It takes a concerted effort to deal with our fears and break through barriers to communication (i.e. "nobody wants to talk about it."). We don't always have the energy or have the stomach for it.

Yet, again, we have the opportunity to come up with new ways to approach these things. They are not all fixed situations, really.

Take garbage, as one example. In Nature, everything is recycled, pretty much, so there is no such thing as garbage. Water and leaves are good examples of things where it's easy to see the cycles.

Before the advent of modern industry, you could grab an orange from a tree, peel and eat it, then drop the rind on the ground where it would decompose. It's not "littering" because it's all part of a natural decomposition and recycling process.

So now we have invented candy wrappers and sidewalks. The wrapper has taken the place of the rind and the sidewalk has taken the place of the ground. It's still in our nature to drop the wrapper (the rind) on the sidewalk once we eat the candy. So, perhaps it makes more sense to blame litter on the existence of the candy wrapper and the sidewalk rather than blame the person who drops the wrapper there. We're only doing the same thing we've done for millions of years. As a result, we have created what we call litter which we now have to clean up and dispose of.

As we "Reduce, Reuse, Repair, Repurpose, or Recycle," we are producing less and less garbage, per person, every day. As we eat more and more natural, unprocessed foods, the entire issue of garbage changes and becomes less of an issue.

That's just one example of many as to how something that seems, at first, to be an ugly problem can be seen in a new light. If anything, I believe that we as a society, or even as an entire world, are in the process of reexamining many of the things on this list. The old problem only looks like a problem if we stay stuck in our old ways of thinking about it.

This definitely goes for issues related to gender identity and sexuality. After all, these issues can stir up very deep feelings within us! If we distance ourselves from people who remind us of these issues, we may be cutting ourselves off from our very route to eventual resolution, leaving us vulnerable to political exploitation instead.

Our challenge, then, is to take the risk to get to know those who are different from ourselves, to help us see them as unique human beings. If we can do that, we are more likely to work out ways to coexist in harmony, rather than see others as just another problem to fight over.

Steering a Course

I want to go back to say a few things related to what I wrote about in "The Curve." In that section, I referred to a breakeven or balance point (around 2000 to 2004), but I didn't say much about what I see happening after that.

Although I drew the curve reaching up toward the New Age line at the top,[123] that doesn't necessarily mean that everything is smooth sailing after those years. If the late 1960s was our first try or a "practice run" to reaching the New Age level, we certainly left a lot of unfinished business behind! Now, much of what was left undone is right back in front of our faces.

We have work to do on sexism, racism, class stratification, and right treatment of the planet on which we live. Some of this work is very difficult! It's tempting to postpone it or just hope for easy fixes. But current events here at the start of this century are leaving us with little choice. Our best bet is to face them and work on resolving them.

Although the election in 2016 might seem to be a major victory for regressive sentiments, I see it differently. I see the results as more of a wake-up call to roll up our sleeves and get to work on the underlying issues. To me, it is hypocritical for us to work for the empowerment of people of color, women, and LGBTIAQ folks, along with protecting the environment, and yet assume that others (e.g., white folks, men, and straight or cis gender people), are doing just fine on their own.

That's not how it works because nobody is really the "enemy" in the first place. If anything, the enemy has been some common beliefs in our culture, that we've carried forward from the past. For example, as I pointed out earlier, patriarchy is not men. Patriarchy has been a theme, a belief system, that has been held historically by most of us. As we untangle and retire it, we are destined to help all people to live life with value and respect.

When we step back and look at the really big picture, what we face might at first seem overwhelming. How can we ever resolve climate change, overpopulation, civil war, economic injustice, and so on? Aren't we supposed to be free of all that in the New Age? Ah, but perhaps just resolving these things themselves is not our ultimate goal after all. Rather, they might just be focal points for what we're really working on.

What if we take the next step and think of our planet as a whole as a laboratory for personal growth and spiritual evolution? What if our true goal is to expand our capacity for love of each other and love for all of nature, of which we are an integral part? That sounds pretty good to me. So, are you willing to join me?

While you're pondering that question, let's go for a little drive and have some fun.

---

[123] Or more formally "asymptotic to."

Driving

In the driver's seat
I'm not a gatherer
I'm a hunter!

I have no prey
in mind, mind you

But I will not stand
to be hemmed in.

I want space,
Freedom!
Speed!
To fly along,
to soar!

And that car in front of mine
is foolishly
suffocating me
instead.

I will overtake them
at the next opportunity.

So what if I get there
three minutes
ahead of time.

That's not the point!

In driving
It's the journey!
Not the destination.

Father's Day

It was around Father's Day 2012. I was up in the Boston area at home and the rest of my family was at our house in New Jersey. For some reason, I wasn't able to travel down there at the time, so my sister set up a Skype connection. I had to download the software because I had never used Skype before.

My father had had a series of strokes and was already in an assisted living center at the time. They had brought him up to the house in a van and wheeled him up to the back deck on a ramp. He was sitting at the head of the slatted wood table we had out there, with his back to the back door that goes into the kitchen, having his dessert. They put a laptop computer down on the table, with the screen facing him.

So there I was, staring at my computer screen, with the camera at the other end directly facing my father as he sat at the table. I could only see the waist and torso of my siblings as they walked behind him, clearing the dishes from the main meal and serving dessert. The connection was not that great, as the WiFi router they had was all the way at the other end of the house. So the picture froze up at times, then suddenly jumped to life again as the signal was restored. The sound had some gaps as well.

But there we were, focused on each other, on our respective screens, face to face, having a direct conversation. Everything else was rendered to a background of gentle irrelevant commotion. There was a kind of odd privacy to it, although the others were there all around him. His normal speaking voice was never that loud, but I could hear him well enough.

I wished him a happy Father's Day and we talked about a few things. Then my father did something that he rarely ever did. That is, he opened up to me about some deep feeling. In a pretty much normal tone of voice, he said something like, "I'm sorry about some of the things I did." I had not expected this. After a few moments, I said, "Well, I forgive you." We talked a little more after that, then my brother and sisters leaned down into the picture to say goodbye, and we closed the connection.

I did visit him at the house that fall, but in early December, I got a call from my sister on a Saturday afternoon to tell me that he had passed away that morning. He had a burst aortic aneurism. We all knew from the previous ultrasounds that it was bound to happen, we just didn't know exactly when. Apparently, it was quick and relatively painless for him. When I received the call, I was up in New Hampshire, at a UU youth con. That turned out to be a good place to be, surrounded by youth and other adults, most of whom knew me well and responded with love and support.

So, how did I come to forgive him? Over a very long time, I had come to understand that he had no idea what to do about those things he did, way back when I was a child.

When he was about six, his family had moved from the Washington, D.C., area to New York City. He and his brother spoke in southern accents, which was not at all well received in New York. So he had also been a "new kid in school" in a way. His father had discarded all their toys as punishment one day, so he and his brother had secretly rescued them from the trash and hid them under the floorboards of their apartment. Then, soon after the Great Depression started, his parents divorced. This was rare in the early 1930s, so I can only imagine the shame that my father felt.

His father forbid him to have a bicycle because he said it was "too dangerous." So my father obtained on old rusty one, secretly kept it at a friend's house, sanded down all the rust, repainted it, fixed up the mechanism, and rode it around during the day while his father was away at work.

His father chose a college for him; he didn't really have a say in the matter. The Depression was still lingering on in 1938 when he started freshmen classes at RPI. The news from Europe was that trouble was brewing.

While he was at college, the rooming house in which he was living burned to the ground while he was at class one day. He lost everything he had in the fire. He once told me that it was impossible to describe the sinking feeling in his stomach when he came around the corner that afternoon to go "home," only to find that the entire building was completely gone. Somewhere there is a photograph of him, standing in front of the empty lot where the building had been.

Before he graduated in 1942, World War II had already started. He got his degree as an aeronautical engineer, so he worked long hours in an aircraft plant, designing parts for fighter planes. When the war was over, they drafted him, so that the US could show the world that we still had a trained army of considerable size, even after releasing everyone who had been in combat. There was really nothing for them to do in the Army, so it was a big waste of time for him.

Within one year of his release from the service, he married my mother and a few years after that, I was born. In all that time, the whole idea of therapy, or even asking for any kind of help with emotional issues was considered unacceptable to most people. It was considered shameful to admit any kind of psychological trouble. The fear was that you'd be labeled mentally ill and have trouble getting a job.

It all made some sense to me, years later, that he had become a father without any opportunity to process what he himself had been through. Couple that with the isolation my family seemed to experience in the suburbs, and it's little wonder that he had no idea what to do with his temper.

Over the years, I had learned how to acknowledge that I had been terribly hurt by his actions, yet realized that blaming him or holding a grudge against him was of little use. He had struggled to do his best, after all, and I was thankful that he had finally had the courage to apologize, now that we were both much older.

Now and Then

Twenty years ago, I couldn't do what I am doing now. And I doubt that twenty years from now, I could do this the way I'm doing it now, either. I mean, what will wearing a dress mean by then?

Twenty years ago, who would have been ready for what I'm doing? Perhaps a very few people. I certainly was not ready. If you had told me what I'd be doing today, I would have had trouble believing you. I certainly would have been too frightened to try it.

As I write this, twenty years ago was 1996. Just by one related measure, same-sex marriage rights didn't start in Massachusetts until 2004 and didn't become a national policy until 2015. The entire world of trans folk has come a long way as well, although there is still much work to do. So, we've come a long way already.

But, what can I say about twenty years from now? One thing seems likely. The whole area of expanding gender diversity will have changed. I was at a lecture about gender identity last year, and the language had changed so much that the slides on the screen didn't match the handouts anymore, and it had only been three weeks since the handouts were printed!

We were told, "the language we're using today will be embarrassing ten years from now, and insulting twenty years from now." The same thing has happened to language regarding race. Our attitudes toward race are undergoing a revolution right now. We are in the midst of rejecting the mascots for sports teams that refer to native peoples of North America, for one example. This is not for the purpose of being politically correct, it is for recognizing the basic dignity of all people and their heritage.

Rights for trans people are still being argued in legislatures and courts. I expect that we will make steady progress on this over the next few years. Twenty years from now, it will probably seem strange that we used to discriminate as we have up until now.

Right now, my wearing a dress or a skirt is a symbol, as well as something that helps me feel happy inside. I'm breaking through boundaries. I'm demonstrating that a man (me) can wear clothes that were considered traditional only for women in this culture.

But it's clear that what women wear is also changing. What will we call "women's clothes" twenty years from now? After all, in the early 1950s, adult women did not wear pants. Doing housework? You wore a dress or a skirt anyway. Then, in the 1960s, that started to change rapidly.

As we "mix up" our clothing, it will become more symbolic of who we are as individuals rather than which of the old gender binary groups we belong to.

Poem 23

I bought a chair
It's modern
It's white
It swivels

I bought a house, too
And a desk
And a stew pot

I own them
But they are not mine
Not really.

I get to enjoy them
While I am here
But I am just borrowing them
from Mother Nature

Even my own body
Is mine only for now
Someday, when it stops working,
I will have to leave it behind.

I will probably outlive my car
But my house
will probably outlive me

My house is 100!
The people who built it
Lived and died
A long time ago.
It will probably
Still be here
After I've lived and died
A long time ago, too.

So, do I own it?
No.

I just get to change the walls
Without asking the landlord.

How I Made This Book

I first had the idea to make a book when I was going over the numerous photographs I had taken over the previous decade (2003 to 2013) with my digital camera and later my iPhone. I had taken a number of what I call "art shots" during that time and wanted to make a nice book with a few of them. I looked into using iPhoto and checked out a photo album enterprise at a kiosk in a local mall, but nothing seemed right. Their pre-planned design themes might be nice for people who wanted something easy, but I wanted more control of the page layout, the location of my commentary, and other features. So I dropped the idea for awhile.

Then, while at Dance Camp in the summer of 2014, I bought a tie-dye dress at the used clothing store there. As I returned to my cabin while wearing it, I realized that I wanted a photo of myself. A group of teens was walking by, so I handed my iPhone to one of them and asked them to take a photo of me. They took just one.

When I looked at the photo, I liked it a lot. I started thinking about using it for the cover of my book of photographs. Over the next few months, I pondered how to get started on the project. I had written a few poems and short essays, so I started to think that perhaps I could include a mixture of these along with selected photos.

During that time, I learned that the Harvard Book Store[124] had a device called the "Espresso Book Machine." You could send in PDF files (one of the cover and one for the content) and they would produce a book for you, custom-made in the size you requested. There was one catch, however. Although the cover could be printed in color, the pages had to be in monochrome (black and white).

As much as I appreciate monochrome photographs and films, I love color! So I decided to make my first book consist of essays and poems only and see how that went. Then perhaps I could make a more visual book later on, as that would be more expensive, and I didn't have the means to start right off with high-quality color printing on good-quality paper.

As I started to write my essays and gather my poems, I decided to have a book made, even though I had only just started. I didn't know how to use Illustrator or other graphic design software, so I made the cover as a layout in FileMaker Pro. It was the only way I knew how to get white text for the title superimposed on top of the photo! (I couldn't figure out how to use Pages to do that.)

I had the Harvard Book Store make a book with six pages of content and thirty-four more blank ones since the machine had a forty-page minimum.

I went down to pick it up, and there, in my hands, was my first book! There was a practical reason to do this, of course. I knew from designing software and producing

---

[124] The store in Harvard Square, Cambridge, Mass.

videos that things seldom come out as you expect them to, so I "made one to throw away" just to learn about the little quirks in the process.

But another reason I did this was to feel what it would be like to actually hold my book in my own two hands. To make it seem more real to me that I was, in fact, creating a book. This is my first book, if you don't count my senior study at Goddard College.

This proved to work very well for me. I left the book I had just made out on the table next to my computer. There it sat, with my own image looking out at me, while I used my computer for paying bills, reading email, and other tasks. Sitting there, it served as a gentle reminder that as soon as I got the chance, I would put more time into creating more pages and editing the whole thing together.

And yet, there was still another reason. By this time in my life I had figured out that I had spent way too much time struggling to create things alone. Making videos alone, working on inventions alone, and so on.

I had begun to realize that, in my life, I had many more ideas than time available to bring more than a few of them to life. Sometime in the recent past, friend had said to me, in so many words, "Look, there are plenty of people who want to make things, who need the work, but don't know what to make. You're a person with lots of ideas of what to make and not enough time to make them all, so why don't you get together with some of those other people and collaborate?"

So, I began to think that I wanted a more collaborative process. I thought of the way I've written software (or more specifically, designed databases) for the last two decades. I've used what they call "agile" development techniques.

Here's how it works: A client and I get together, do some research as to what is needed and make an overall plan. Then, I implement the smallest but most useful piece of that plan and get people using it as soon as possible. Right away, I get an idea of what it is like to work with that client, they get an idea of what it's like to work with me and what it costs to get something useful produced, and then we plan for the next piece.

At any point, if we decide not to continue, we at least both have had some benefit. That is, I get paid and they have something that works, that their employees can keep using after I've gone. But more often than not, we establish a good working relationship and proceed to flesh out the whole system.

The employees benefit because there is no giant transition to navigate. Instead, there is a gradual process of learning how to use the software, and I get to participate in that, both in training them and learning about their experience in using it, so that I can do a better job of tailoring things to their actual (rather theoretical) needs as we go along.

If you want to understand the alternative, you can look up the "waterfall" method, typically used when designing software for big government contracts.

So, based on that model, I decided to make a series of partly finished books, each a little further along than the previous one, and take them around to show my friends. Perhaps I would even make a few copies of each version so that I could lend them out, have people read them, and get back to me with their impressions, comments, and suggestions. I would then take their feedback under consideration, perhaps change a few things, keep other things as they were, and proceed.

This turned out to be a great idea. For the most part I got great feedback! People liked what they read and begged me to notify them as soon as my book was ready for sale! This really helped me stay optimistic and keep working on writing it. After all, writing and then publishing one's first book is a daunting task! It has taken me years from my first ideas to actually have this book in final condition. It's easy to get discouraged at times, so having some support from others, including family members, friends, and even strangers, has helped a lot!

Human Nature

I was born
looked around
everything
was ready for me

A house
a car
heat in winter
toy wood blocks

Picture book farms
never saw a real one
Canned soup lunch
meat counter dinner

Took it for granted
Only said thanks
over big turkey meal
in November

Then teen years shock!
car exhaust lead?
oil heat crisis?
garbage burned smog?

All hidden from view
out of sight, out of mind
We turned to see
but hard to face

When life is easy
who wants it
harder again?

Nature was our servant
burned what we wanted
the sky was our dump
side effects ignored

Bigger screen TV
leaf blower screaming
will not heal anything
We went just so far
Now we change

Time to watch
the sunrise
feel the rain
walk in the woods
plant a garden

Repeat after me:

The health of the soil
is *our* health

The purity of the water
is *our* purity

The clarity of the air
is the clarity of my mind

It's a Wrap

By now, my mother has definitely read more drafts of this book, all the way through, than anyone else.[125] I am so grateful that she has helped in this way, suggesting changes, finding errors, and reminding me of a few details about my childhood.

After writing about my father's life, I realized that I had not said much about hers. And yet, her role in my family of origin is certainly just as important!

My mother was born about half a year before my father was. Although her parents did not divorce, she also had a father who was prone to open outbursts of anger when she was young, occasionally stomping out of the house with the words "I'm leaving!" and slamming the door behind him. Of course, he just needed some time alone to cool off by taking a walk outdoors, but for a young child, this was quite terrifying!

She had to live through the Great Depression during her teen years, just as my father did. When it was time for college, her father insisted that she go to engineering school. There were terrible financial problems in his family of origin, so he thought she should have a solid career, even though most women were expected to marry and become homemakers. She demurred, as she didn't think she would do well with the math that would be required. They eventually agreed that she would attend Barnard College. Later, she transferred to the Columbia School of Business to finish her undergraduate degree there.

After graduating, she commuted to work in New York City, then worked at a bank until after the war was over. A few years later, soon after she met my father, tragedy struck. The older of her two younger brothers died of an illness he had acquired while in the Navy during the war. She had only one brother left. The family was devastated!

Two years later, I was born. As with my father, my mother had no time to work through the trauma she had experienced. She was faced with raising a family without the self-confidence to stand up to my father during his angry outbursts.

At the suggestion of one of my sisters, she decided to try therapy, starting in her mid-70s! She has been able to restore much of her self confidence and come to terms with some of the trauma she experienced long ago.

Recently, she wrote to me to apologize for her inability to be a strong advocate for me and my siblings while we were growing up. Mom, I definitely forgive you! As with my father, you were doing the best you could in a difficult situation. Since then, it has been my responsibility, in turn, to seek out ways to heal my own pain from the past.

§ § §

---

[125] Including my professional editor, who only got to read it for the first time when it was nearly finished.

Earlier, in "Family Matters,"[126] I introduced my wife, my stepdaughter, and my son. After my stepdaughter went to college and left the house to live on her own, I began to realize that being active parents was the main activity my wife and I had had in common. When that phase of our lives was over, we found ourselves desiring distinctly different ways of living. A few years later, we decided to separate and divorce. We employed a mediator to help us through the process, which went well. We still live in the same town, visit each other frequently, and get along better now that we each live in our own households. Although our marriage is over, I don't regret getting married in the first place; I think it was a good decision at the time.

My stepdaughter married and she and her husband (now separated) have a daughter of their own. I started to refer to myself as a step-grandfather, but friends of mine said, "Forget the'step' part; you're a grandfather!" I get to see my granddaughter frequently and enjoy interacting with her as she grows and discovers the world.

My son and I have built a solid relationship since I first met him. He has amazing energy and sometimes, I wonder how I can keep up! We have continued to grow closer as both of us have committed to connect with each other. Like me, he has set out to create his own business, and I expect that he is going to be very successful.

§ § §

After reflecting on the lives of those who are closest to me, I realize how fortunate I am, despite the hardships and challenges I've faced. The most important thing has been my health, which has been very good. My father lived past the age of 90 and my mother is now living well into her 90s as I write this, so I think I have many more years to look forward to. I'm also fortunate that my parents and grandparents were able to earn enough to pass some of their savings on to the next generation.

I am grateful that I have an aptitude for technical work that has paid well enough for me to make my own living. I think of people who have to work two or three jobs, just to make ends meet, who are not likely to have the time or resources to ever write a book! I think about how many places there are in this world beset by violence, poverty, and other harsh living conditions. I think about all the bigotry and discrimination I escaped by being born where I was and who I am when it comes to my background. I am truly grateful for all of this.

But I am not just the result of my environment and the opportunities afforded to me. I grew up with the constant fear that, despite what I had, I was messing it all up. I thought everything that went wrong was ultimately my fault, including problems with my education, social life, and relationships. Often feeling hopeless, I could have just sat and sulked, and indeed there were times when I did just that.

However, along the way, I found the courage and perseverance within me to get up, set out, find the resources, do the hard work, and change my life. As much as I'm

---

[126] See page 122

thankful to others for helping me, I now know it's a good idea to appreciate myself for all that I've done and the results that I've achieved so far.

I think there has to be a balance. A balance between opportunity and effort. Success requires both. Of course, even with both, sometimes success eludes you because of some other error or flaw or misfortune. This is another reason why I don't believe in blame.

So, I did this. I had opportunity and help from others, yes. But in the long run, I did it. I have moved my life forward, developed solid friendships, taken risks, and have now written this book. I look forward to doing more interesting and exciting things, as well as time to relax and connect with my friends with as much love as possible. To me, money and career are good to have, but good friends are the most important.

§ § §

Back in my essay "Sex and Drugs and Rock 'n' Roll" (page 89), I promised to say more about autogynephilia. I realize that by using this term to describe a facet of my own sexuality, I'm stepping into a very important controversy. The controversy arose from an assertion that trans people are motivated by only two factors, homosexuality or autogynephilia, stemming from a theory put forth by Ray Blanchard and others a few decades ago.[127]

I have not done any statistically valid research on this, but based on my own experience and from conversations I've had with various trans people, I find this theory hopelessly limiting and offensive. It presumes that in all cases, being trans is essentially a self-deception and therefore is never genuine. The individual is presumed to transition only in order to better attract romantic partners, or because they are attempting to fulfill an erotic fantasy by taking hormones and undergoing surgery.

Although I have described myself as having autogynephilia and as "not trans," please don't use my experience to deny someone else of their own legitimate desire to transition. From what I can tell, every person and every trans story is unique. There is some research that supports this, which of course is ongoing.[128]

§ § §

---

[127] Or, for trans men, autoandrophilia.

[128] I found a good summary in the book *Becoming Nicole*, by Amy Ellis Nutt, Chapter 14

OK, the movie is over now. The credits are about to roll. The house lights are coming up. I invite you to go ahead and read the poem on the last page, after the Table of Contents, then stand up and stretch. Perhaps take a breath or two. Then I invite you to return to page 4 and read the first poem over again.

After all, it's still all about love.

Credits

Author	Glenn C. Koenig
Cover design	Glenn C. Koenig
Cover photographer	(unidentified)
Cover photo location	Camp Robin Hood Freedom, NH[129]
Cover photo dress	Beautiful Tie Dye by Refractions (purchased used, from the Store at Dance Camp)
Book design	Glenn C. Koenig
Editor	Kate Victory Hannisian, of Blue Pencil Consulting
Editing Assistants	Jan Larivee
	Mehera Hathaway
Advisors	Charlotte Pierce
	Virginia Towler
	Barbara Helfgott Hyett
Beta Readers	Helen C. Koenig
	Lauretta F. Koenig
	Kathy Whitham
	Susan Kline
	Karen Watts
	Adrienne J. Burnette
	Rob Kanzer
	Nat Duranceau
Resources	IPNE[130]
Publishing on Demand	Ingram Spark
Distribution	Ingram Spark
	Glenn C. Koenig

---

[129] See www.camprobinhood.com

[130] Independent Publishers of New England, ipne.org

Table of Contents

What Is Love? ·   4
I Don't Blame You ·   6
Not Everything   7
Day One   8
I Deserved My Mother's ·   10
Living in the 1950s   11
The Unexpected   14
Early On   18
The Erection   20
The World Outside   21
Blue and Gray   22
Two Paths of Fear   23
The New House   24
Gravel Road ·   26
Patriotic   28
Housework   29
School Sucks   30
School Triumphs   33
Recess   35
The Ocean Liner   36
Tree Tops   37
Boys and Girls   38
Little League   40
A Nasty Surprise   42
Swimming Lessons   44
The Swimming Lesson   46
Boxing Lessons   49
The Bonfire   51
Patriarchy ·   52
Boy Scouts   53
The Future   54
Playing with Numbers   55
Compost Pile   56
Racism, Invisible   57
Blame Culture   59
High School   60
Down for the Count   61
Interpretation ·   65
The Garage   66
The Latest Thing   67
Life Path and the World Around Us   68

A Shock to the System   69
The Price of Integrity   72
Do Not Read ·   74
Higher Education   75
The Dawn   78
Uncle Sam Calls   79
College?   85
At Goddard   87
Sex and Drugs and Rock 'n' Roll   89
Dance Class   92
Feminism   94
The Decline of Civilization   96
Asking for Help   97
Suburban Life   98
A Job's a Job   101
Charging Ahead   103
Making a Living   105
Emotional Growth   107
Days of Darkness   108
At the Bottom   111
A Great Loss   113
The Spirit   115
Seeking ·   117
The Inventor Gene   118
My Own Two Feet   120
Family Matters   122
Prophecy   127
Change   129
The Curve   131
Border Crossing ·   136
Size Matters   137
Fashion Trumps Everything!   141
What is Science?   143
I Start Asking   146
Shopping for Clothes   150
As a Woman   152
Private Lives   157
Walking at Night ·   158
The Big Question   160
The Power of Women   163
Armpits   166
Fat Girls   169
Lying Awake ·   170

Us and Them   171
Youth   172
Parents   174
Educational Change   176
The Glass Ceiling   177
The Softness   181
Little by Little   182
Social Media ·   185
Prohibition   186
Abortion Rights for Men   188
The Three Faces of Homophobia   190
Lost Men   193
Words ·   198
Tragedy   199
The Ugly   203
Steering a Course   205
Driving ·   206
Father's Day   207
Now and Then   209
Poem 23 ·   210
How I Made This Book   211
Human Nature ·   214
It's a Wrap   216
Credits   220
(untitled poem) ·   224

(untitled poem)

It's my birthday tomorrow
A friend gave me a piano
last week
The movers moved it
right away.

I had to move all my stuff
out of the stairwell
and the front hall
and the dining room corner
where they put it.

Now the living room is a mess
and the dining room table
is cluttered
and I have some guests
coming for dinner
tomorrow.

What shall I do?
At least I
have a piano.

CPSIA information can be obtained
at www.ICGtesting.com
Printed in the USA
FFOW01n1736081017
40758FF